Green Arrow and Black Canary

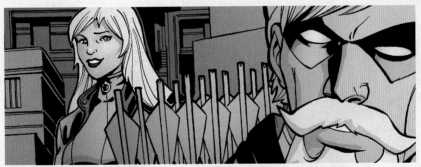

Family Business

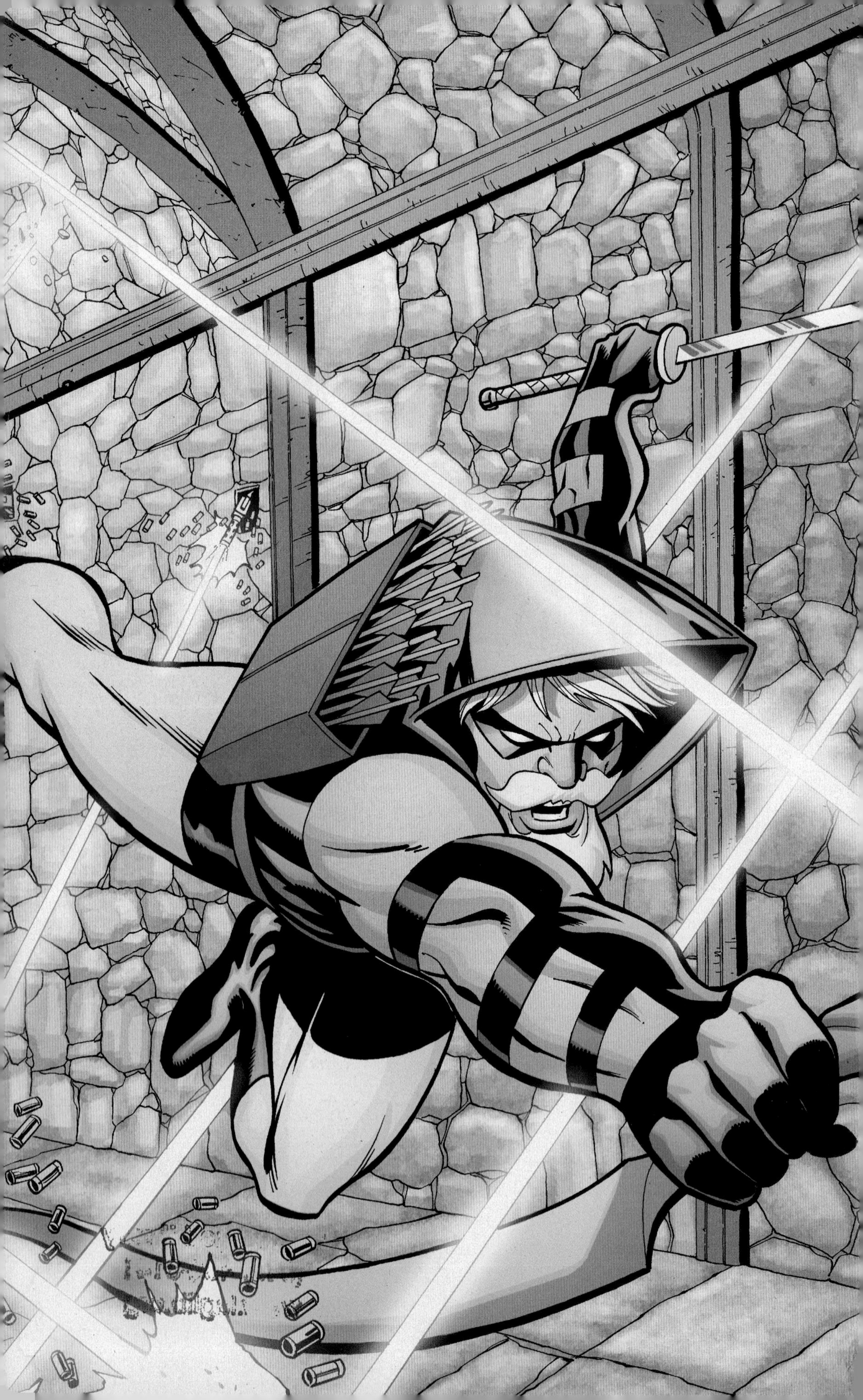

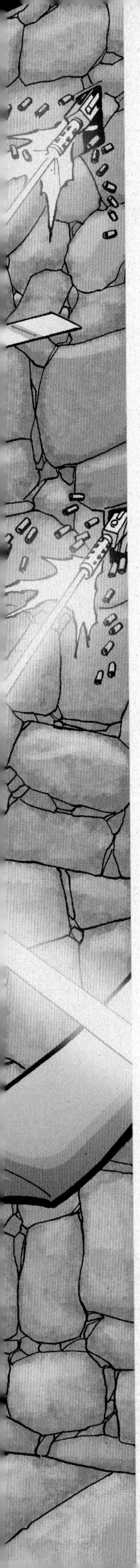

Green Arrow and Black Canary

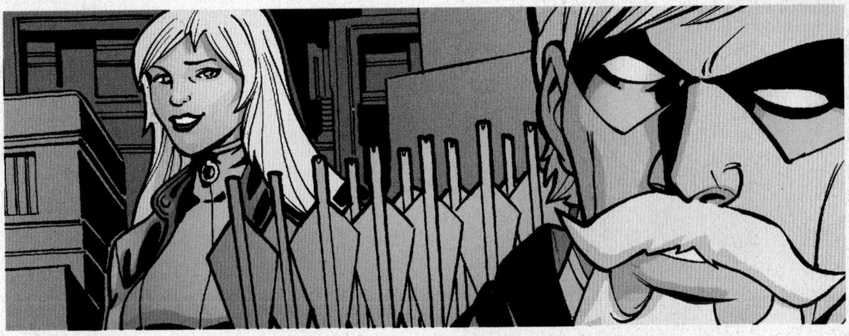

Family Business

Judd Winick
Writer

Mike Norton
Cliff Chiang
André Coelho
Wayne Faucher
Rodney Ramos
Artists

David Baron
Colorist

Pat Brosseau
Travis Lanham
Jared K. Fletcher
Steve Wands
Sal Cipriano
Letterers

Cliff Chiang
Original Series Covers

Dan DiDio Senior VP-Executive Editor

Mike Carlin Editor-original series

Elisabeth V. Gehrlein Assistant Editor-original series

Bob Joy Editor-collected edition

Robbin Brosterman Senior Art Director

Paul Levitz President & Publisher

Georg Brewer VP-Design & DC Direct Creative

Richard Bruning Senior VP-Creative Director

Patrick Caldon Executive VP-Finance & Operations

Chris Caramalis VP-Finance

John Cunningham VP-Marketing

Terri Cunningham VP-Managing Editor

Amy Genkins Senior VP-Business & Legal Affairs

Alison Gill VP-Manufacturing

David Hyde VP-Publicity

Hank Kanalz VP-General Manager, WildStorm

Jim Lee Editorial Director-WildStorm

Gregory Noveck Senior VP-Creative Affairs

Sue Pohja VP-Book Trade Sales

Steve Rotterdam Senior VP- Sales & Marketing

Cheryl Rubin Senior VP-Brand Management

Alysse Soll VP-Advertising & Custom Publishing

Jeff Trojan VP-Business Development, DC Direct

Bob Wayne VP-Sales

Cover art by Cliff Chiang

GREEN ARROW AND BLACK CANARY: FAMILY BUSINESS

DC Comics, 1700 Broadway, New York, NY 10019
A Warner Bros. Entertainment Company
Printed in Canada. First Printing.

ISBN: 978-1-4012-2016-7

SFI CERTIFIED SOURCING Fiber used in this product line meets the sourcing requirements of the SFI program. www.sfiprogram.org PWC-SFIOOO-260

PREVIOUSLY...

After many years, Green Arrow and Black Canary's on-again/off-again romance has finally led to their tying the knot. Unfortunately the wedding — with a reception that included the biggest super-villain ambush in history — ended with a casualty. Even under the eyes of the wedding guests — the World's Greatest Superheroes — Green Arrow was kidnapped and replaced by the shape-changing criminal Everyman... whom Black Canary was forced to kill in self-defense!

Black Canary, Speedy and Green Arrow's son, Connor Hawke, tracked down and rescued Green Arrow from Paradise Island, but during their escape, a mysterious beam from an unknown source struck down Connor. With the greatest scientific technology available, Hawke's life was saved, but he was now comatose.

Heartbroken but needing to move on, Green Arrow and Black Canary were really finally married in a small private ceremony and are now ready to embark on a much needed honeymoon... after they deal with what happens next...

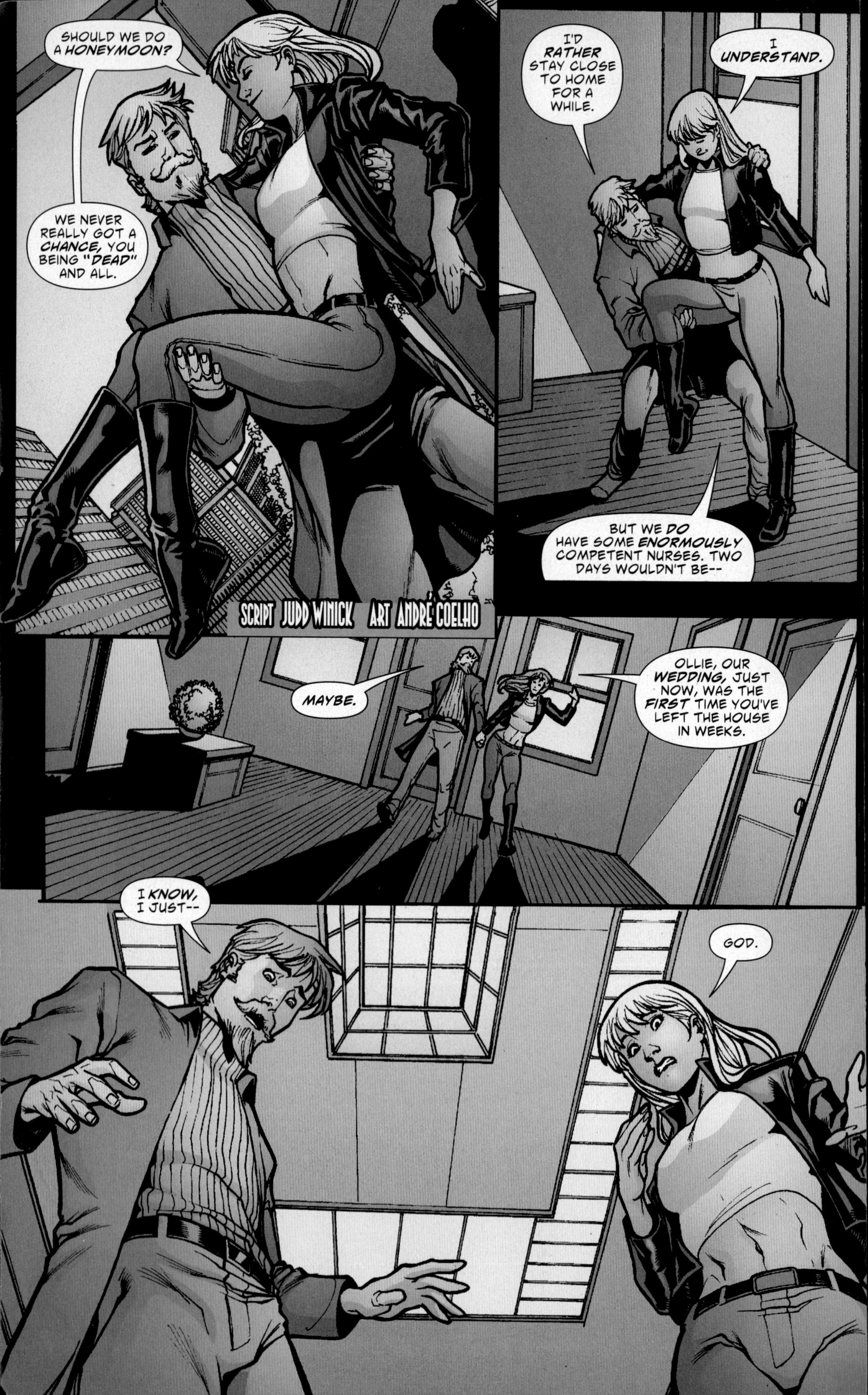
SHOULD WE DO A HONEYMOON?
WE NEVER REALLY GOT A CHANCE, YOU BEING "DEAD" AND ALL.
SCRIPT JUDD WINICK ART ANDRÉ COELHO
I'D RATHER STAY CLOSE TO HOME FOR A WHILE.
I UNDERSTAND.
BUT WE DO HAVE SOME ENORMOUSLY COMPETENT NURSES. TWO DAYS WOULDN'T BE--
MAYBE.
OLLIE, OUR WEDDING, JUST NOW, WAS THE FIRST TIME YOU'VE LEFT THE HOUSE IN WEEKS.
I KNOW, I JUST--
GOD.

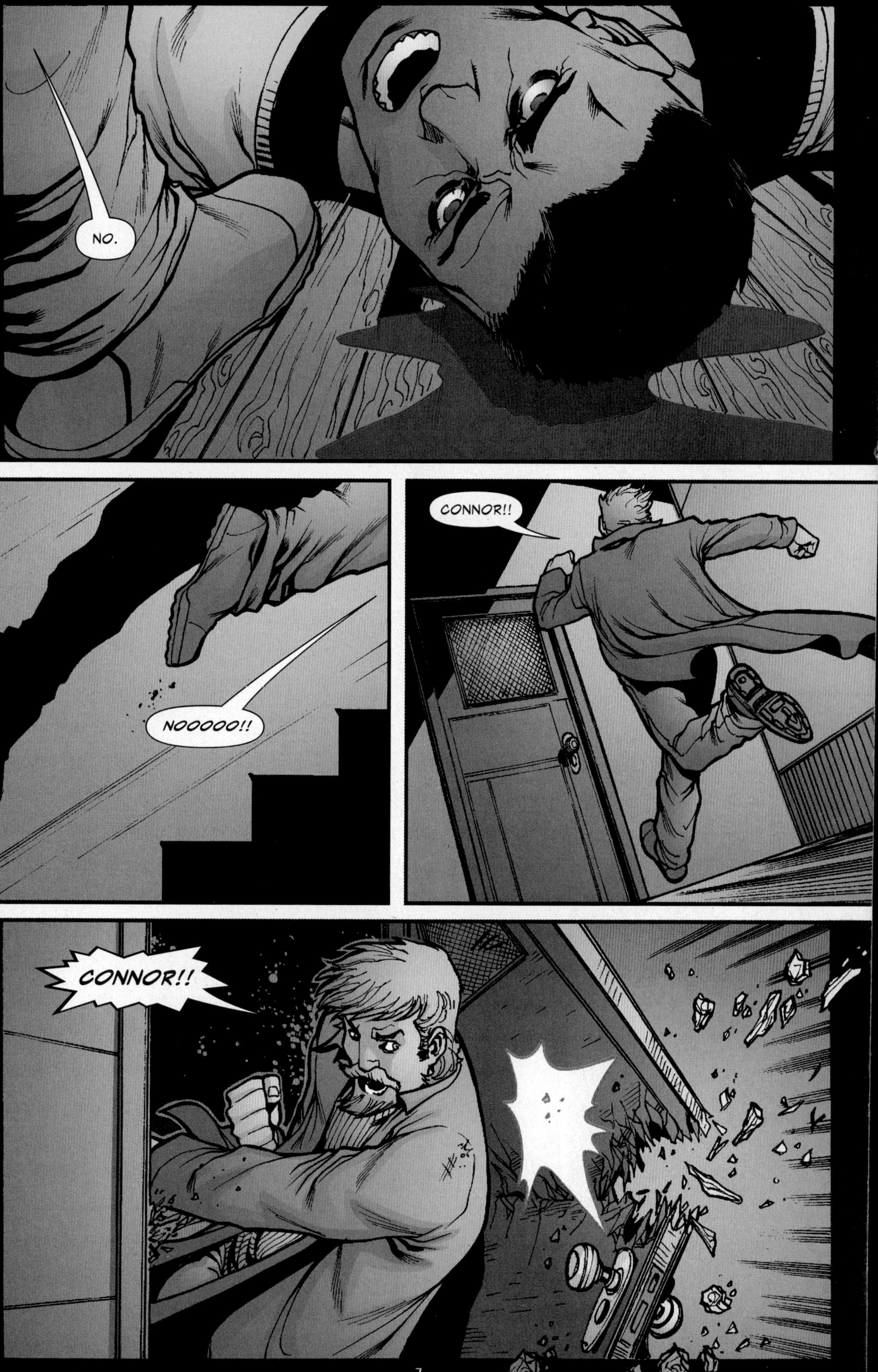
NO.
NOOOOO!!
CONNOR!!
CONNOR!!

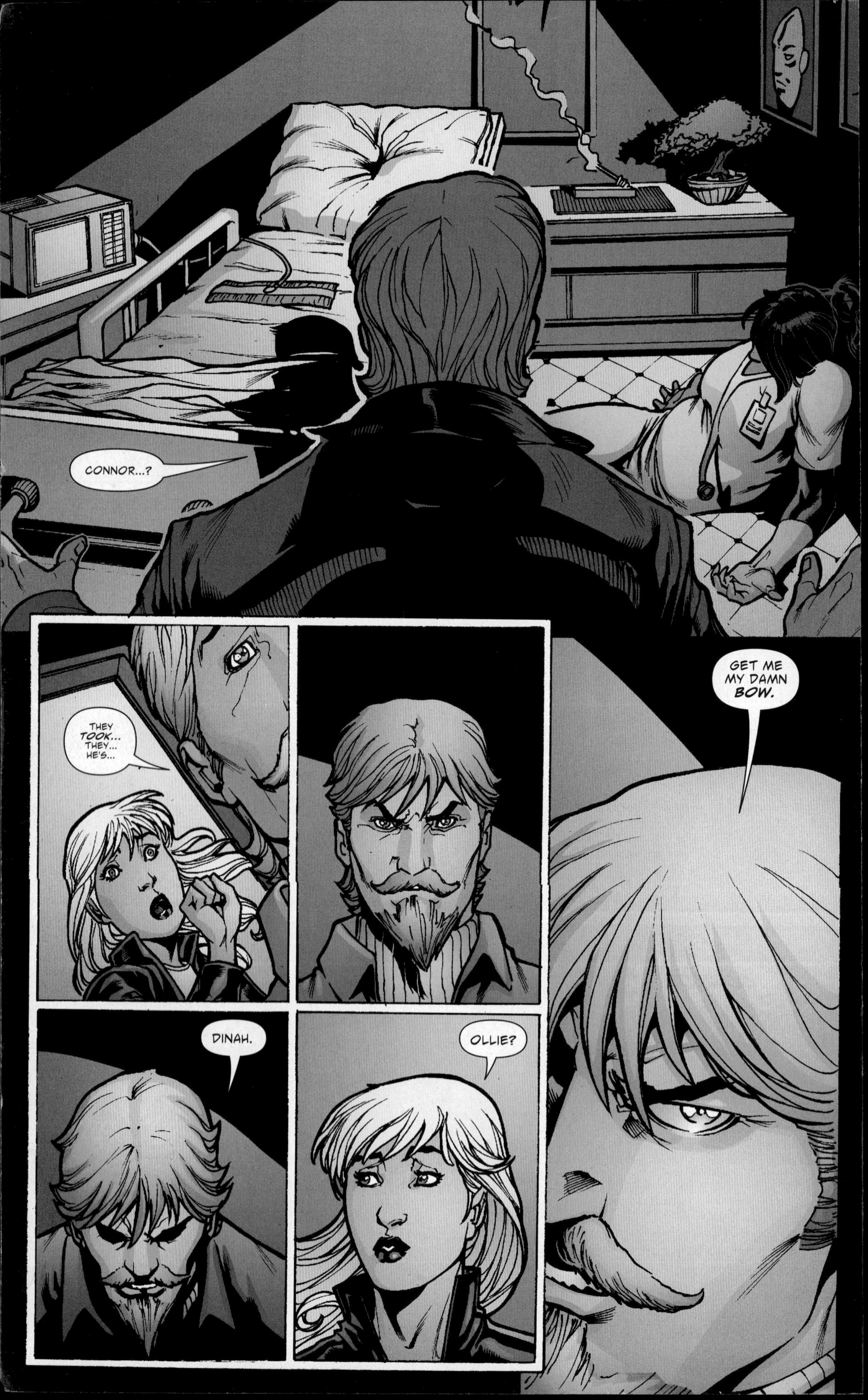
CONNOR...?
THEY TOOK... THEY... HE'S...
GET ME MY DAMN BOW.
DINAH.
OLLIE?

GREEN ARROW AND BLACK CANARY 6

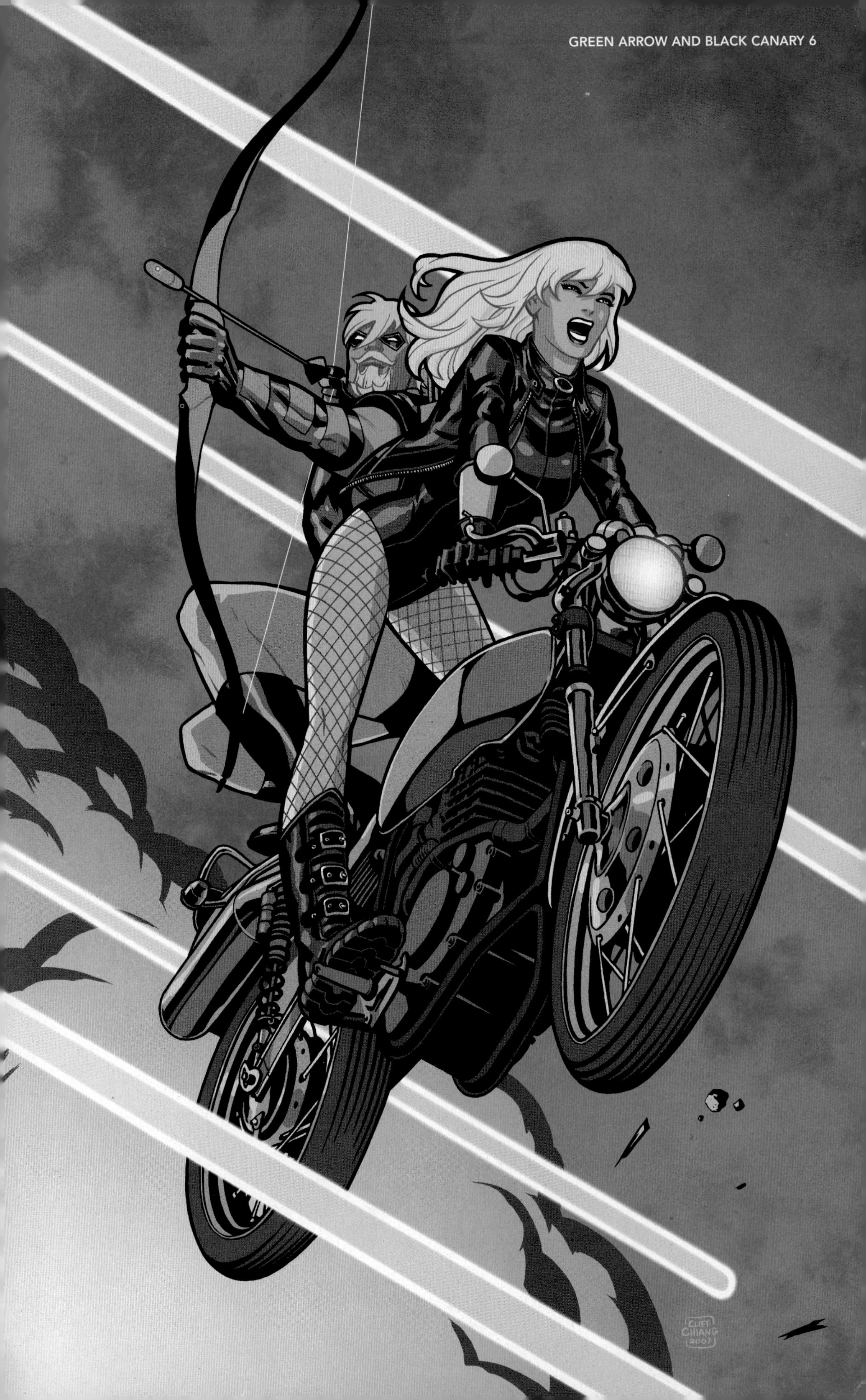
CLIFF CHIANG 2007

HAYSTACK

PART 1: FIRST NEEDLE

JUDD WINICK
STORY

CLIFF CHIANG
ART

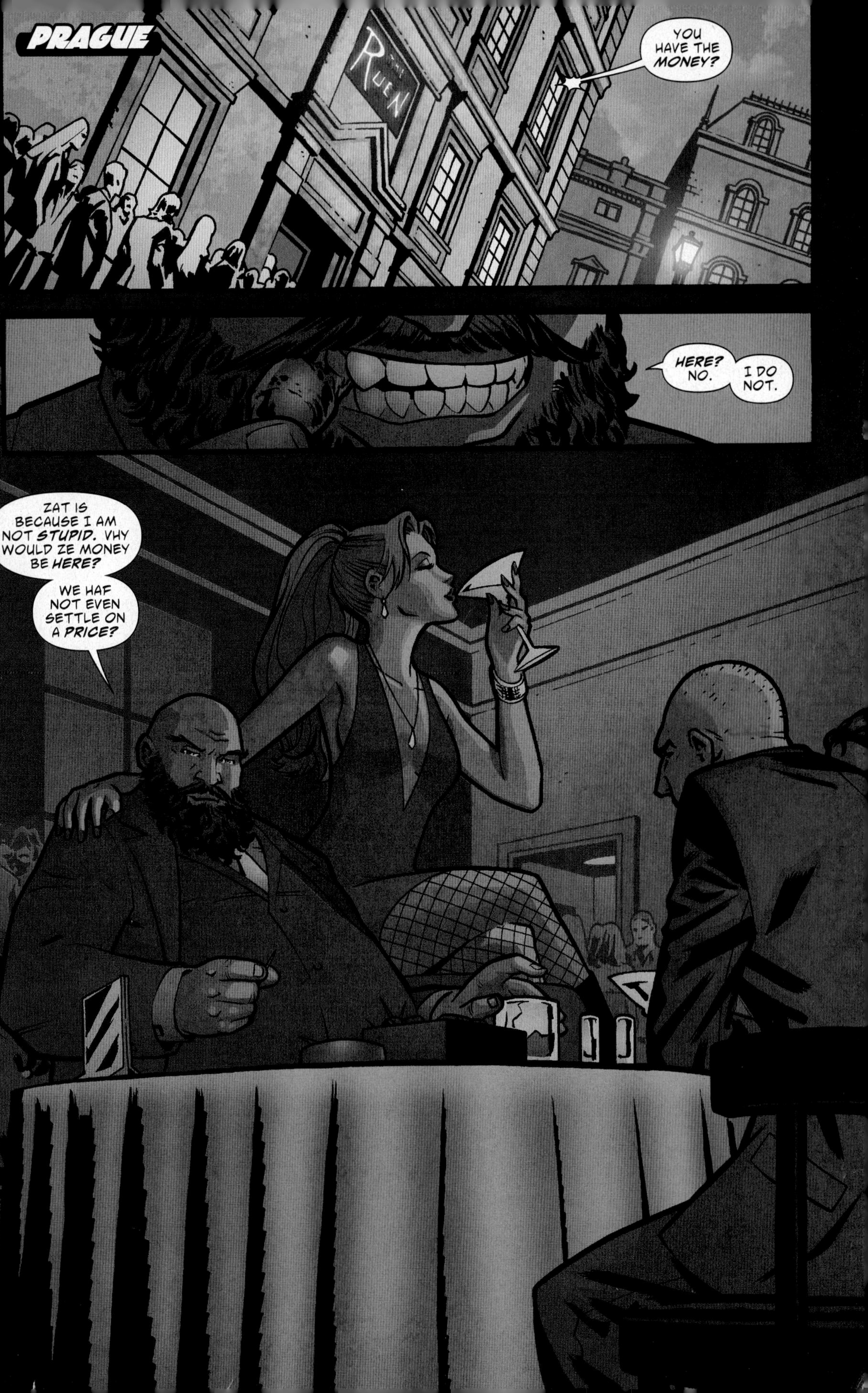
PRAGUE
THE RUEN
YOU HAVE THE MONEY?
HERE? NO.
I DO NOT.
ZAT IS BECAUSE I AM NOT STUPID. VHY WOULD ZE MONEY BE HERE?
WE HAF NOT EVEN SETTLE ON A PRICE?

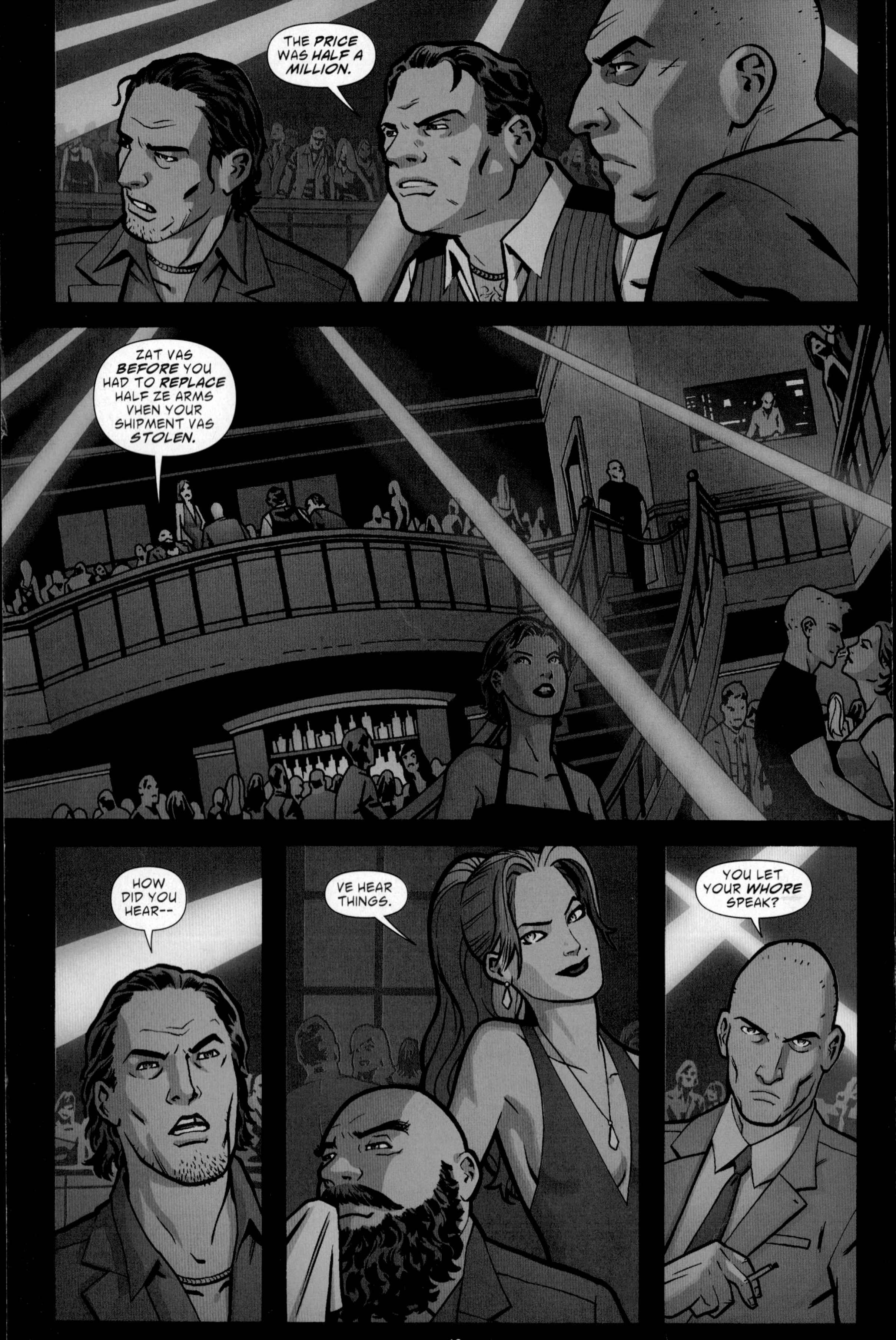
THE PRICE WAS HALF A MILLION.
ZAT VAS BEFORE YOU HAD TO REPLACE HALF ZE ARMS VHEN YOUR SHIPMENT VAS STOLEN.
HOW DID YOU HEAR--
VE HEAR THINGS.
YOU LET YOUR WHORE SPEAK?

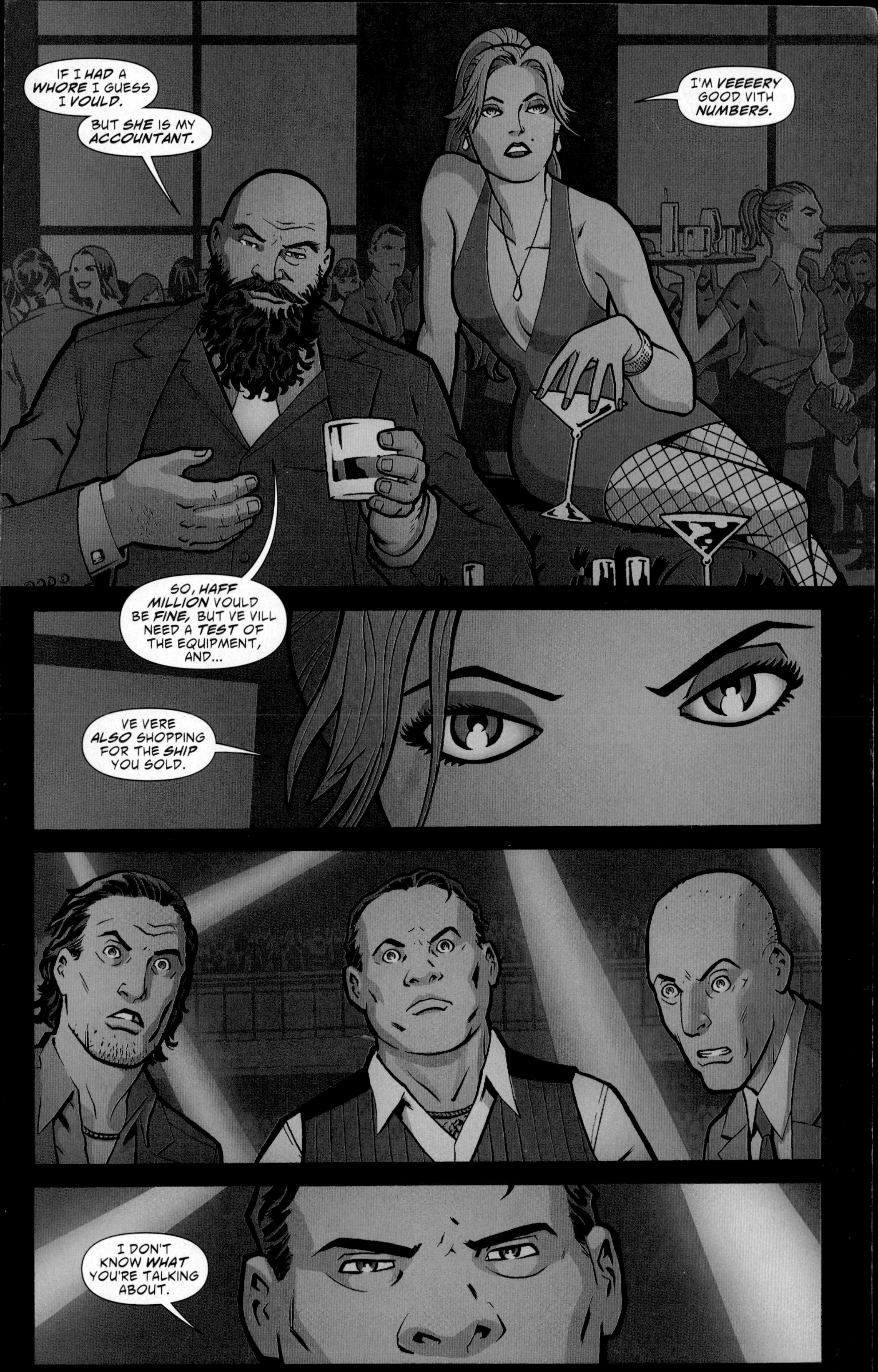
IF I HAD A WHORE I GUESS I VOULD.
BUT SHE IS MY ACCOUNTANT.
I'M VEEEERY GOOD VITH NUMBERS.
SO, HAFF MILLION VOULD BE FINE, BUT VE VILL NEED A TEST OF THE EQUIPMENT, AND...
VE VERE ALSO SHOPPING FOR THE SHIP YOU SOLD.
I DON'T KNOW WHAT YOU'RE TALKING ABOUT.

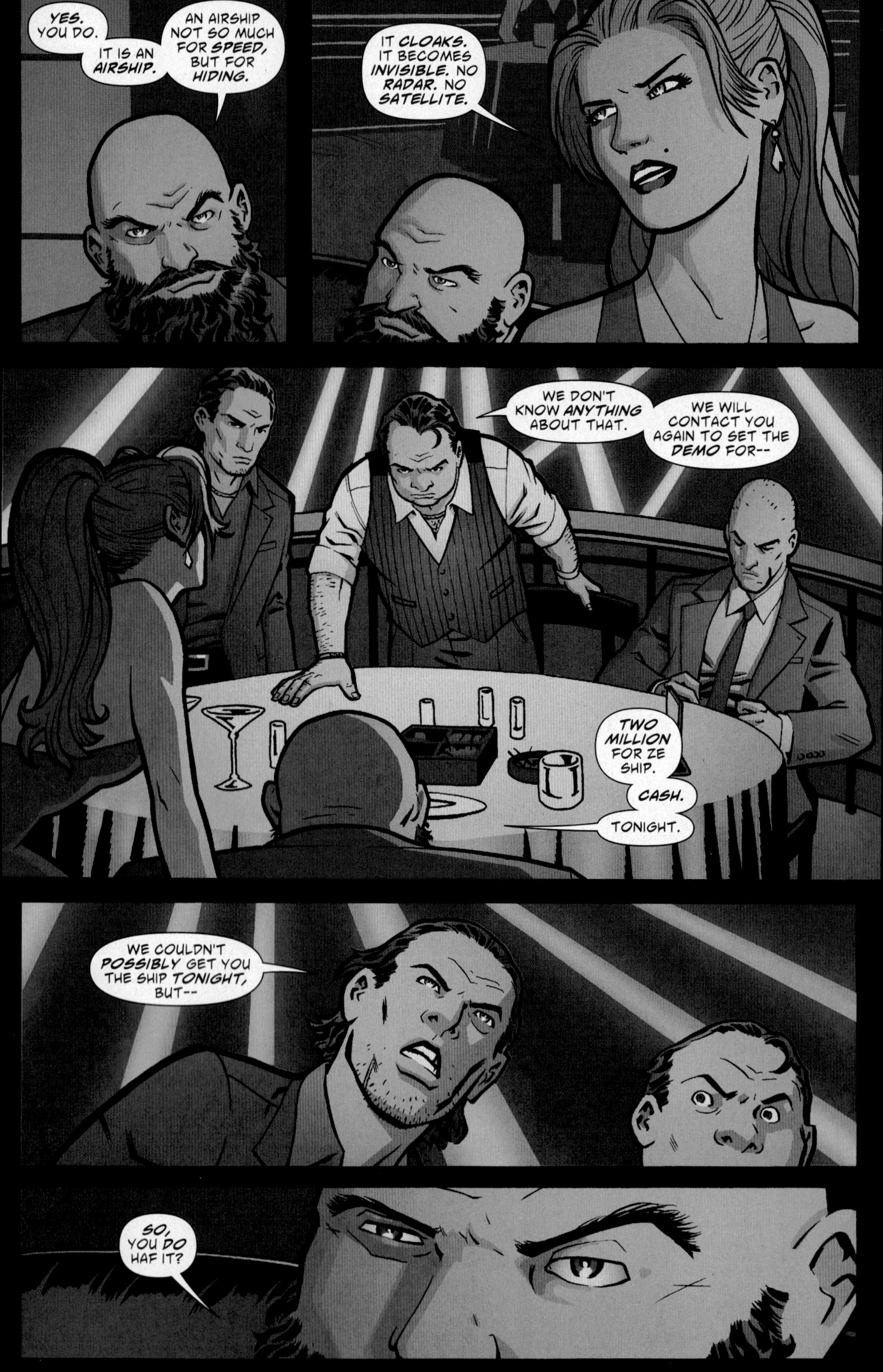
YES. YOU DO.
IT IS AN AIRSHIP.
AN AIRSHIP NOT SO MUCH FOR SPEED, BUT FOR HIDING.
IT CLOAKS. IT BECOMES INVISIBLE. NO RADAR. NO SATELLITE.
WE DON'T KNOW ANYTHING ABOUT THAT.
WE WILL CONTACT YOU AGAIN TO SET THE DEMO FOR--
TWO MILLION FOR ZE SHIP.
CASH.
TONIGHT.
WE COULDN'T POSSIBLY GET YOU THE SHIP TONIGHT, BUT--
SO, YOU DO HAF IT?

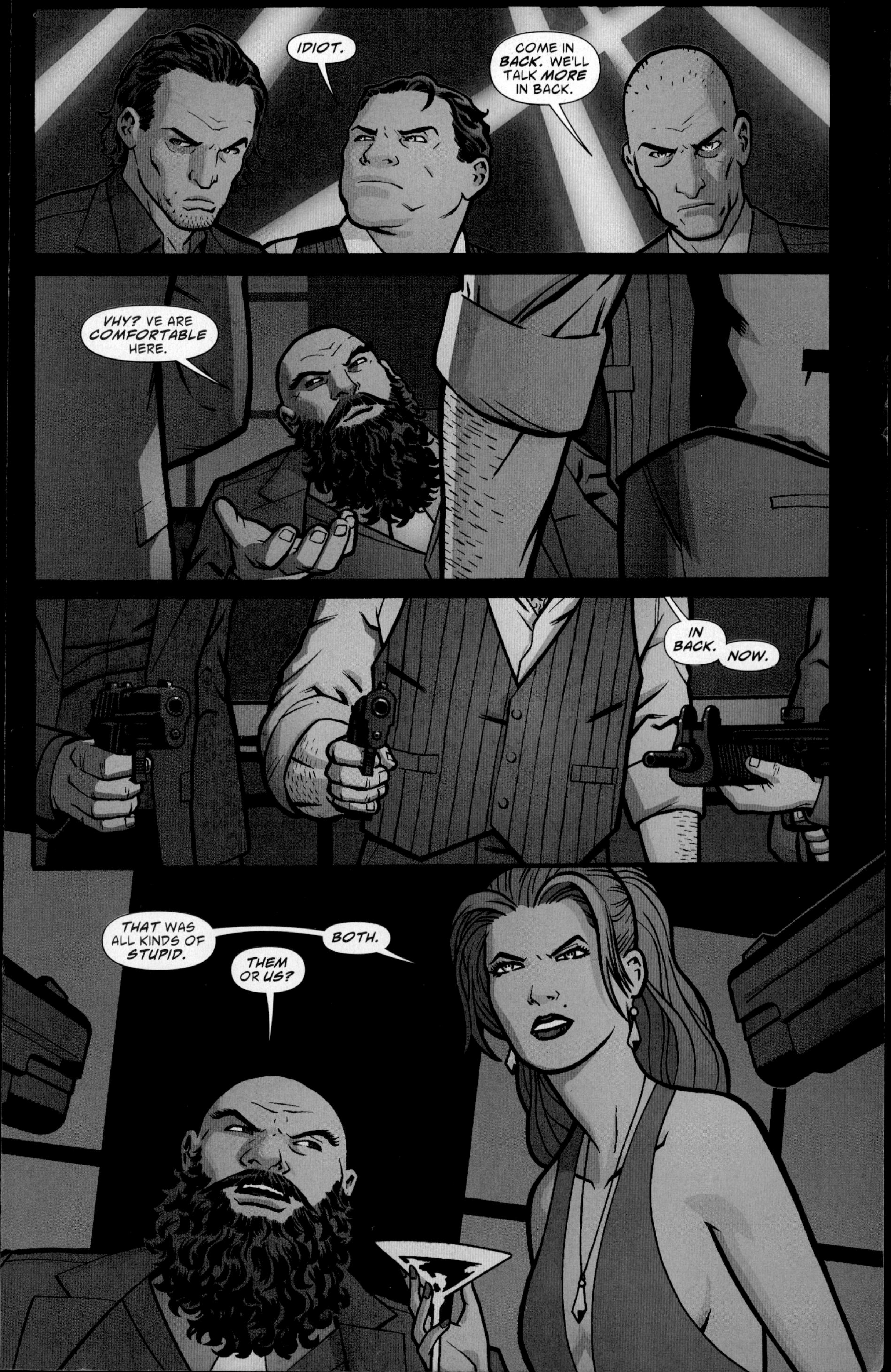
IDIOT.
COME IN BACK. WE'LL TALK MORE IN BACK.
VHY? VE ARE COMFORTABLE HERE.
IN BACK. NOW.
THAT WAS ALL KINDS OF STUPID.
THEM OR US?
BOTH.

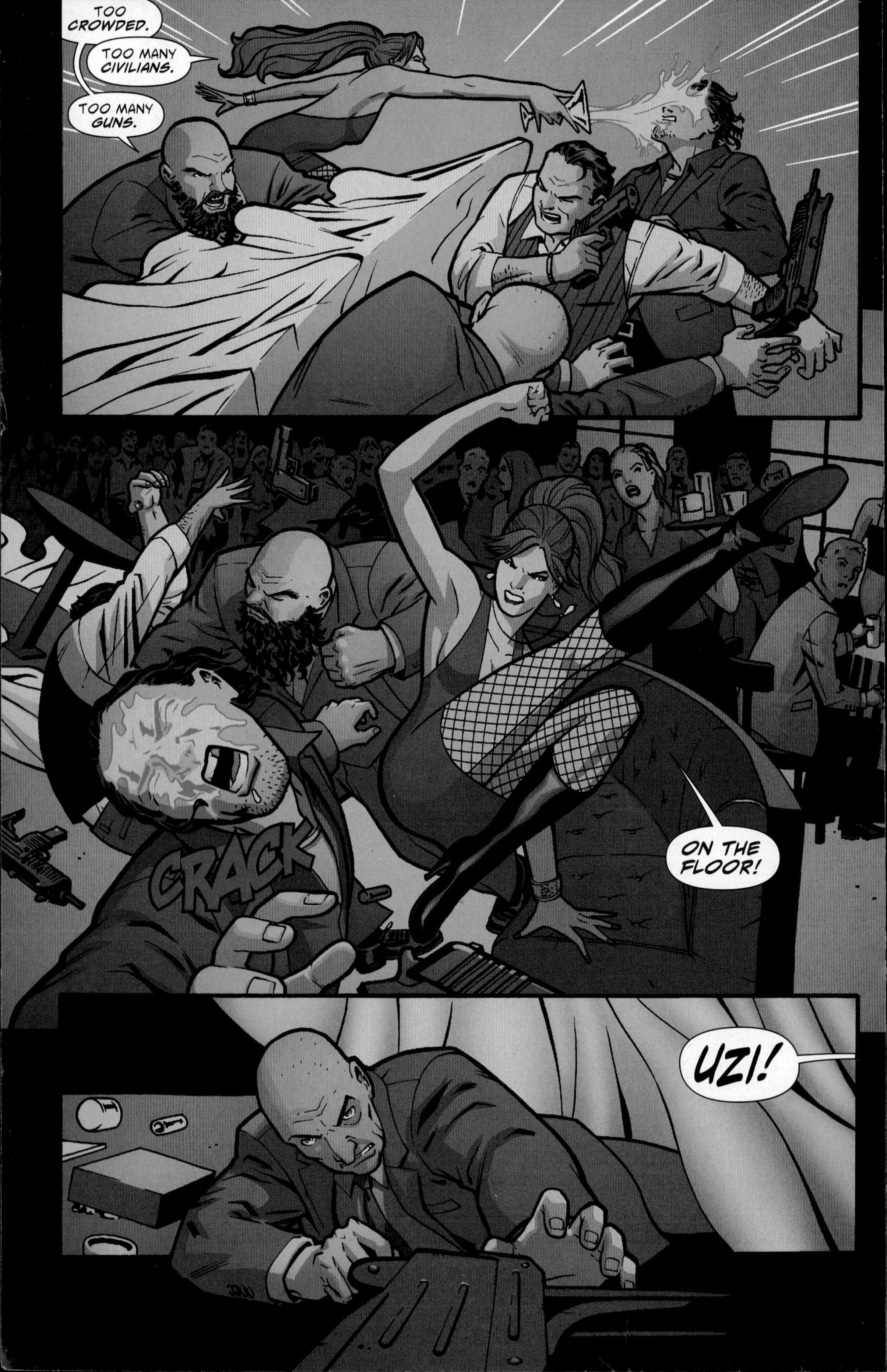
TOO CROWDED.
TOO MANY CIVILIANS.
TOO MANY GUNS.
CRACK
ON THE FLOOR!
UZI!

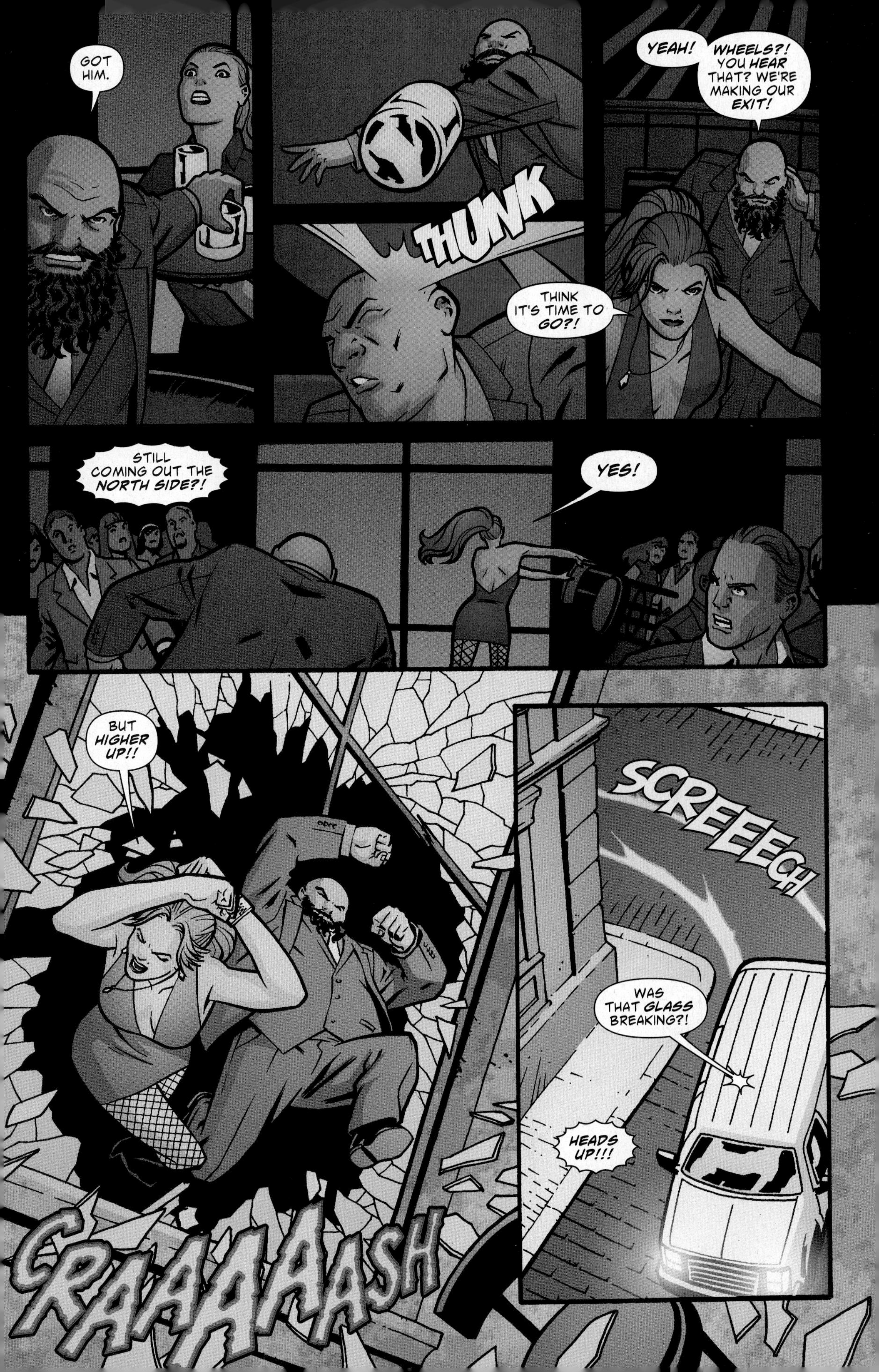
GOT HIM.
THUNK
THINK IT'S TIME TO GO?!
YEAH!
WHEELS?! YOU HEAR THAT? WE'RE MAKING OUR EXIT!
STILL COMING OUT THE NORTH SIDE?!
YES!
BUT HIGHER UP!!
CRAAAAAASH
SCREEEECH
WAS THAT GLASS BREAKING?!
HEADS UP!!!

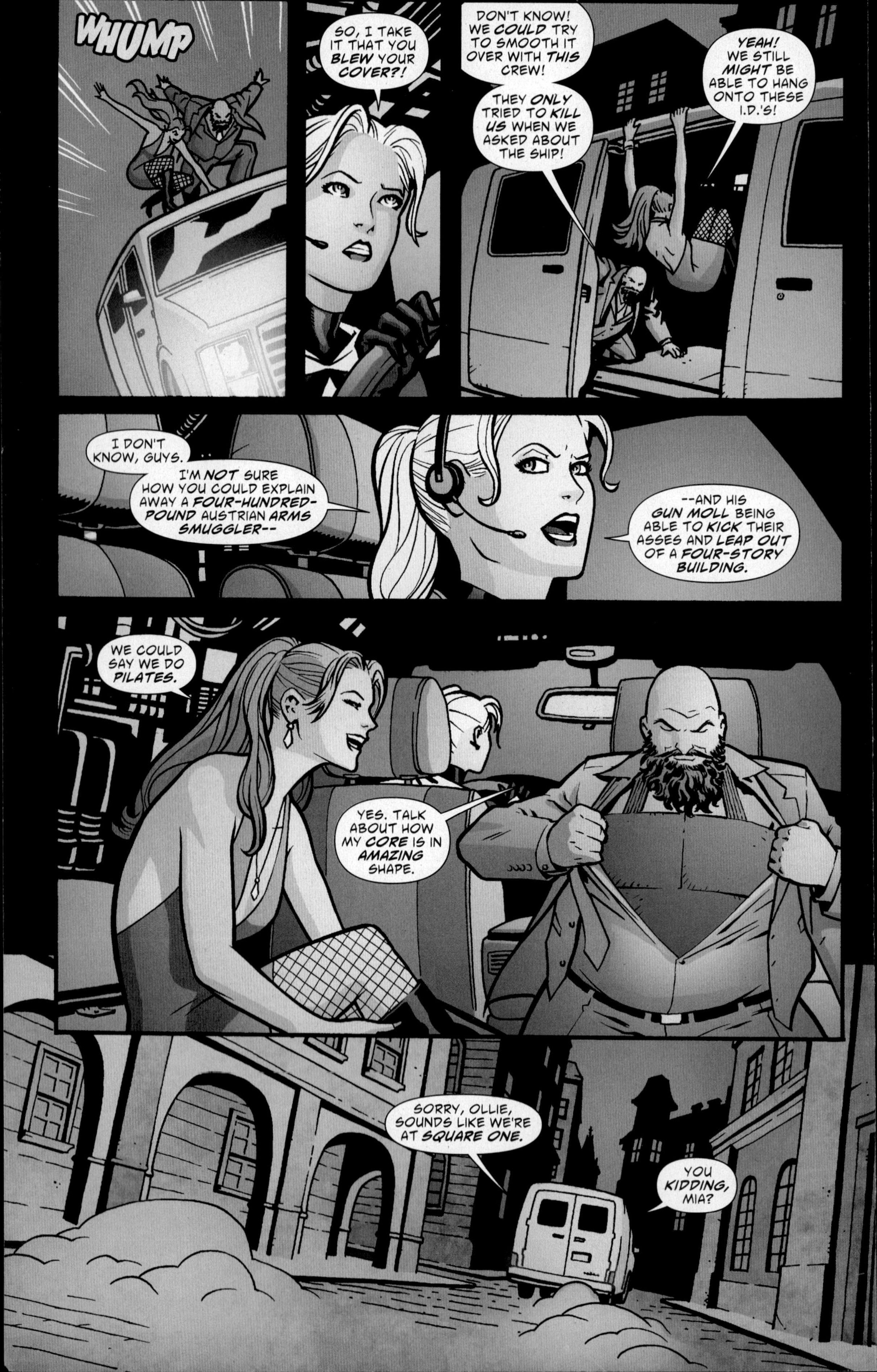
WHUMP
SO, I TAKE IT THAT YOU BLEW YOUR COVER?!
DON'T KNOW! WE COULD TRY TO SMOOTH IT OVER WITH THIS CREW!
THEY ONLY TRIED TO KILL US WHEN WE ASKED ABOUT THE SHIP!
YEAH! WE STILL MIGHT BE ABLE TO HANG ONTO THESE I.D.'S!
I DON'T KNOW, GUYS.
I'M NOT SURE HOW YOU COULD EXPLAIN AWAY A FOUR-HUNDRED-POUND AUSTRIAN ARMS SMUGGLER--
--AND HIS GUN MOLL BEING ABLE TO KICK THEIR ASSES AND LEAP OUT OF A FOUR-STORY BUILDING.
WE COULD SAY WE DO PILATES.
YES. TALK ABOUT HOW MY CORE IS IN AMAZING SHAPE.
SORRY, OLLIE, SOUNDS LIKE WE'RE AT SQUARE ONE.
YOU KIDDING, MIA?

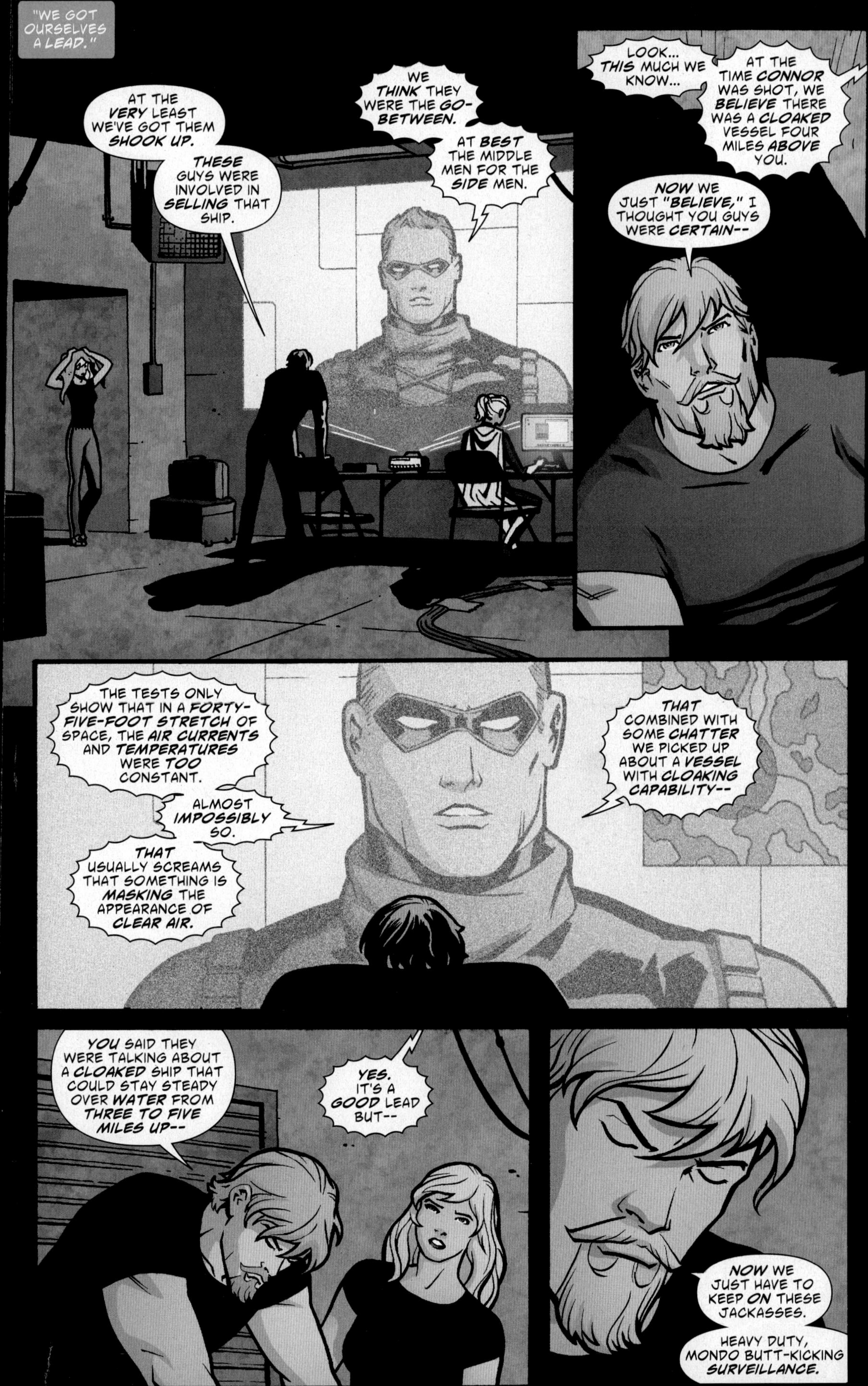
"WE GOT OURSELVES A LEAD."
AT THE VERY LEAST WE'VE GOT THEM SHOOK UP.
THESE GUYS WERE INVOLVED IN SELLING THAT SHIP.
WE THINK THEY WERE THE GO-BETWEEN.
AT BEST THE MIDDLE MEN FOR THE SIDE MEN.
LOOK... THIS MUCH WE KNOW...
AT THE TIME CONNOR WAS SHOT, WE BELIEVE THERE WAS A CLOAKED VESSEL FOUR MILES ABOVE YOU.
NOW WE JUST "BELIEVE," I THOUGHT YOU GUYS WERE CERTAIN--
THE TESTS ONLY SHOW THAT IN A FORTY-FIVE-FOOT STRETCH OF SPACE, THE AIR CURRENTS AND TEMPERATURES WERE TOO CONSTANT.
ALMOST IMPOSSIBLY SO.
THAT USUALLY SCREAMS THAT SOMETHING IS MASKING THE APPEARANCE OF CLEAR AIR.
THAT COMBINED WITH SOME CHATTER WE PICKED UP ABOUT A VESSEL WITH CLOAKING CAPABILITY--
YOU SAID THEY WERE TALKING ABOUT A CLOAKED SHIP THAT COULD STAY STEADY OVER WATER FROM THREE TO FIVE MILES UP--
YES. IT'S A GOOD LEAD BUT--
NOW WE JUST HAVE TO KEEP ON THESE JACKASSES.
HEAVY DUTY, MONDO BUTT-KICKING SURVEILLANCE.

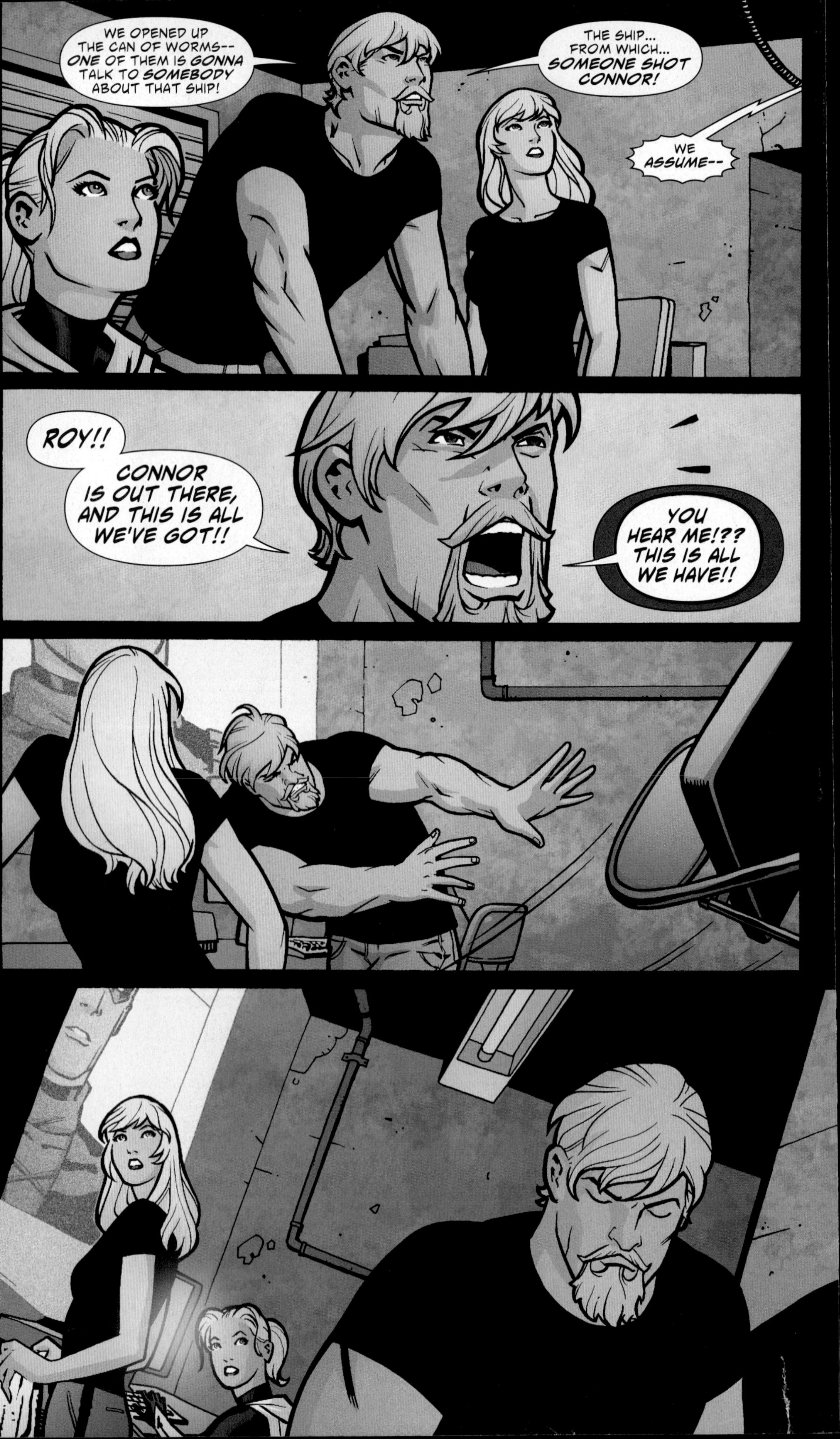
WE OPENED UP THE CAN OF WORMS-- ONE OF THEM IS GONNA TALK TO SOMEBODY ABOUT THAT SHIP!
THE SHIP... FROM WHICH... SOMEONE SHOT CONNOR!
WE ASSUME--
ROY!!
CONNOR IS OUT THERE, AND THIS IS ALL WE'VE GOT!!
YOU HEAR ME!?? THIS IS ALL WE HAVE!!

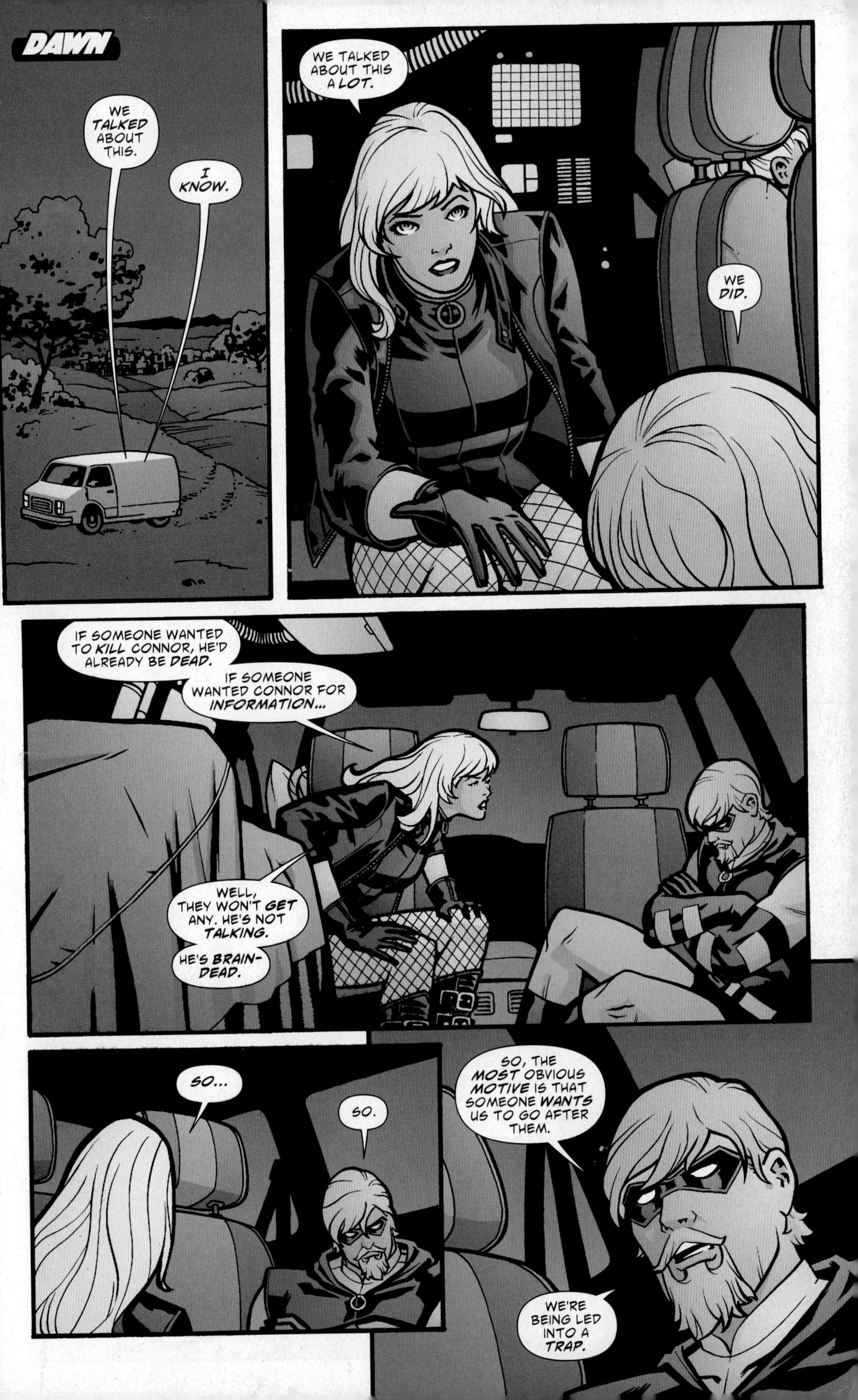
DAWN
WE TALKED ABOUT THIS.
I KNOW.
WE TALKED ABOUT THIS A LOT.
WE DID.
IF SOMEONE WANTED TO KILL CONNOR, HE'D ALREADY BE DEAD.
IF SOMEONE WANTED CONNOR FOR INFORMATION...
WELL, THEY WON'T GET ANY. HE'S NOT TALKING.
HE'S BRAIN-DEAD.
SO...
SO.
SO, THE MOST OBVIOUS MOTIVE IS THAT SOMEONE WANTS US TO GO AFTER THEM.
WE'RE BEING LED INTO A TRAP.

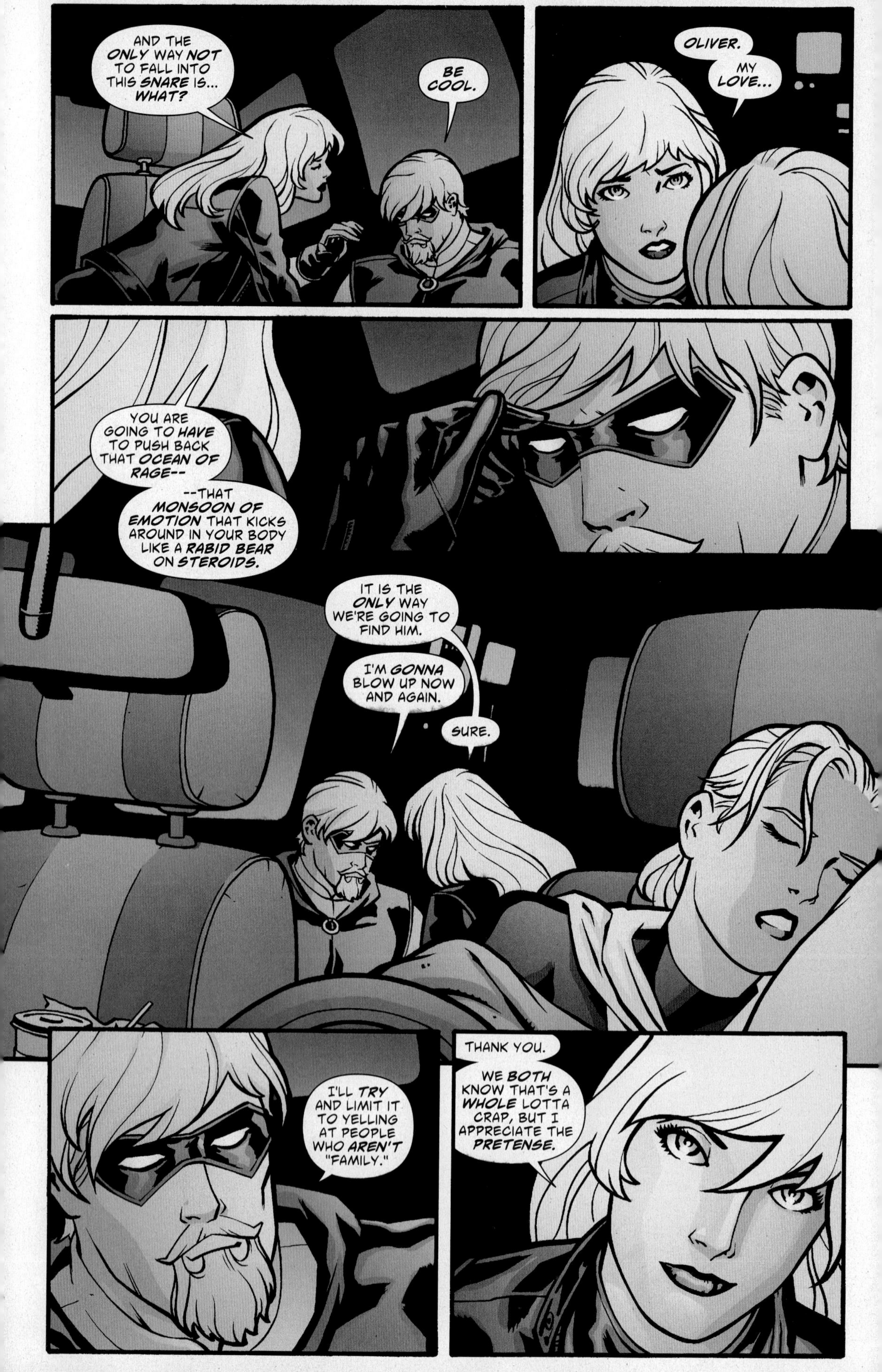
AND THE ONLY WAY NOT TO FALL INTO THIS SNARE IS... WHAT?
BE COOL.
OLIVER.
MY LOVE...
YOU ARE GOING TO HAVE TO PUSH BACK THAT OCEAN OF RAGE--
--THAT MONSOON OF EMOTION THAT KICKS AROUND IN YOUR BODY LIKE A RABID BEAR ON STEROIDS.
IT IS THE ONLY WAY WE'RE GOING TO FIND HIM.
I'M GONNA BLOW UP NOW AND AGAIN.
SURE.
I'LL TRY AND LIMIT IT TO YELLING AT PEOPLE WHO AREN'T "FAMILY."
THANK YOU.
WE BOTH KNOW THAT'S A WHOLE LOTTA CRAP, BUT I APPRECIATE THE PRETENSE.

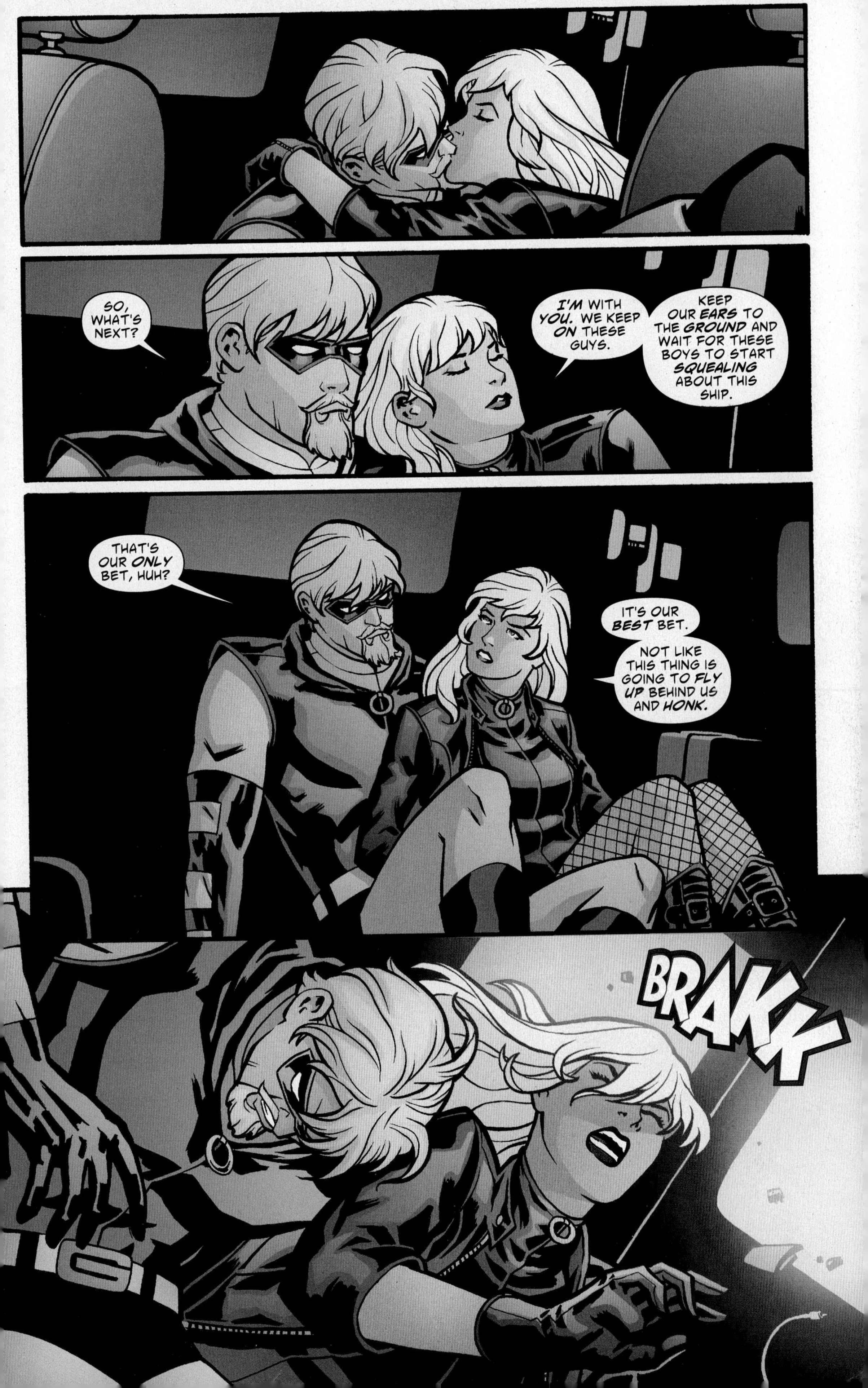
SO, WHAT'S NEXT?
I'M WITH YOU. WE KEEP ON THESE GUYS.
KEEP OUR EARS TO THE GROUND AND WAIT FOR THESE BOYS TO START SQUEALING ABOUT THIS SHIP.
THAT'S OUR ONLY BET, HUH?
IT'S OUR BEST BET.
NOT LIKE THIS THING IS GOING TO FLY UP BEHIND US AND HONK.
BRAKK

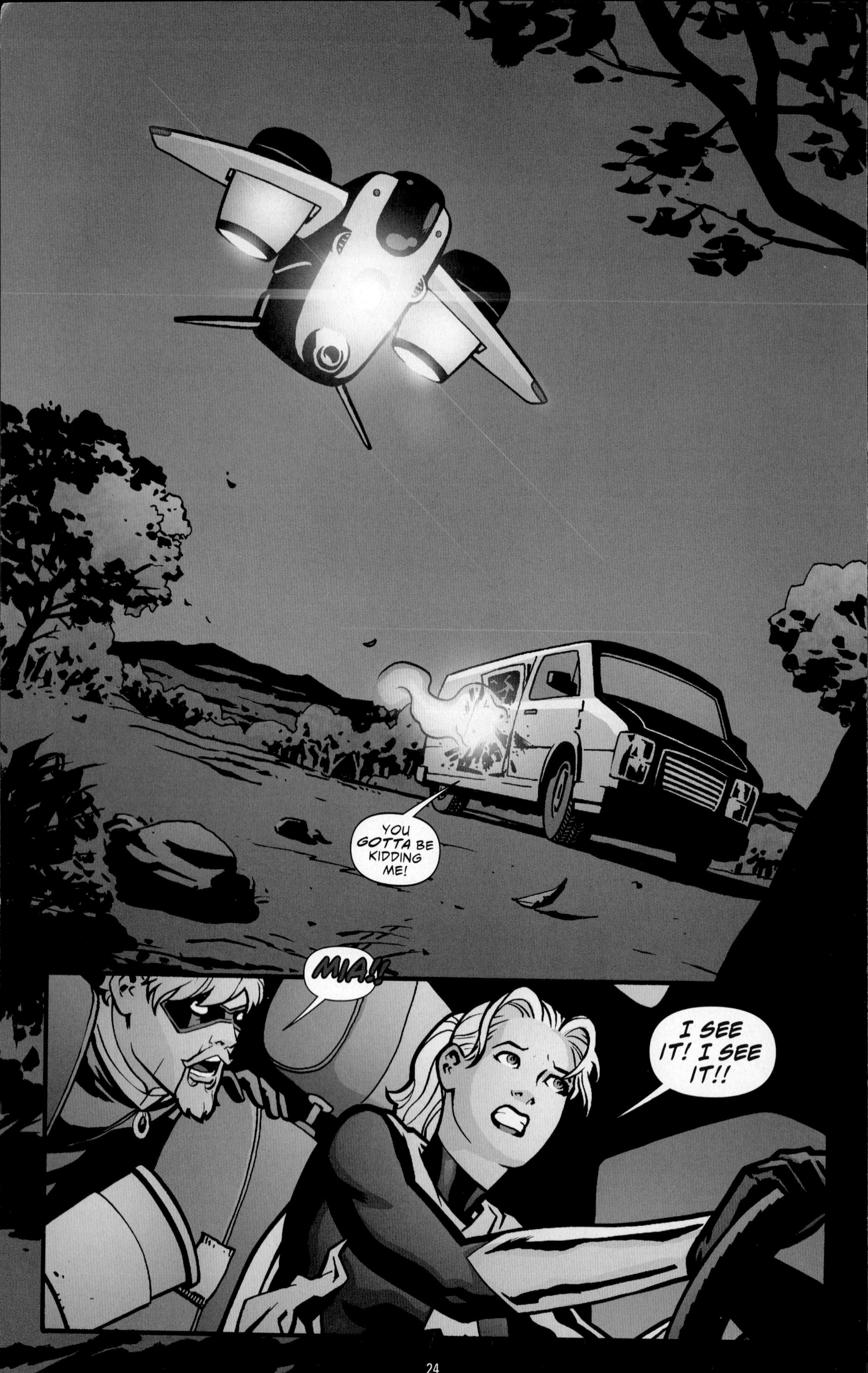
YOU GOTTA BE KIDDING ME!
MIA!!
I SEE IT! I SEE IT!!

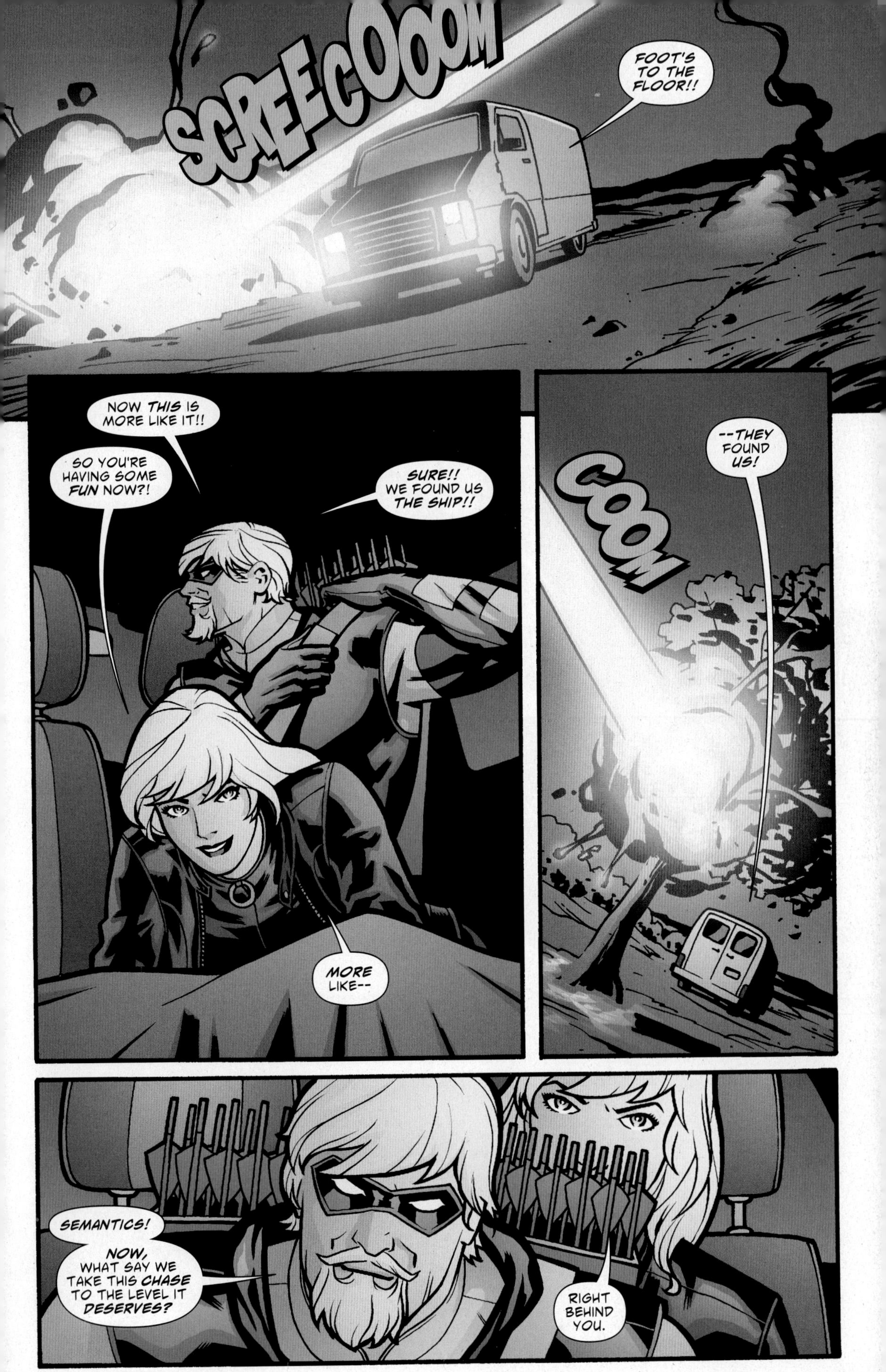
SCREECOOOM
FOOT'S TO THE FLOOR!!
NOW THIS IS MORE LIKE IT!!
SO YOU'RE HAVING SOME FUN NOW?!
SURE!! WE FOUND US THE SHIP!!
MORE LIKE--
COOOM
--THEY FOUND US!
SEMANTICS!
NOW, WHAT SAY WE TAKE THIS CHASE TO THE LEVEL IT DESERVES?
RIGHT BEHIND YOU.

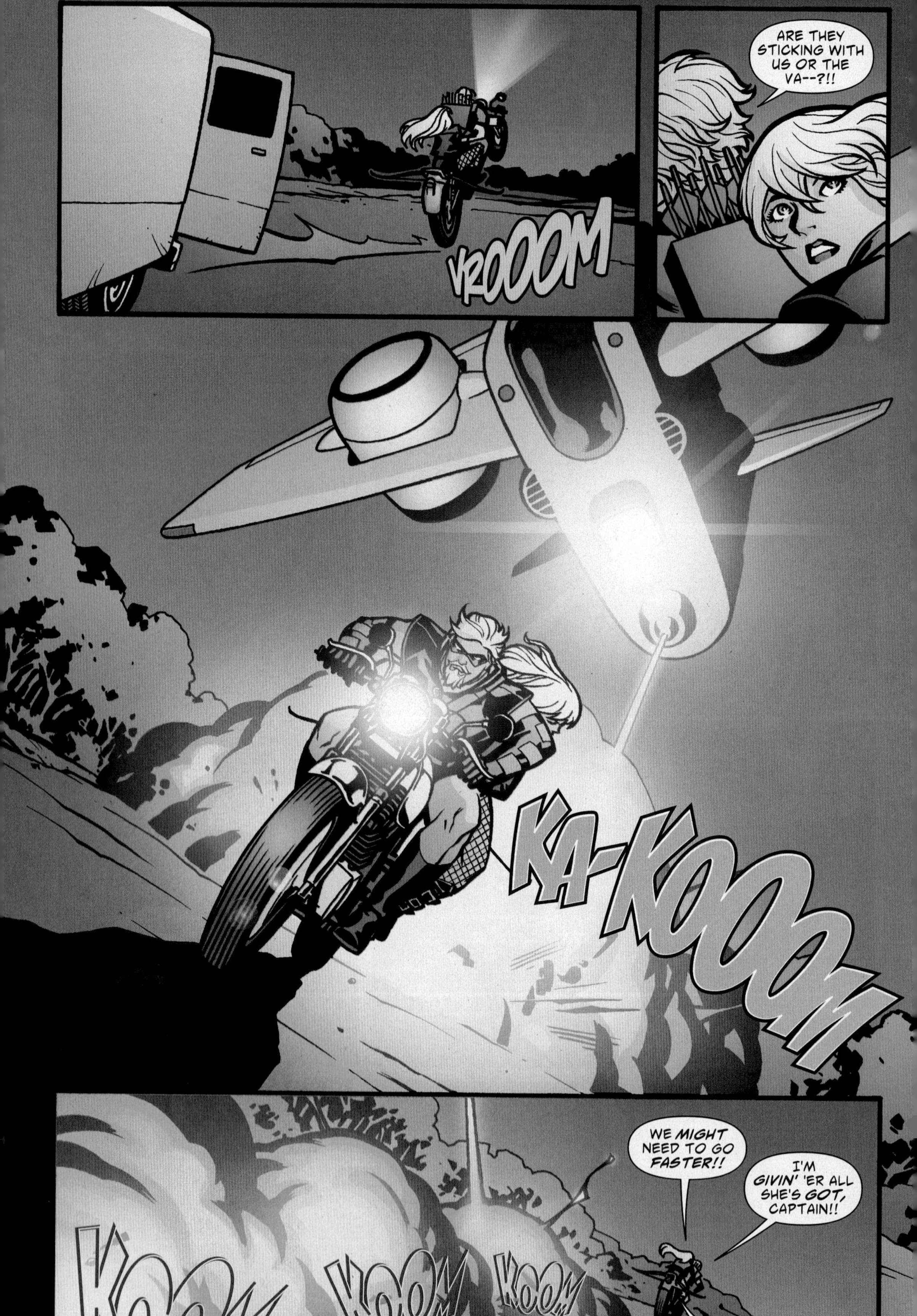
VROOOM
ARE THEY STICKING WITH US OR THE VA--?!!
KA-KOOOOM
KOOOM
KOOOM
KOOOM
WE MIGHT NEED TO GO FASTER!!
I'M GIVIN' 'ER ALL SHE'S GOT, CAPTAIN!!
WELL, THEN WE MIGHT NEED BETTER MANEUVERABILITY!!

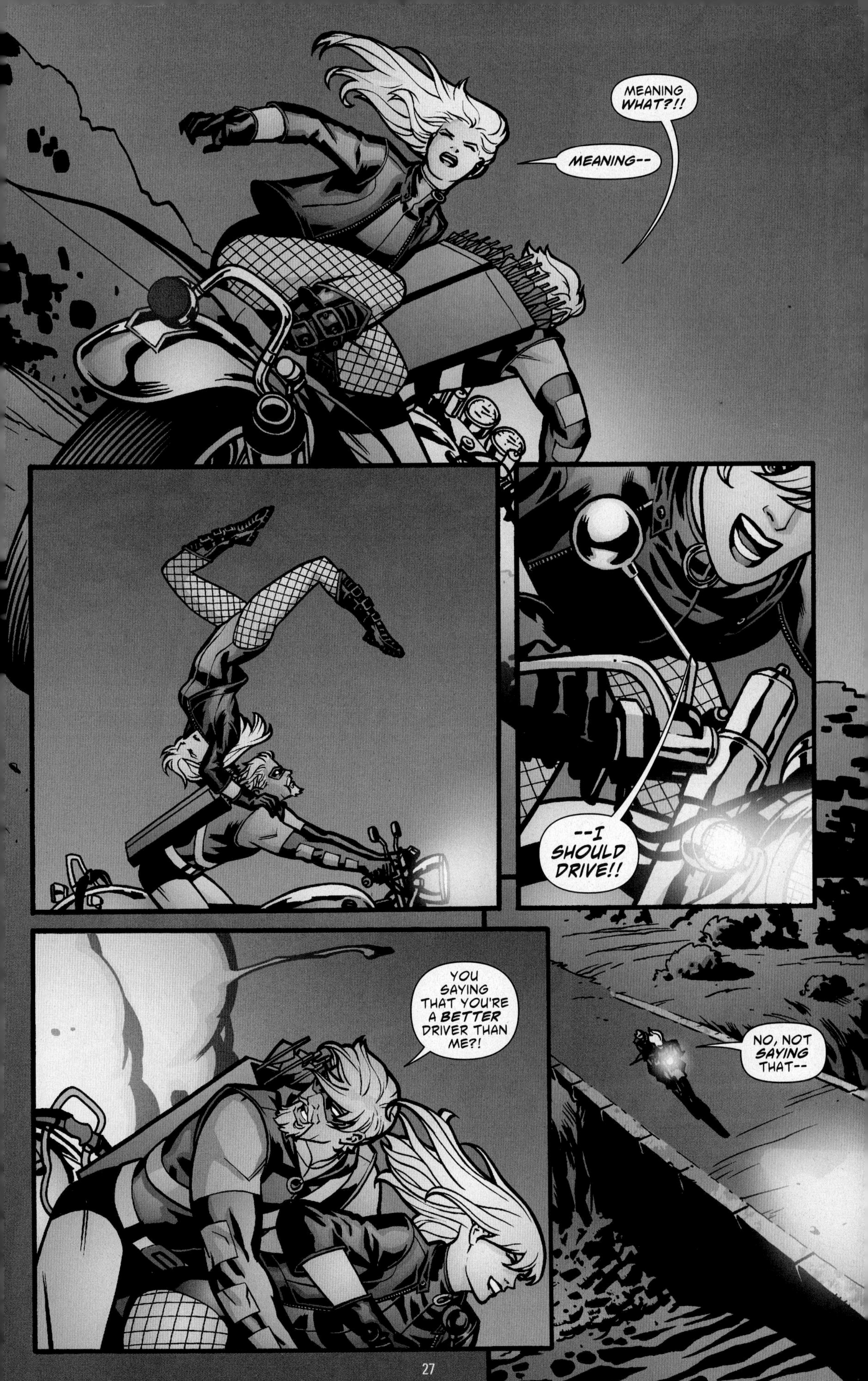
MEANING--
MEANING WHAT?!!
--I SHOULD DRIVE!!
YOU SAYING THAT YOU'RE A BETTER DRIVER THAN ME?!
NO, NOT SAYING THAT--

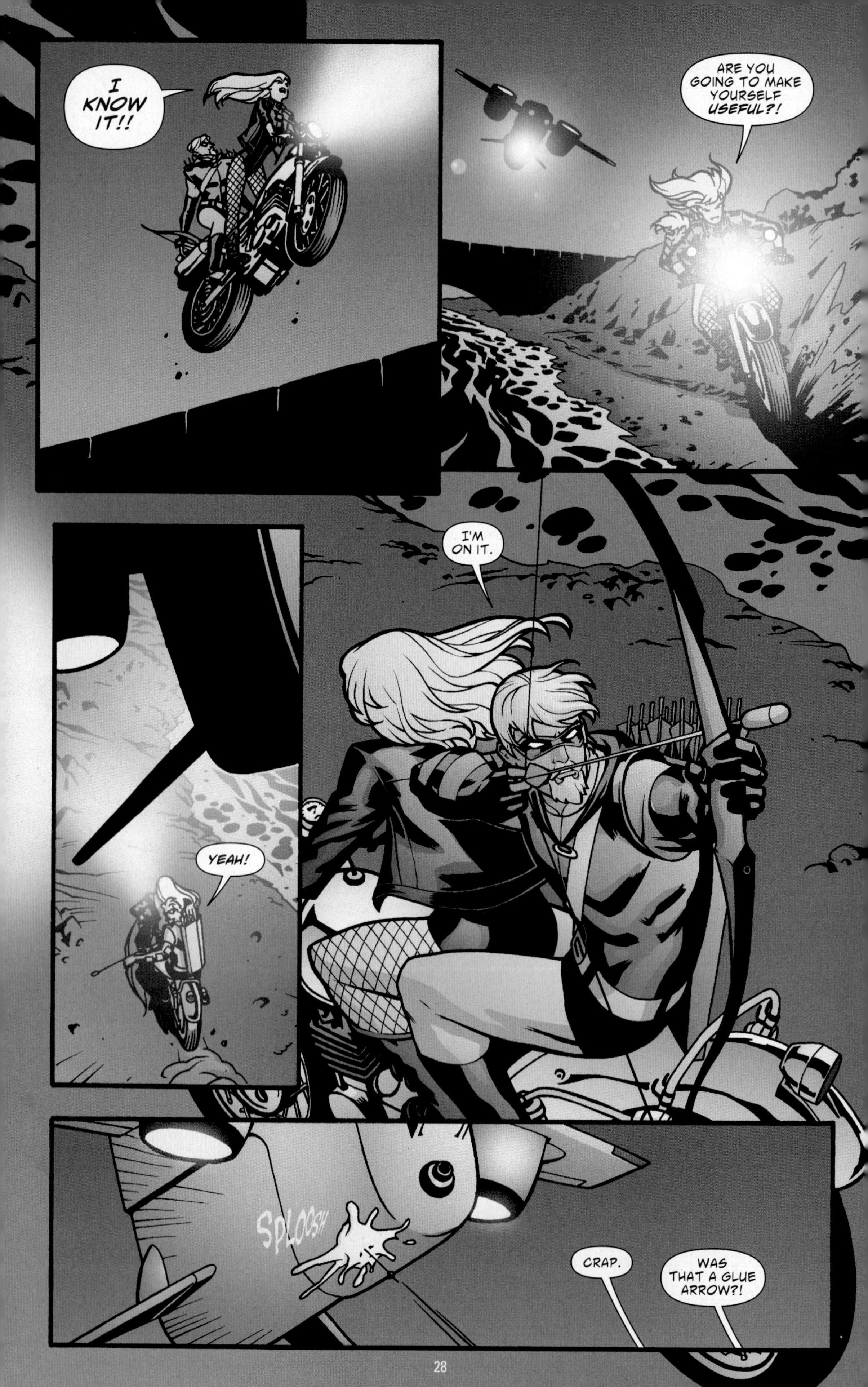
I KNOW IT!!
ARE YOU GOING TO MAKE YOURSELF USEFUL?!
I'M ON IT.
YEAH!
SPLOOSH
CRAP.
WAS THAT A GLUE ARROW?!

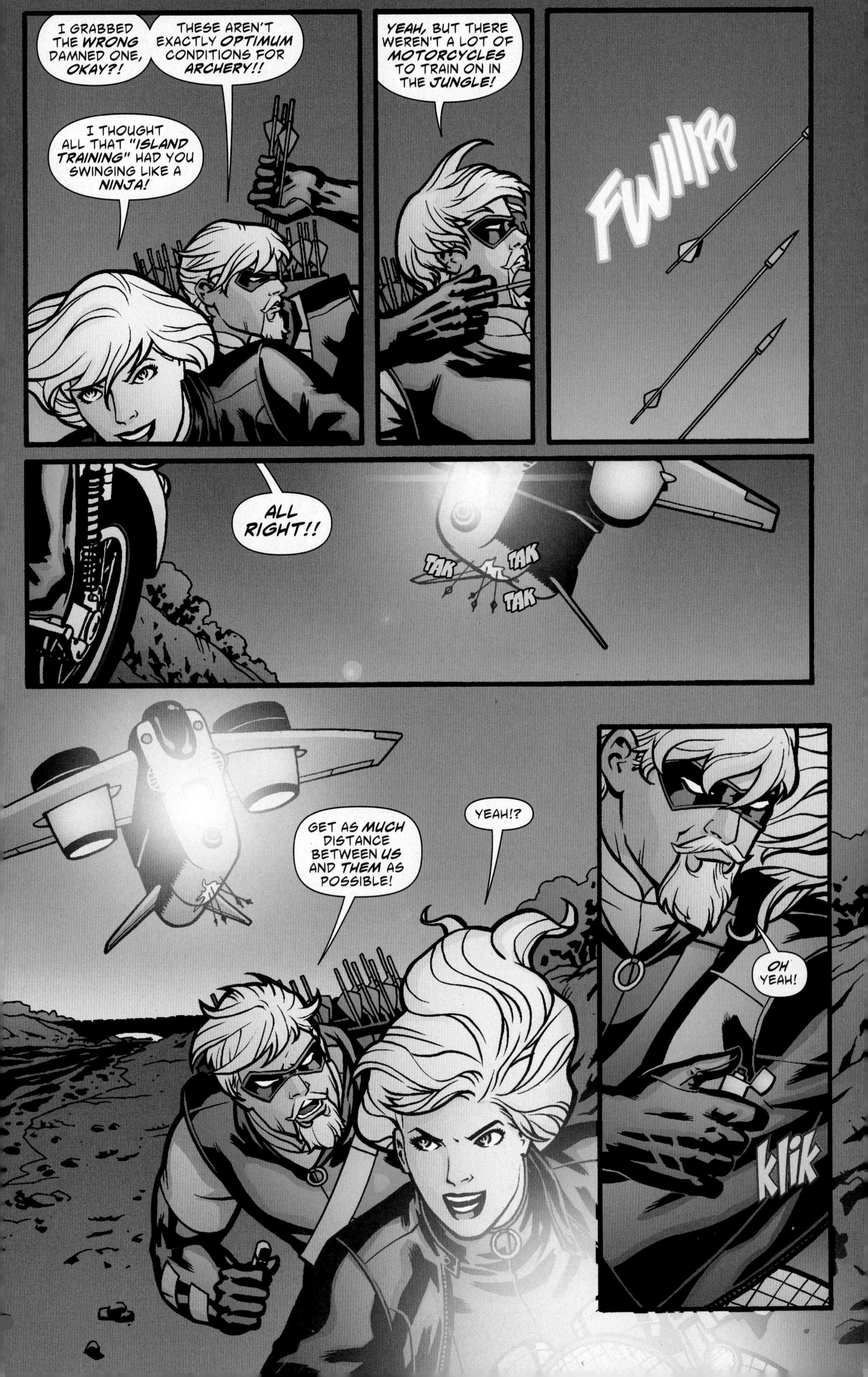
I GRABBED THE WRONG DAMNED ONE, OKAY?!
THESE AREN'T EXACTLY OPTIMUM CONDITIONS FOR ARCHERY!!
I THOUGHT ALL THAT "ISLAND TRAINING" HAD YOU SWINGING LIKE A NINJA!
YEAH, BUT THERE WEREN'T A LOT OF MOTORCYCLES TO TRAIN ON IN THE JUNGLE!
FWIIPP
ALL RIGHT!!
TAK
TAK
TAK
GET AS MUCH DISTANCE BETWEEN US AND THEM AS POSSIBLE!
YEAH!?
OH YEAH!
klik

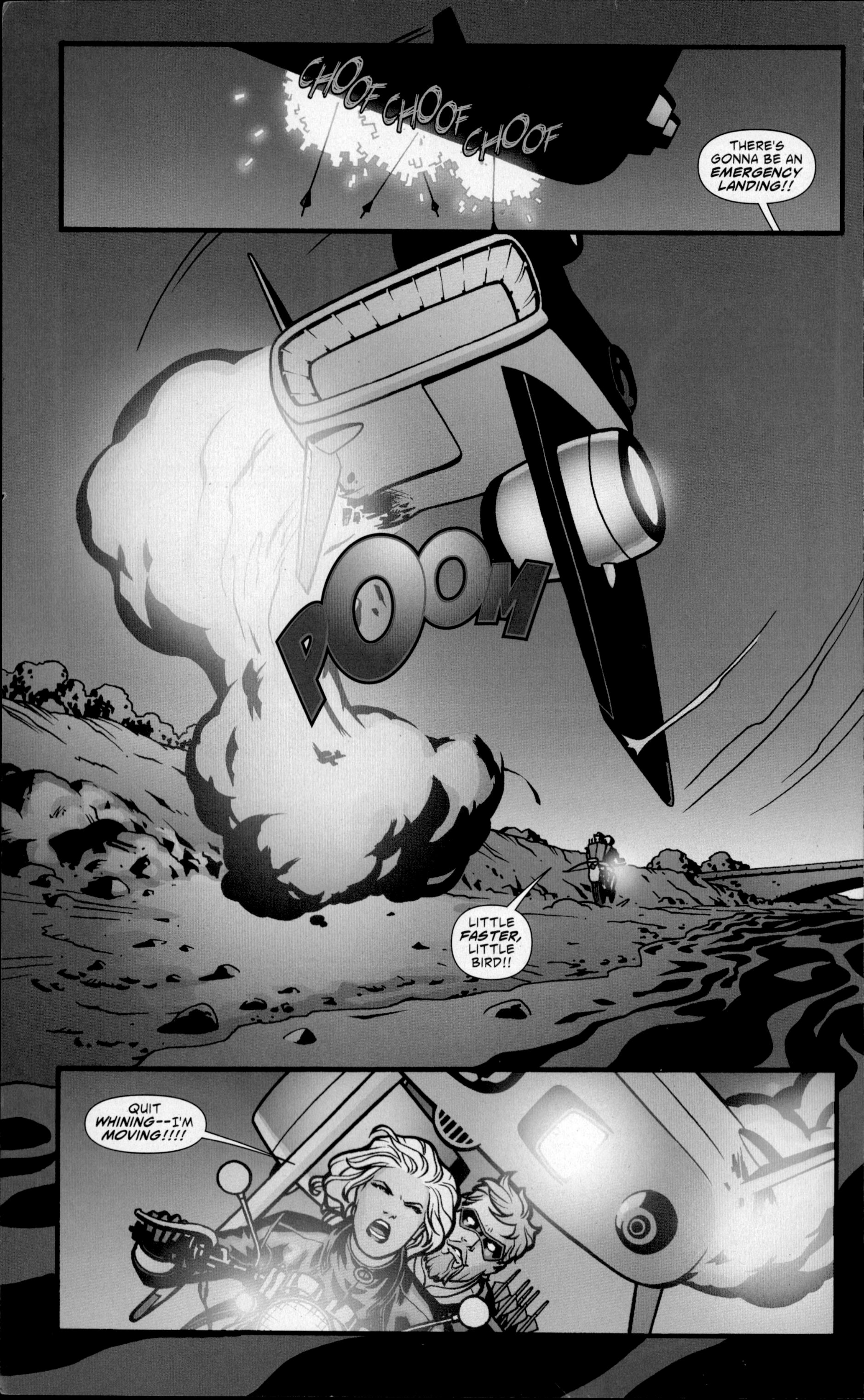
CHOOF CHOOF CHOOF
THERE'S GONNA BE AN EMERGENCY LANDING!!
POOM
LITTLE FASTER, LITTLE BIRD!!
QUIT WHINING--I'M MOVING!!!!

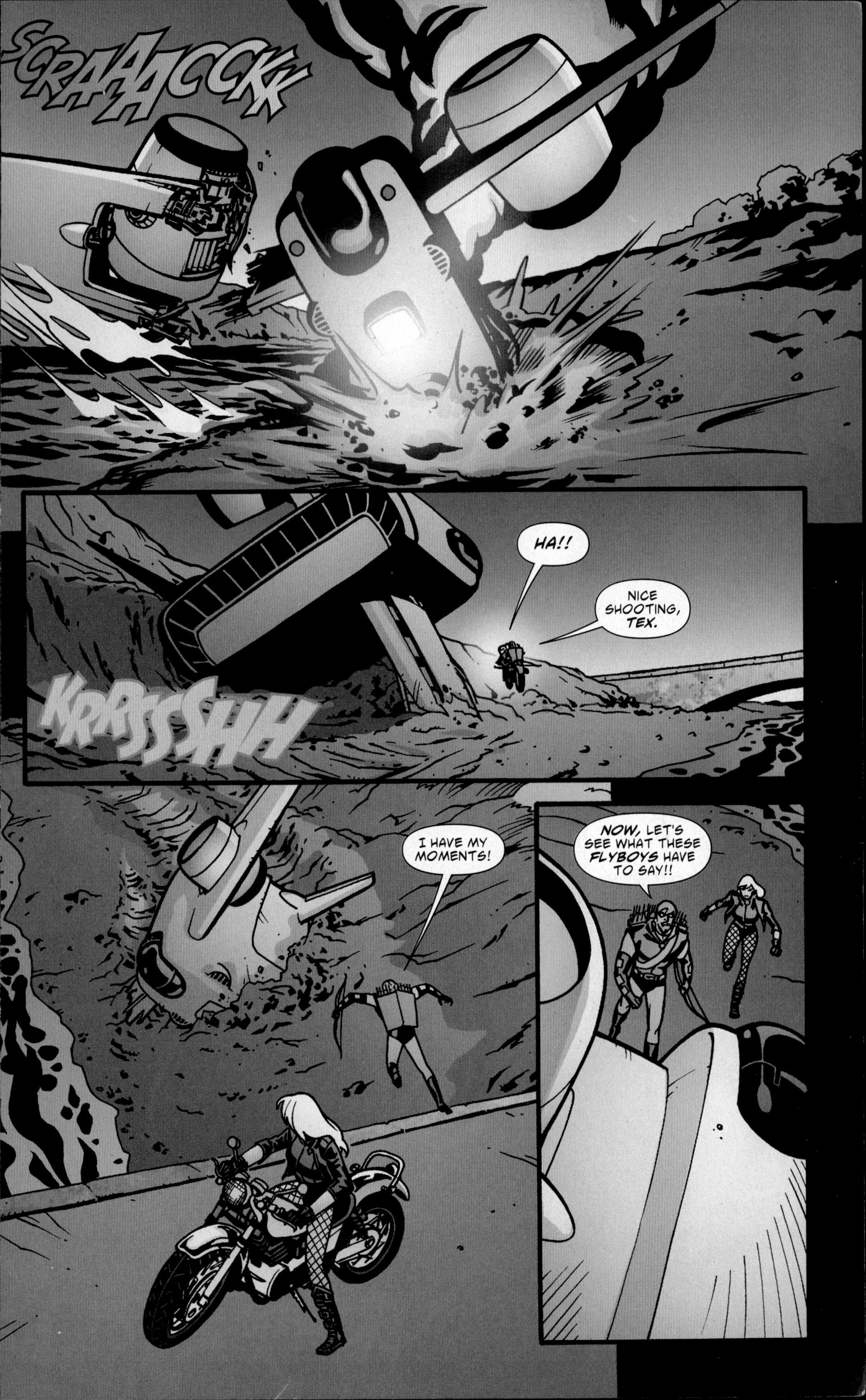
SCRAAACCKK
HA!!
NICE SHOOTING, TEX.
KRASSSHH
I HAVE MY MOMENTS!
NOW, LET'S SEE WHAT THESE FLYBOYS HAVE TO SAY!!

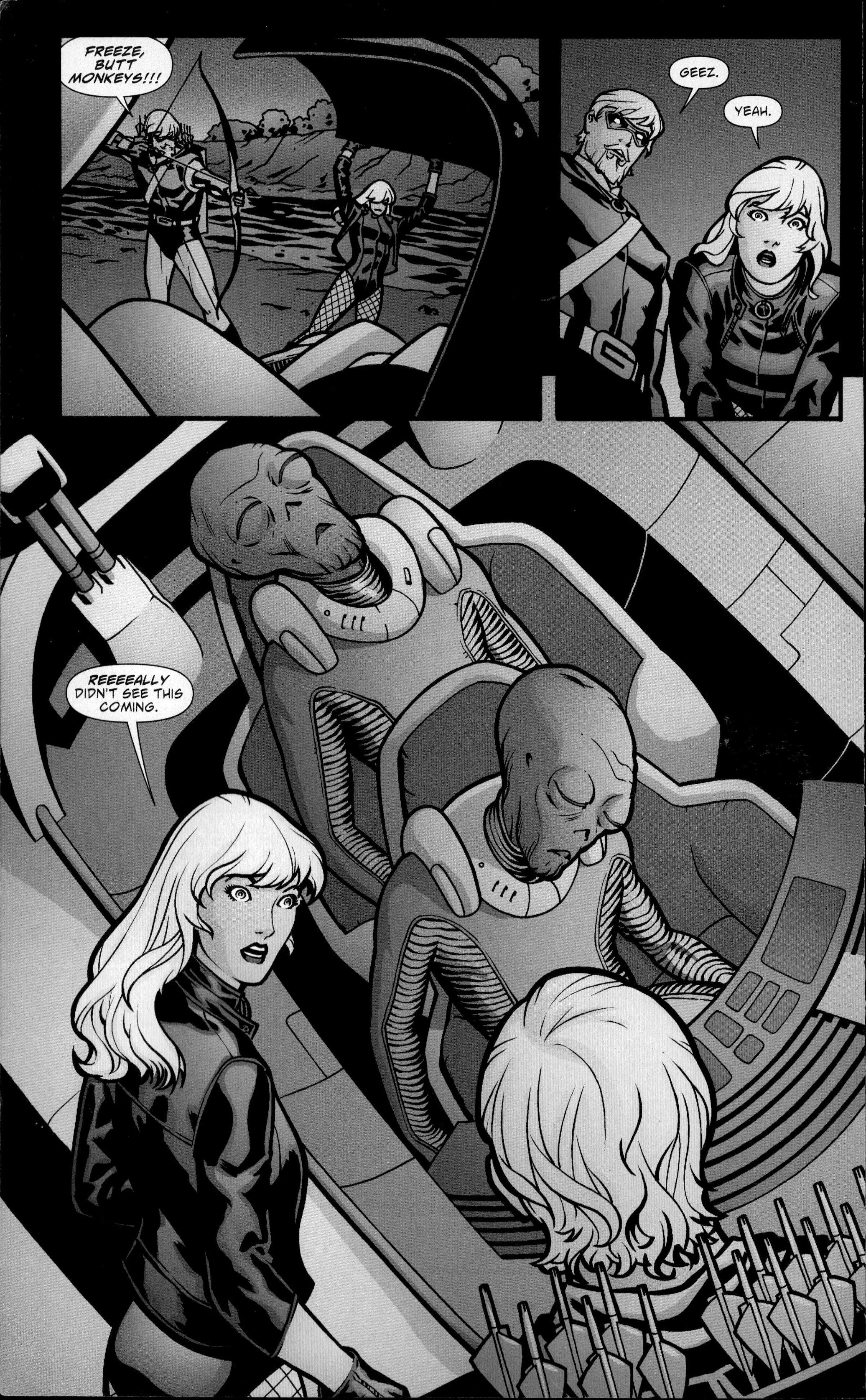
FREEZE, BUTT MONKEYS!!!
GEEZ.
YEAH.
REEEEALLY DIDN'T SEE THIS COMING.

GREEN ARROW AND
BLACK CANARY 7

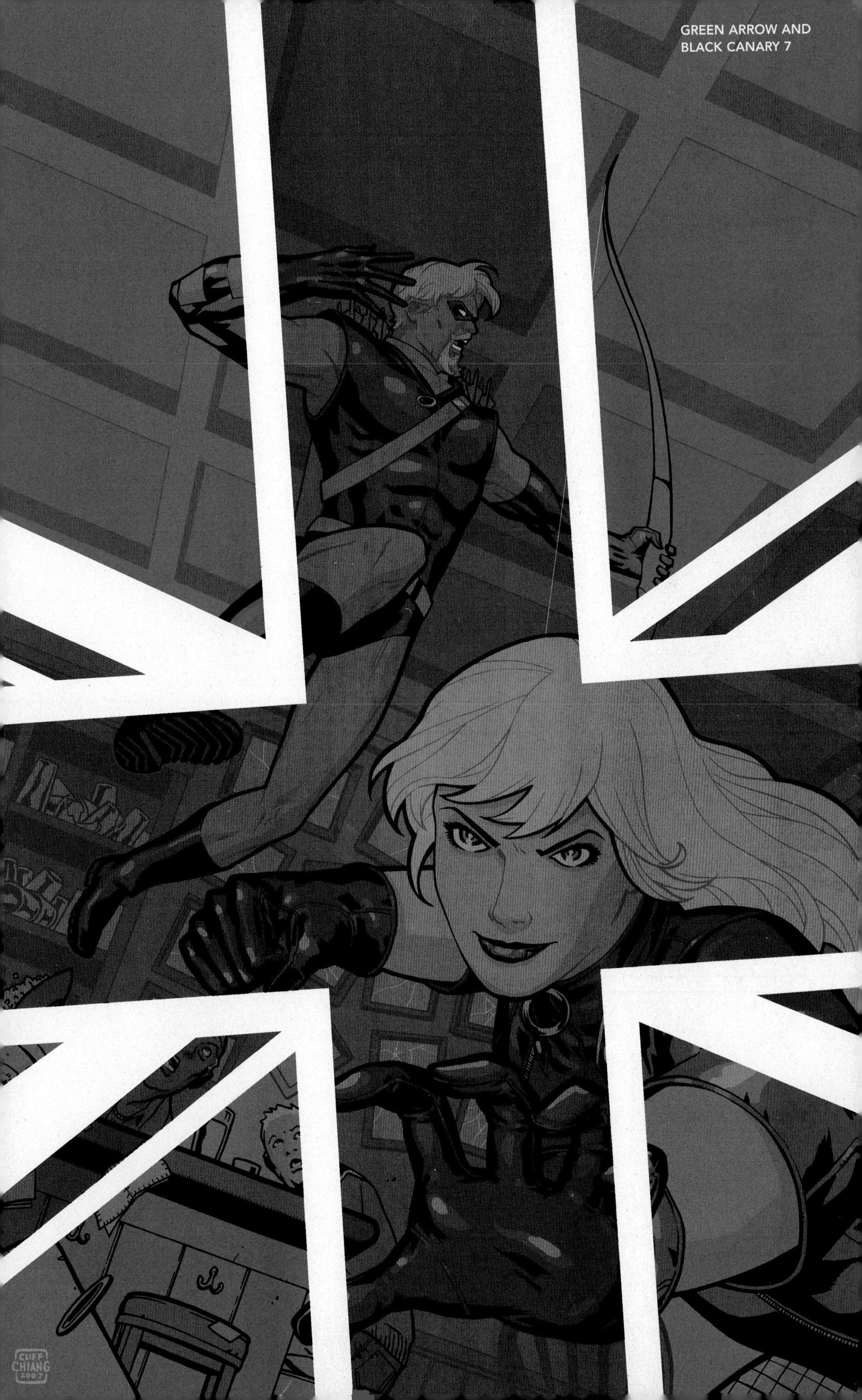
CLIFF
CHIANG
2007

HAYSTACK

PART 2: GREETINGS FROM FAR AWAY LANDS

JUDD WINICK
STORY

CLIFF CHIANG
ART

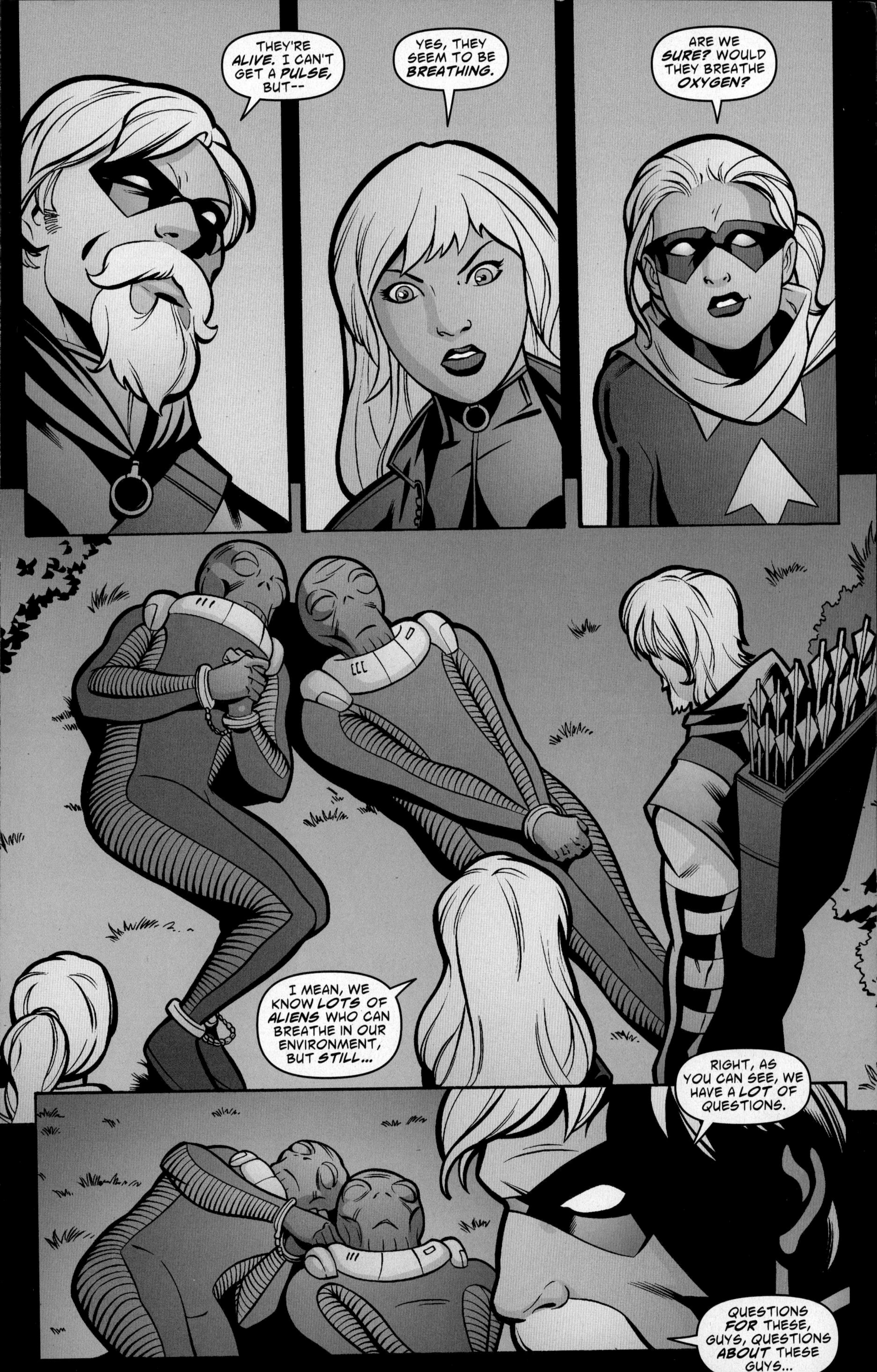
THEY'RE ALIVE. I CAN'T GET A PULSE, BUT--
YES, THEY SEEM TO BE BREATHING.
ARE WE SURE? WOULD THEY BREATHE THE OXYGEN?
I MEAN, WE KNOW LOTS OF ALIENS WHO CAN BREATHE IN OUR ENVIRONMENT, BUT STILL...
RIGHT, AS YOU CAN SEE, WE HAVE A LOT OF QUESTIONS.
QUESTIONS FOR THESE, GUYS, QUESTIONS ABOUT THESE GUYS...

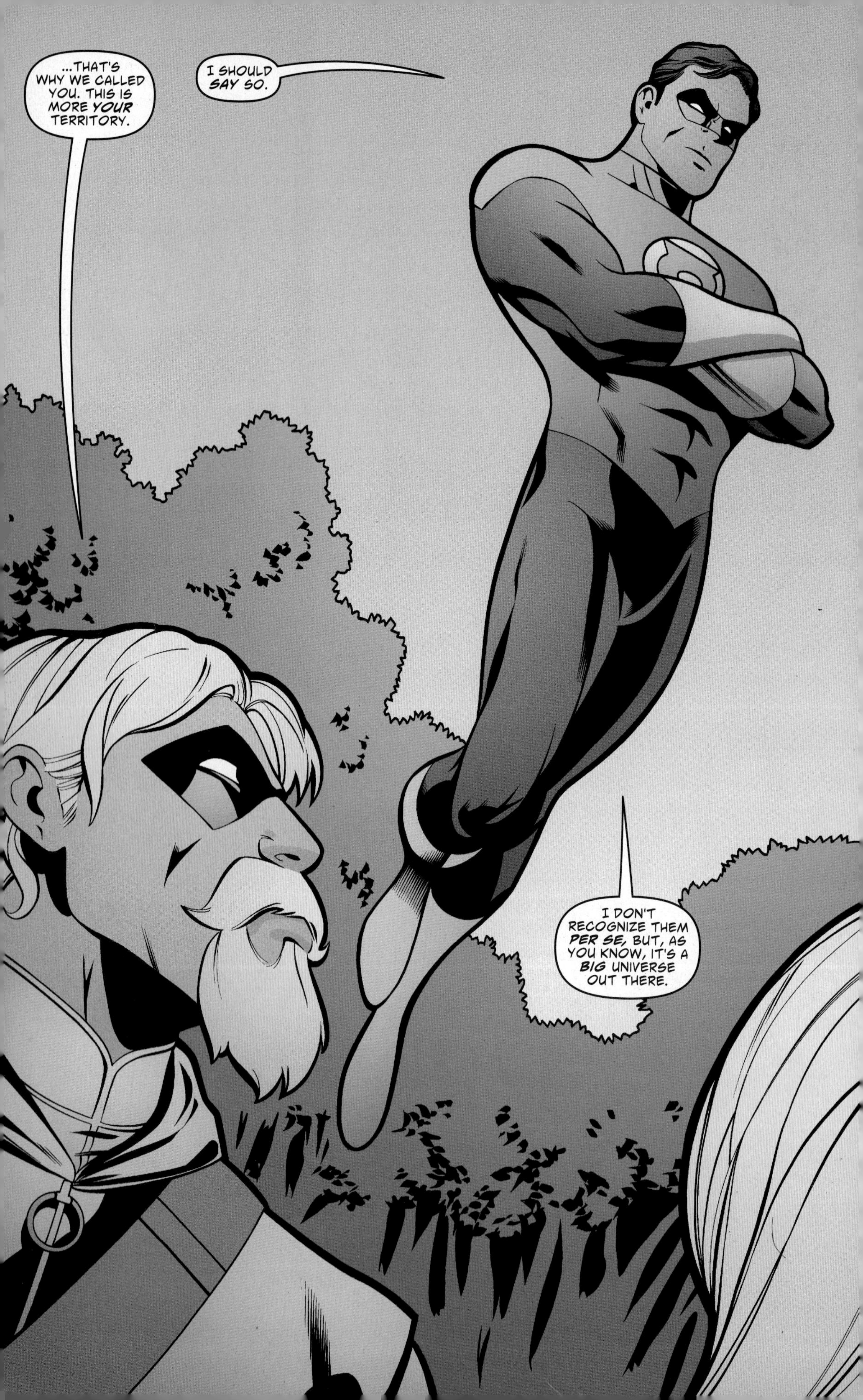
...THAT'S WHY WE CALLED YOU. THIS IS MORE *YOUR* TERRITORY.
I SHOULD *SAY* SO.
I DON'T RECOGNIZE THEM *PER SE*, BUT, AS YOU KNOW, IT'S A *BIG* UNIVERSE OUT THERE.

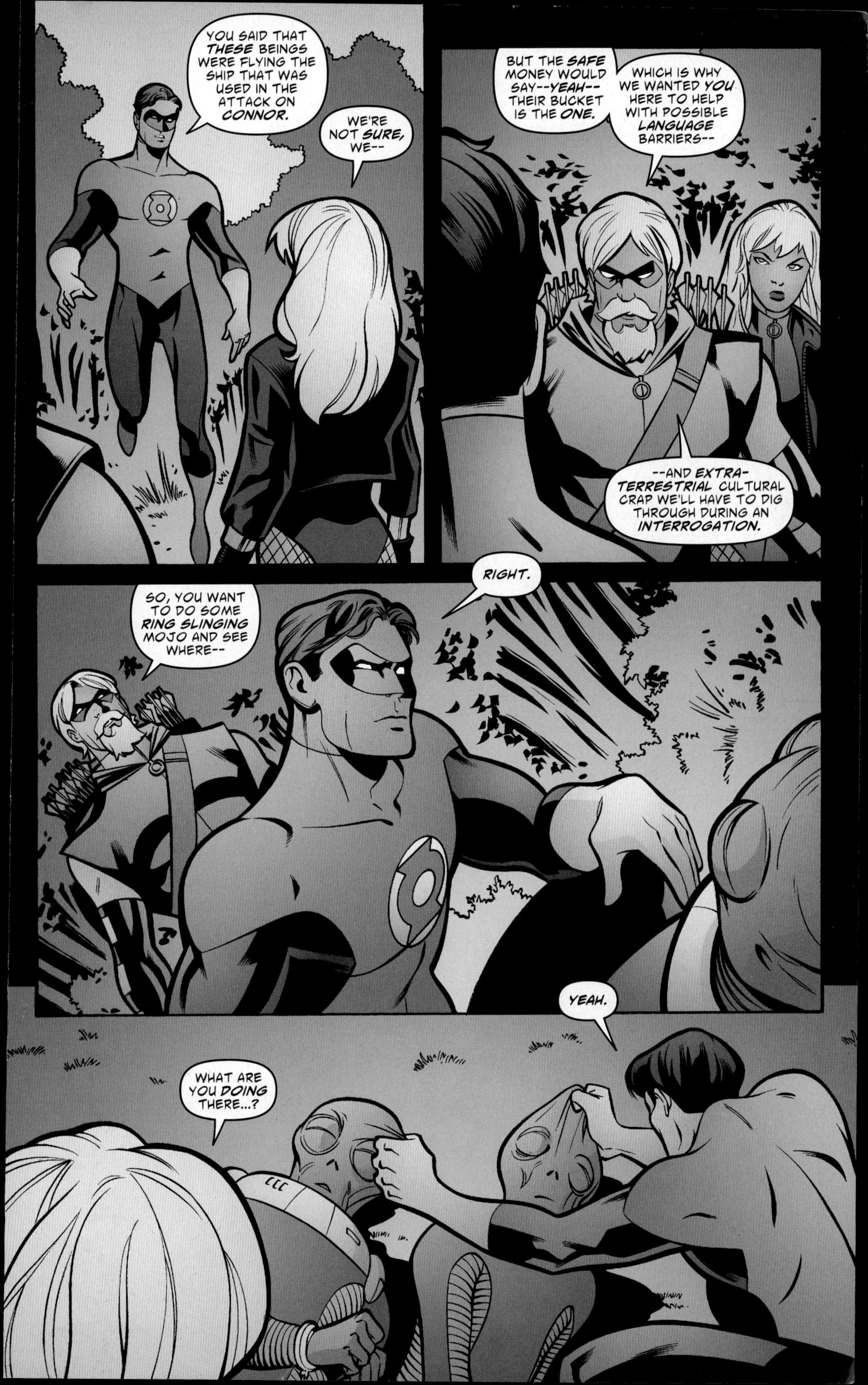
YOU SAID THAT THESE BEINGS WERE FLYING THE SHIP THAT WAS USED IN THE ATTACK ON CONNOR.
WE'RE NOT SURE, WE--
BUT THE SAFE MONEY WOULD SAY--YEAH--THEIR BUCKET IS THE ONE.
WHICH IS WHY WE WANTED YOU HERE TO HELP WITH POSSIBLE LANGUAGE BARRIERS--
--AND EXTRA-TERRESTRIAL CULTURAL CRAP WE'LL HAVE TO DIG THROUGH DURING AN INTERROGATION.
SO, YOU WANT TO DO SOME RING SLINGING MOJO AND SEE WHERE--
RIGHT.
YEAH.
WHAT ARE YOU DOING THERE...?

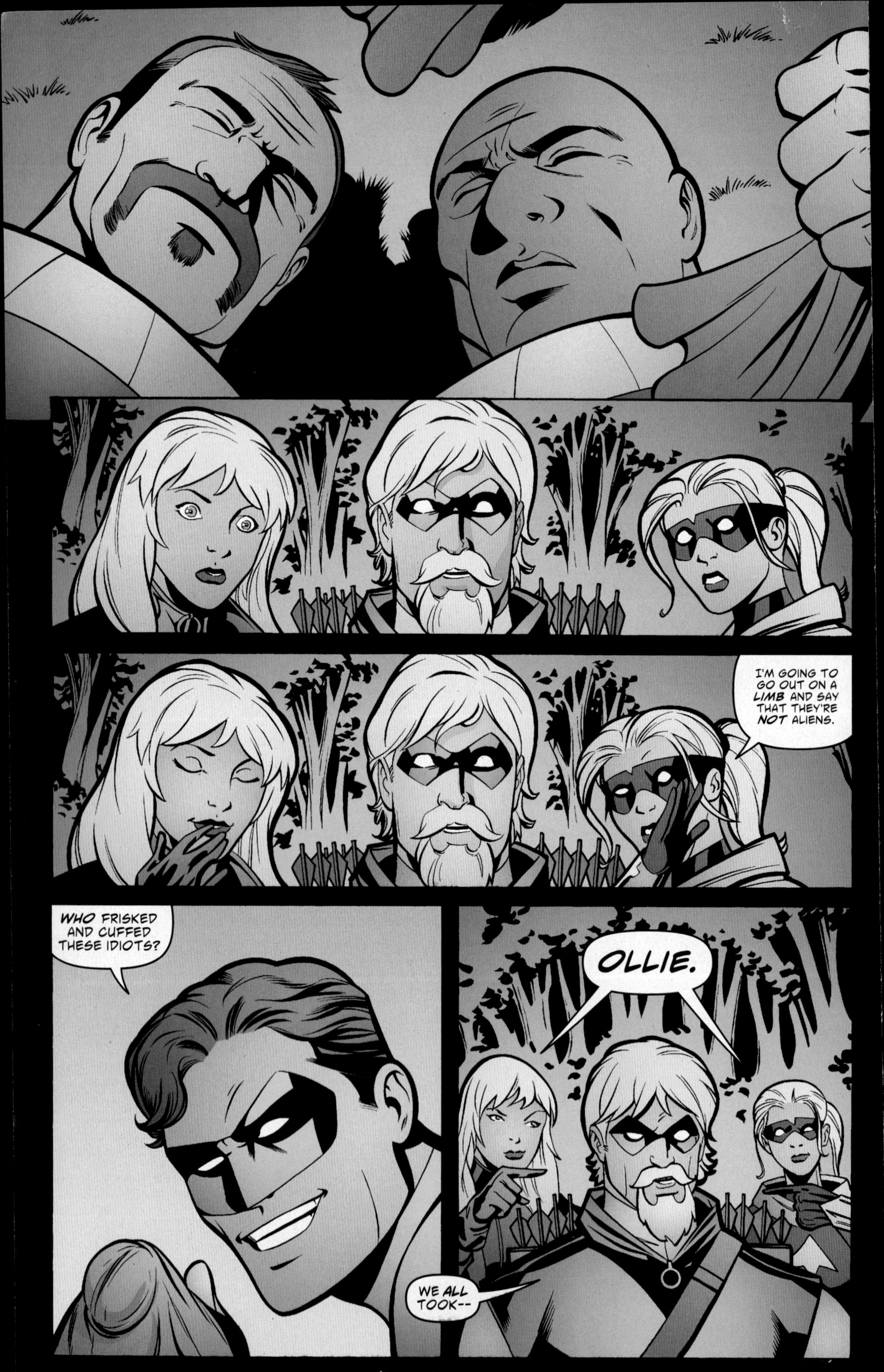
I'M GOING TO GO OUT ON A LIMB AND SAY THAT THEY'RE NOT ALIENS.
WHO FRISKED AND CUFFED THESE IDIOTS?
OLLIE.
WE ALL TOOK--

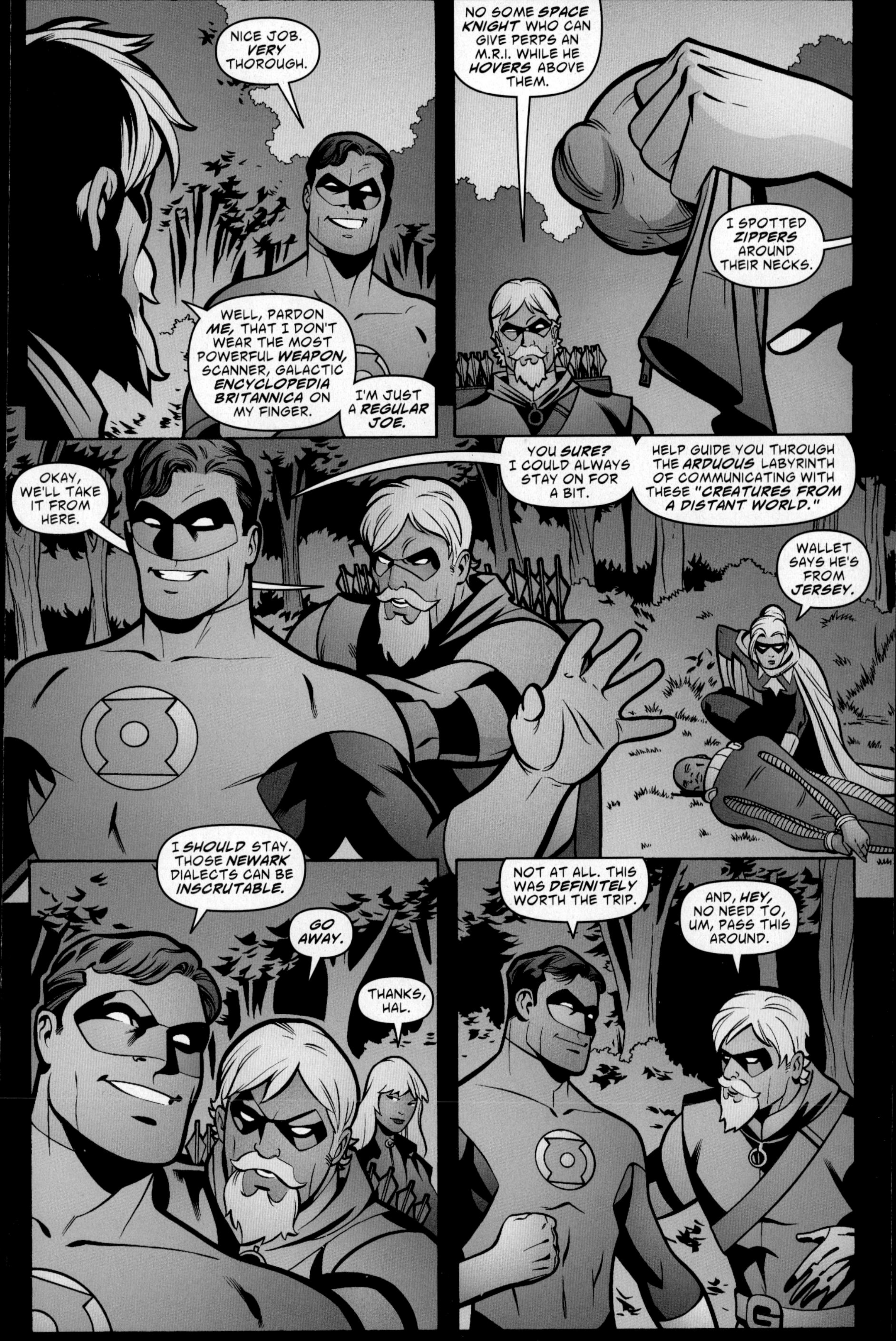
NICE JOB. VERY THOROUGH.
WELL, PARDON ME, THAT I DON'T WEAR THE MOST POWERFUL WEAPON, SCANNER, GALACTIC ENCYCLOPEDIA BRITANNICA ON MY FINGER.
I'M JUST A REGULAR JOE.
NO SOME SPACE KNIGHT WHO CAN GIVE PERPS AN M.R.I. WHILE HE HOVERS ABOVE THEM.
I SPOTTED ZIPPERS AROUND THEIR NECKS.
OKAY, WE'LL TAKE IT FROM HERE.
YOU SURE? I COULD ALWAYS STAY ON FOR A BIT.
HELP GUIDE YOU THROUGH THE ARDUOUS LABYRINTH OF COMMUNICATING WITH THESE "CREATURES FROM A DISTANT WORLD."
WALLET SAYS HE'S FROM JERSEY.
I SHOULD STAY. THOSE NEWARK DIALECTS CAN BE INSCRUTABLE.
GO AWAY.
THANKS, HAL.
NOT AT ALL. THIS WAS DEFINITELY WORTH THE TRIP.
AND, HEY, NO NEED TO, UM, PASS THIS AROUND.

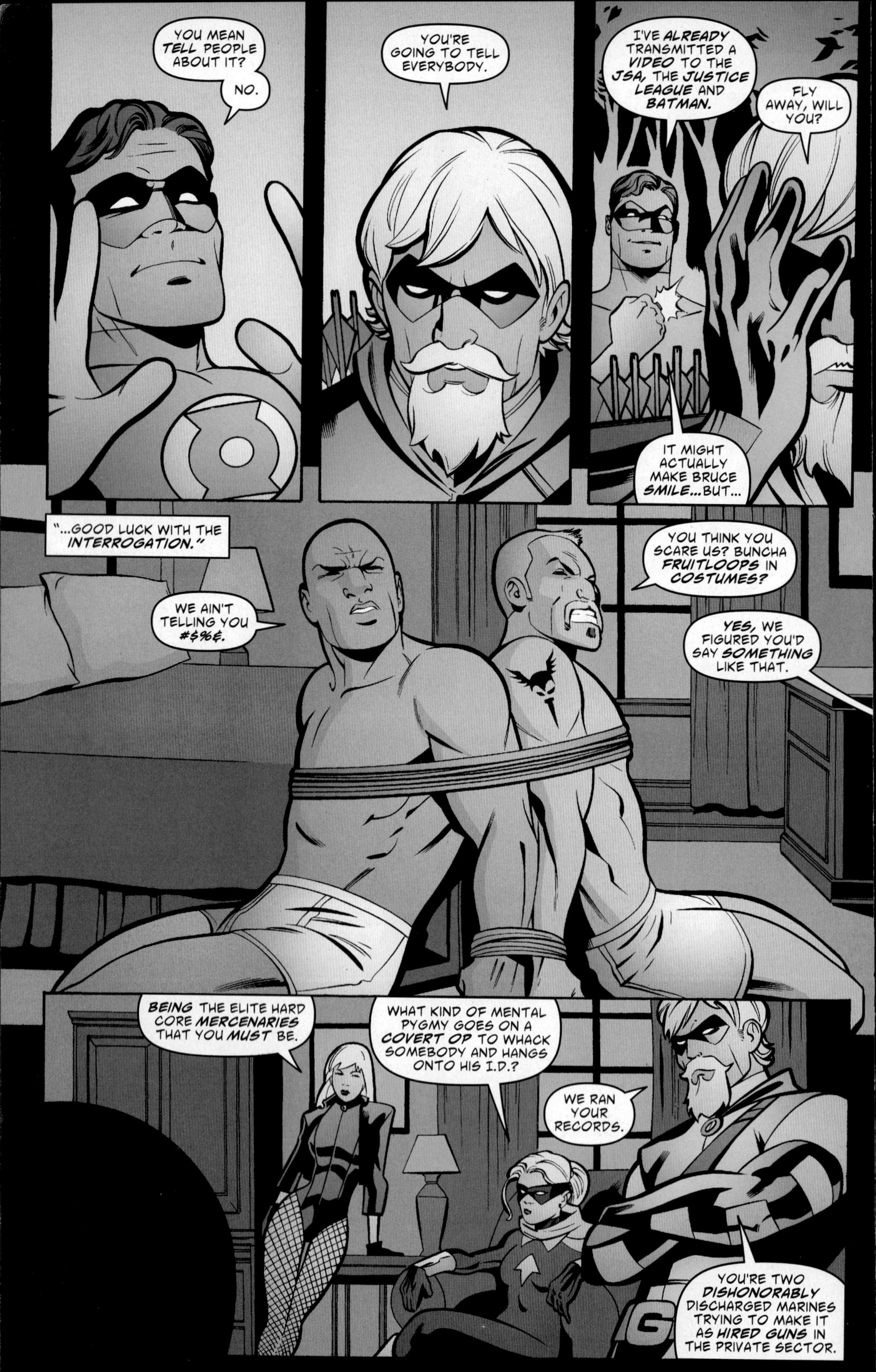
YOU MEAN TELL PEOPLE ABOUT IT?
NO.
YOU'RE GOING TO TELL EVERYBODY.
I'VE ALREADY TRANSMITTED A VIDEO TO THE JSA, THE JUSTICE LEAGUE AND BATMAN.
FLY AWAY, WILL YOU?
IT MIGHT ACTUALLY MAKE BRUCE SMILE...BUT...
"...GOOD LUCK WITH THE INTERROGATION."
WE AIN'T TELLING YOU #$%¢.
YOU THINK YOU SCARE US? BUNCHA FRUITLOOPS IN COSTUMES?
YES, WE FIGURED YOU'D SAY SOMETHING LIKE THAT.
BEING THE ELITE HARD CORE MERCENARIES THAT YOU MUST BE.
WHAT KIND OF MENTAL PYGMY GOES ON A COVERT OP TO WHACK SOMEBODY AND HANGS ONTO HIS I.D.?
WE RAN YOUR RECORDS.
YOU'RE TWO DISHONORABLY DISCHARGED MARINES TRYING TO MAKE IT AS HIRED GUNS IN THE PRIVATE SECTOR.

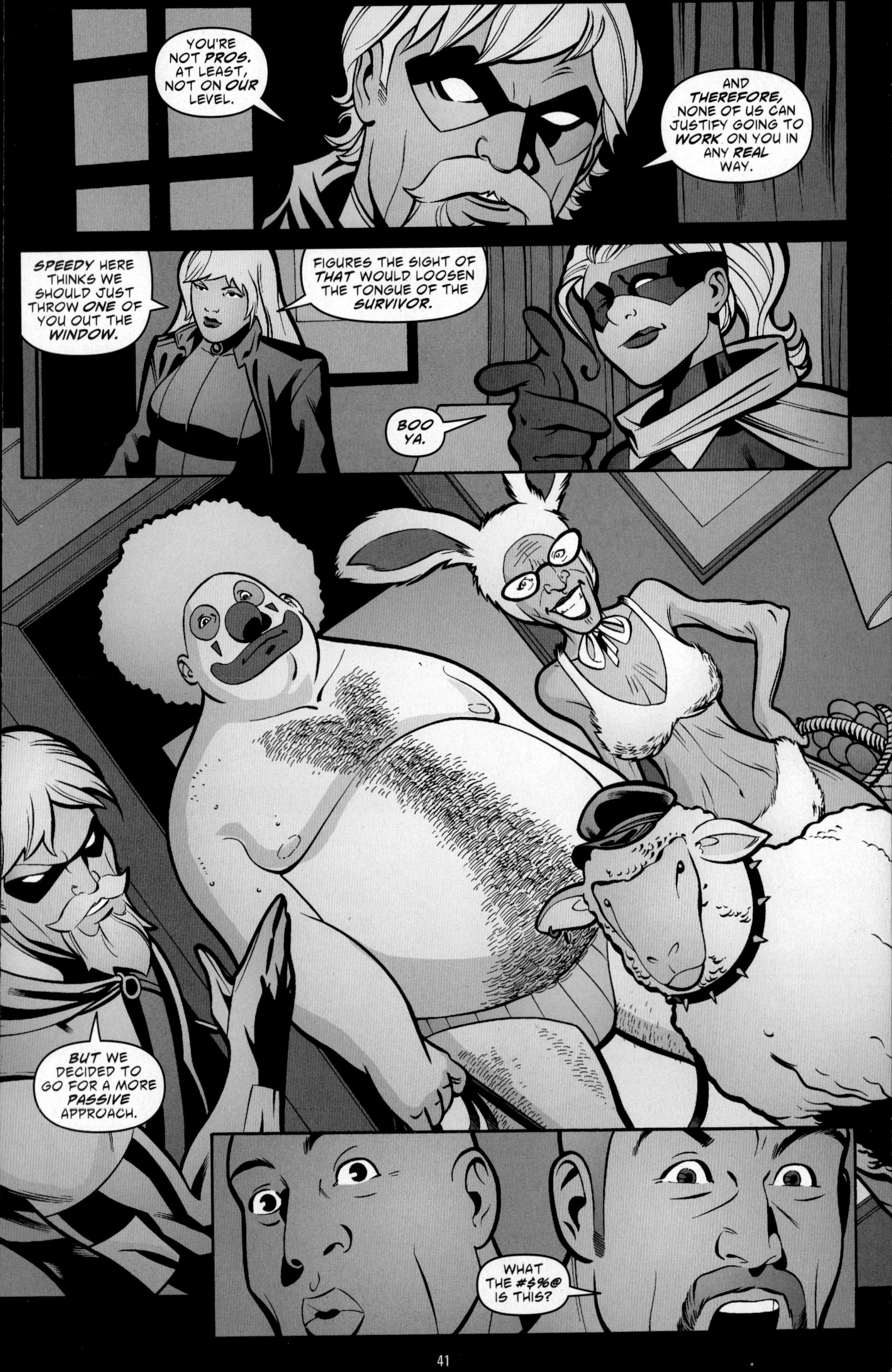

YOU'RE NOT PROS. AT LEAST, NOT ON OUR LEVEL.
AND THEREFORE, NONE OF US CAN JUSTIFY GOING TO WORK ON YOU IN ANY REAL WAY.
SPEEDY HERE THINKS WE SHOULD JUST THROW ONE OF YOU OUT THE WINDOW.
FIGURES THE SIGHT OF THAT WOULD LOOSEN THE TONGUE OF THE SURVIVOR.
BOO YA.
BUT WE DECIDED TO GO FOR A MORE PASSIVE APPROACH.
WHAT THE #$%@ IS THIS?

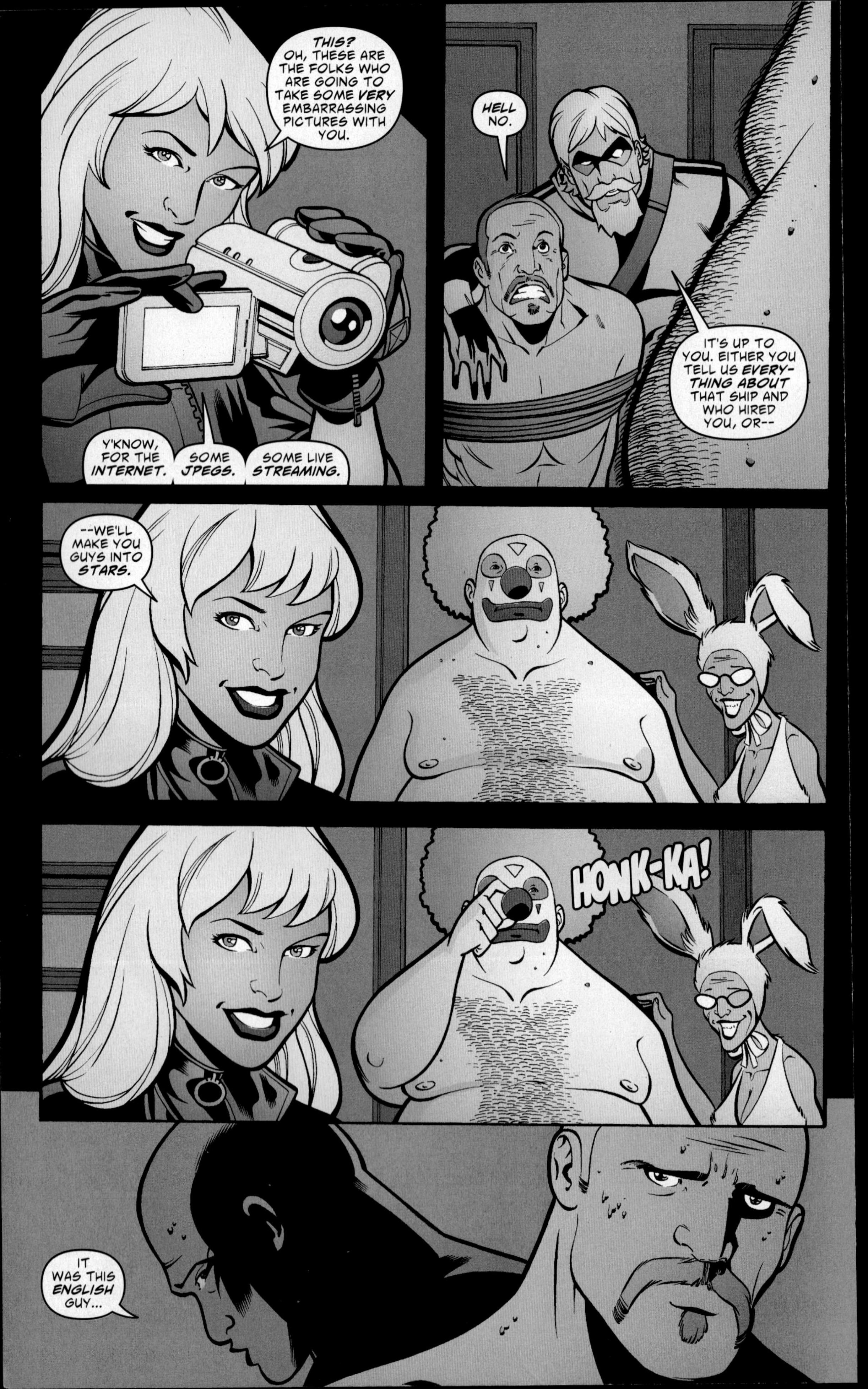

THIS? OH, THESE ARE THE FOLKS WHO ARE GOING TO TAKE SOME VERY EMBARRASSING PICTURES WITH YOU.
Y'KNOW, FOR THE INTERNET.
SOME JPEGS.
SOME LIVE STREAMING.
HELL NO.
IT'S UP TO YOU. EITHER YOU TELL US EVERY-THING ABOUT THAT SHIP AND WHO HIRED YOU, OR--
--WE'LL MAKE YOU GUYS INTO STARS.
HONK-KA!
IT WAS THIS ENGLISH GUY...

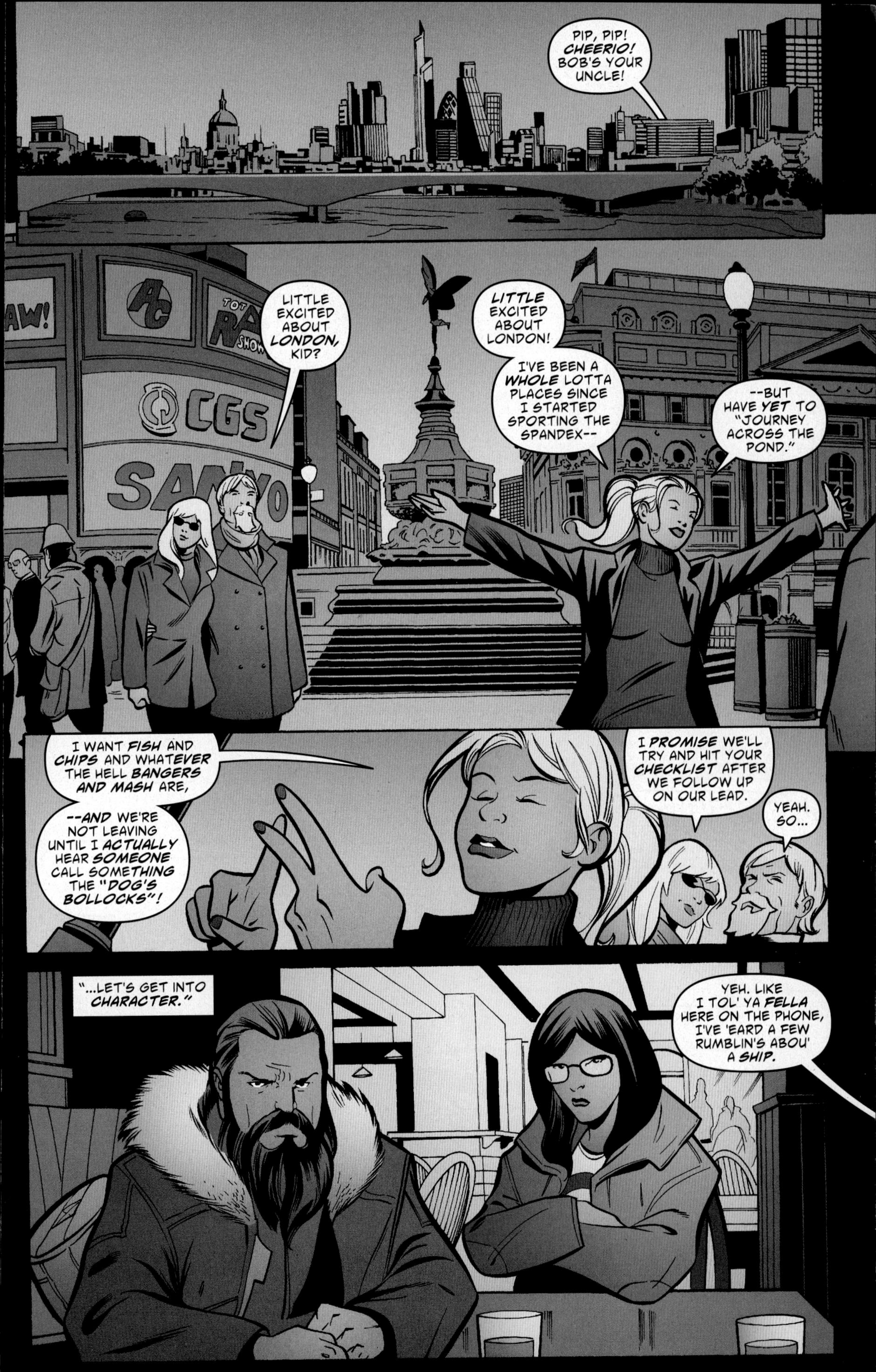
PIP, PIP! CHEERIO! BOB'S YOUR UNCLE!
LITTLE EXCITED ABOUT LONDON, KID?
LITTLE EXCITED ABOUT LONDON!
I'VE BEEN A WHOLE LOTTA PLACES SINCE I STARTED SPORTING THE SPANDEX--
--BUT HAVE YET TO "JOURNEY ACROSS THE POND."
I WANT FISH AND CHIPS AND WHATEVER THE HELL BANGERS AND MASH ARE,
--AND WE'RE NOT LEAVING UNTIL I ACTUALLY HEAR SOMEONE CALL SOMETHING THE "DOG'S BOLLOCKS"!
I PROMISE WE'LL TRY AND HIT YOUR CHECKLIST AFTER WE FOLLOW UP ON OUR LEAD.
YEAH. SO...
"...LET'S GET INTO CHARACTER."
YEH. LIKE I TOL' YA FELLA HERE ON THE PHONE, I'VE 'EARD A FEW RUMBLIN'S ABOU' A SHIP.

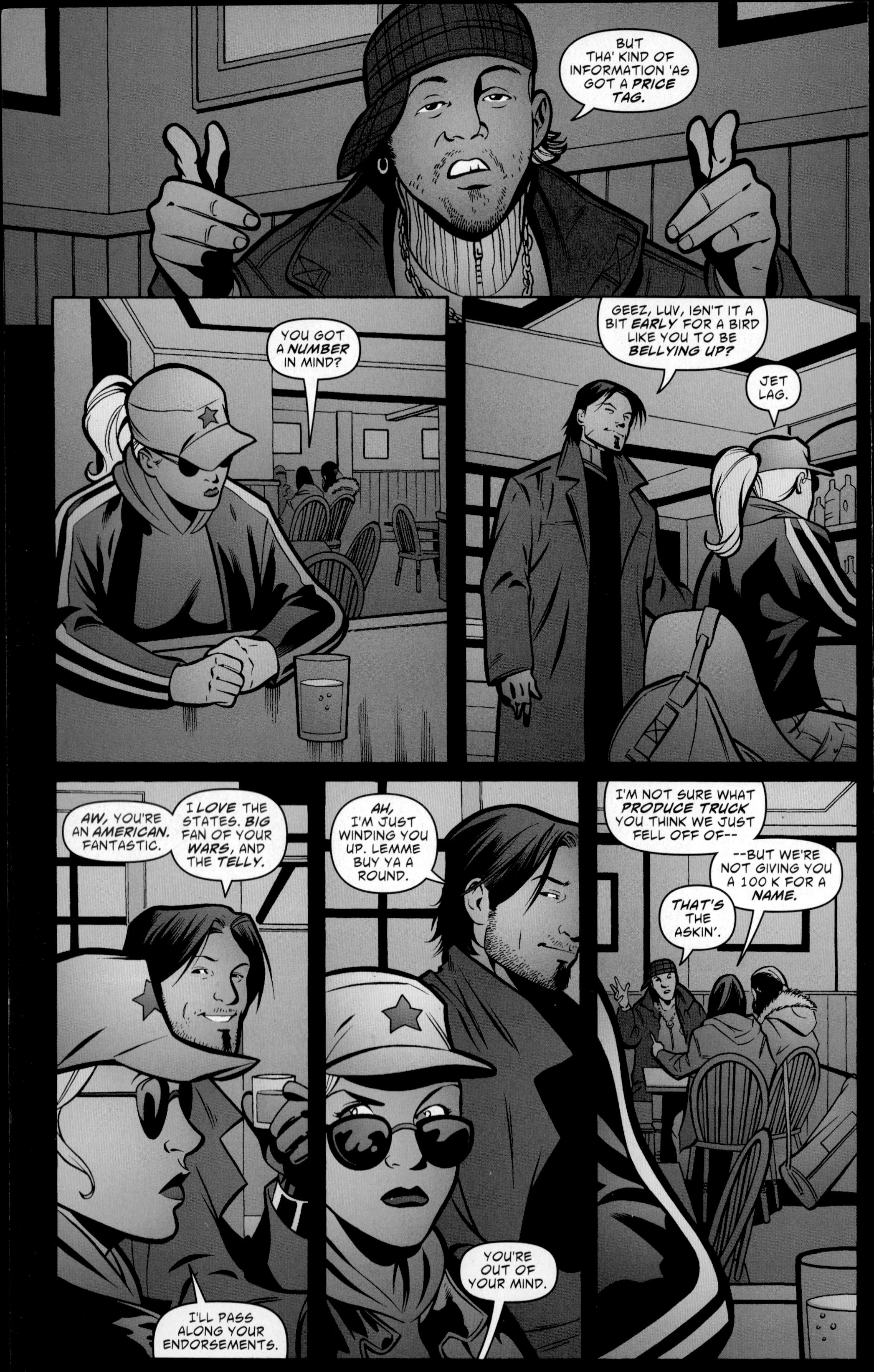

BUT THA' KIND OF INFORMATION 'AS GOT A PRICE TAG.
YOU GOT A NUMBER IN MIND?
GEEZ, LUV, ISN'T IT A BIT EARLY FOR A BIRD LIKE YOU TO BE BELLYING UP?
JET LAG.
AW, YOU'RE AN AMERICAN. FANTASTIC.
I LOVE THE STATES. BIG FAN OF YOUR WARS, AND THE TELLY.
I'LL PASS ALONG YOUR ENDORSEMENTS.
AH, I'M JUST WINDING YOU UP. LEMME BUY YA A ROUND.
YOU'RE OUT OF YOUR MIND.
I'M NOT SURE WHAT PRODUCE TRUCK YOU THINK WE JUST FELL OFF OF--
--BUT WE'RE NOT GIVING YOU A 100 K FOR A NAME.
THAT'S THE ASKIN'.

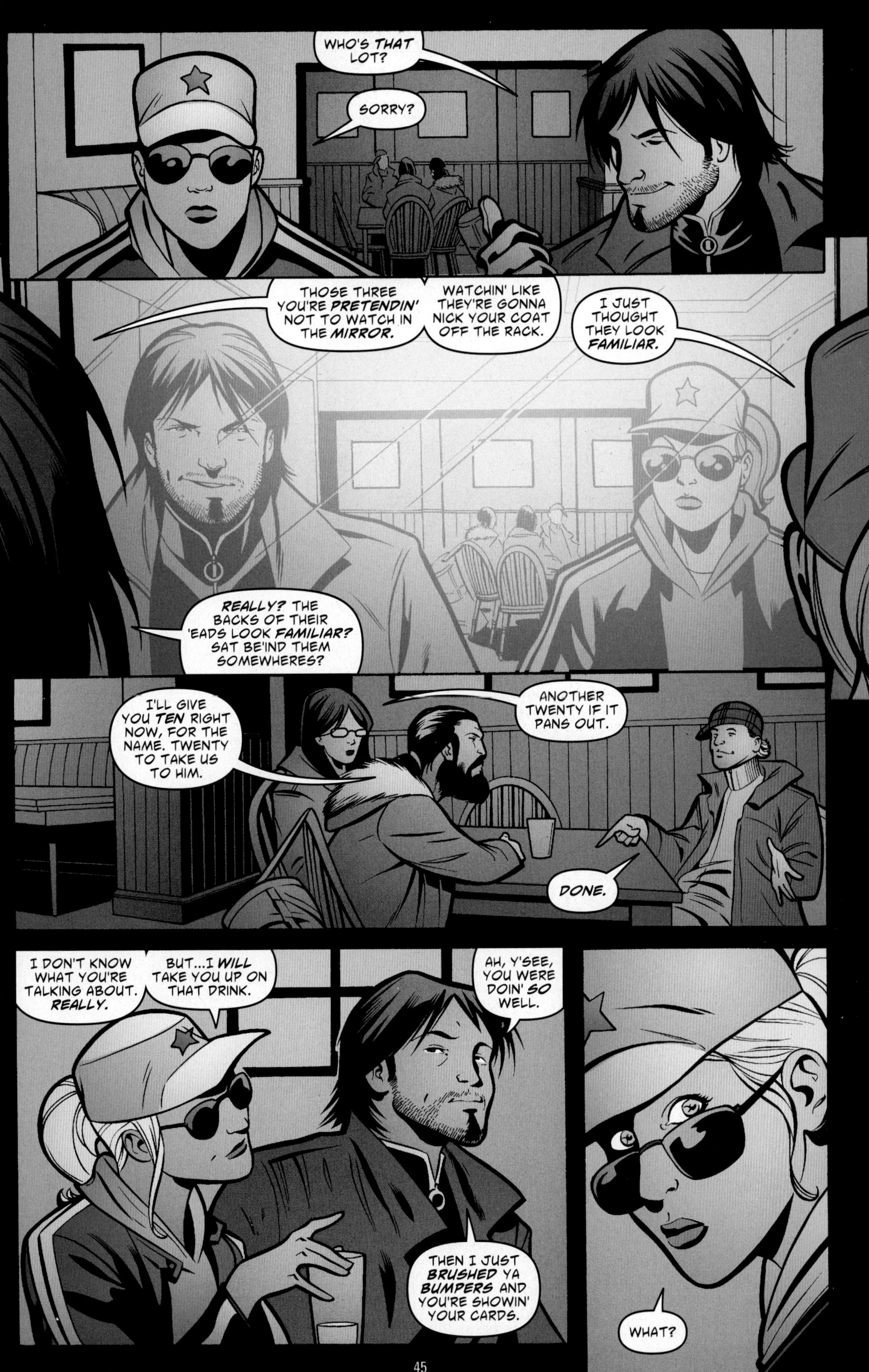
WHO'S THAT LOT?
SORRY?
THOSE THREE YOU'RE PRETENDIN' NOT TO WATCH IN THE MIRROR.
WATCHIN' LIKE THEY'RE GONNA NICK YOUR COAT OFF THE RACK.
I JUST THOUGHT THEY LOOK FAMILIAR.
REALLY? THE BACKS OF THEIR 'EADS LOOK FAMILIAR? SAT BE'IND THEM SOMEWHERES?
I'LL GIVE YOU TEN RIGHT NOW, FOR THE NAME. TWENTY TO TAKE US TO HIM.
ANOTHER TWENTY IF IT PANS OUT.
DONE.
I DON'T KNOW WHAT YOU'RE TALKING ABOUT. REALLY.
BUT...I WILL TAKE YOU UP ON THAT DRINK.
AH, Y'SEE, YOU WERE DOIN' SO WELL.
THEN I JUST BRUSHED YA BUMPERS AND YOU'RE SHOWIN' YOUR CARDS.
WHAT?

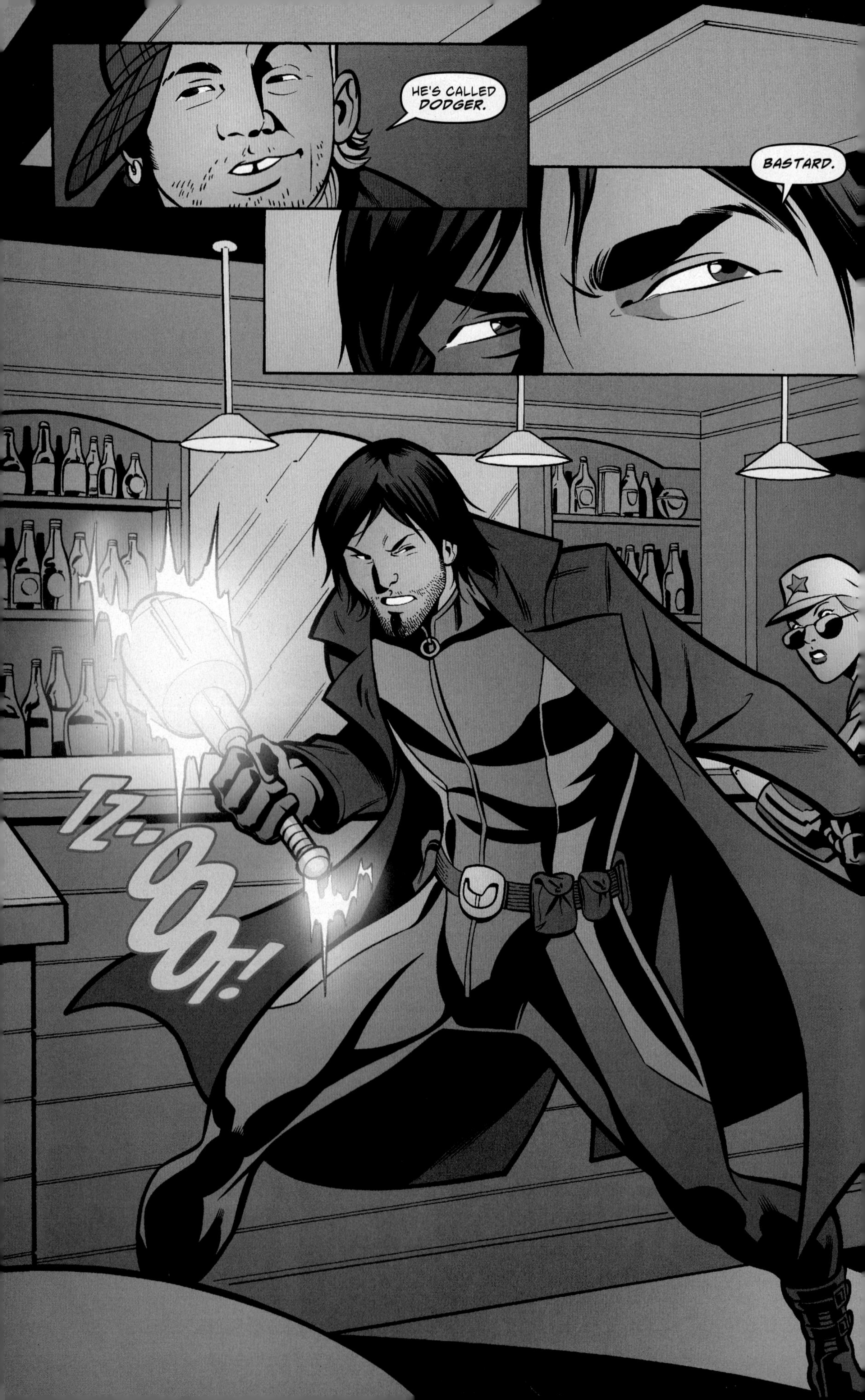
HE'S CALLED DODGER.
BASTARD.
TZ--OOOT!

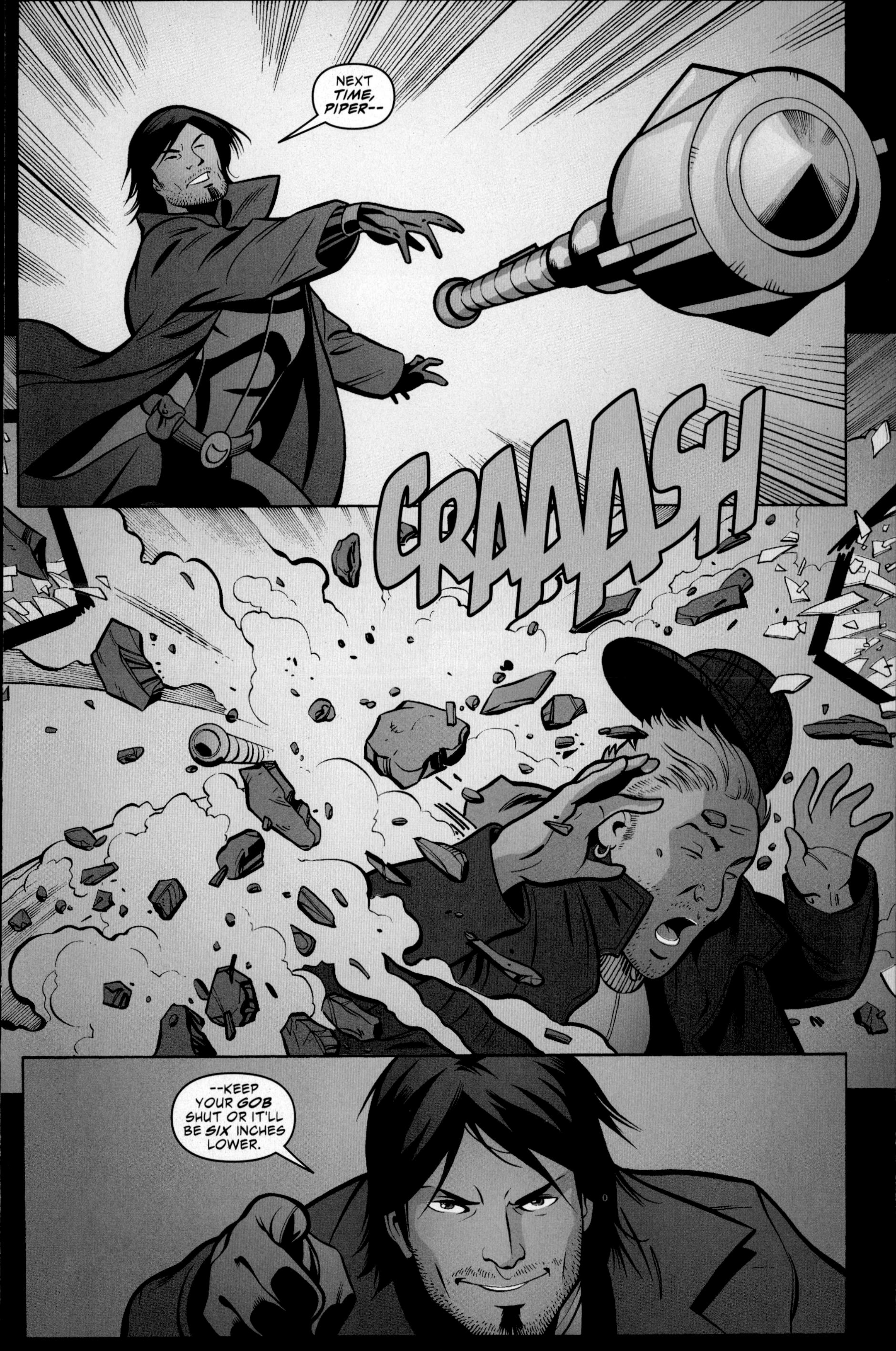
NEXT TIME, PIPER--
CRAAASH
--KEEP YOUR GOB SHUT OR IT'LL BE SIX INCHES LOWER.

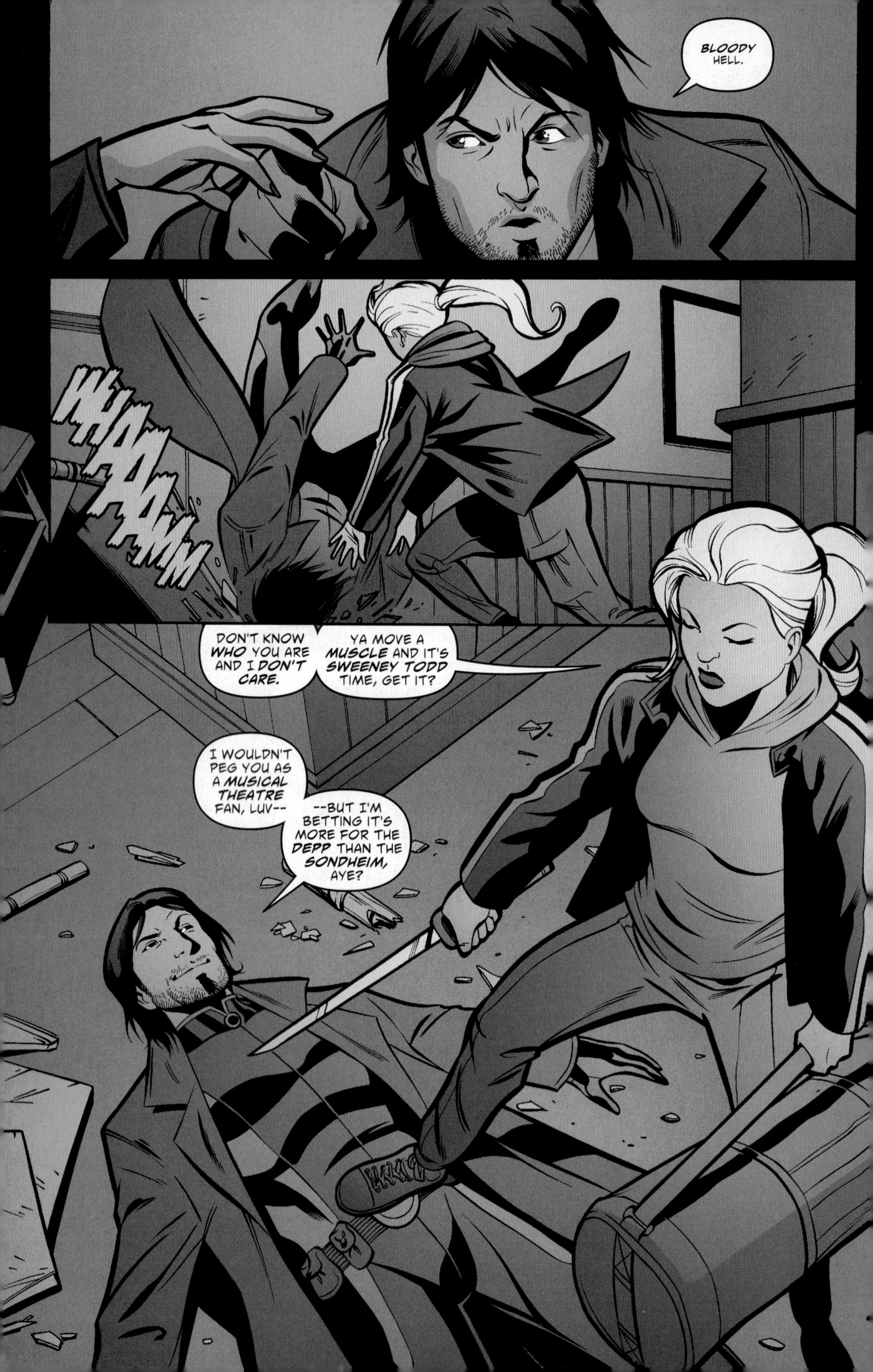
BLOODY HELL.
WHAMM
DON'T KNOW WHO YOU ARE AND I DON'T CARE.
YA MOVE A MUSCLE AND IT'S SWEENEY TODD TIME, GET IT?
I WOULDN'T PEG YOU AS A MUSICAL THEATRE FAN, LUV--
--BUT I'M BETTING IT'S MORE FOR THE DEPP THAN THE SONDHEIM, AYE?

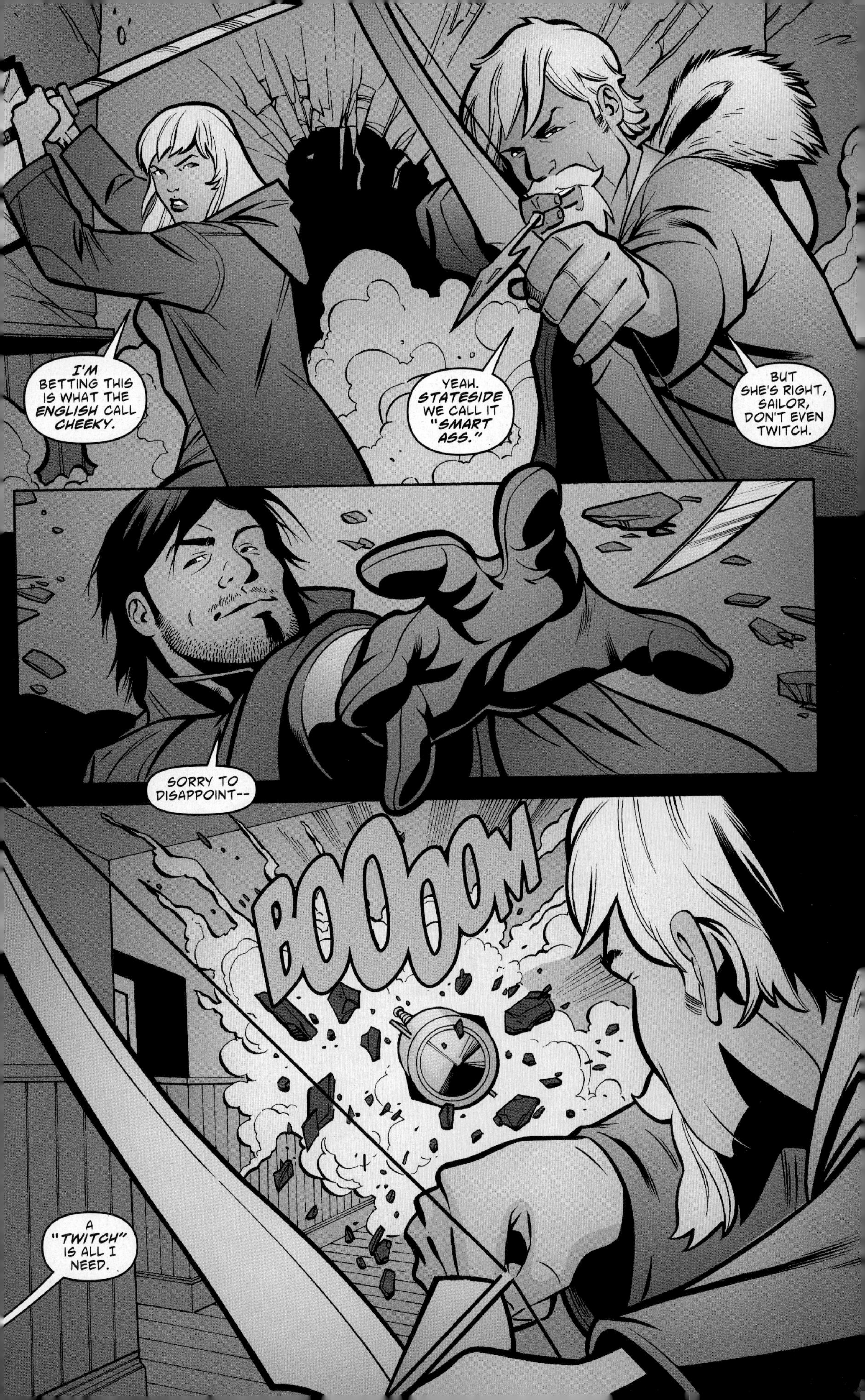

I'M BETTING THIS IS WHAT THE ENGLISH CALL CHEEKY.
YEAH. STATESIDE WE CALL IT "SMART ASS."
BUT SHE'S RIGHT, SAILOR, DON'T EVEN TWITCH.
SORRY TO DISAPPOINT--
BOOOOOM
A "TWITCH" IS ALL I NEED.

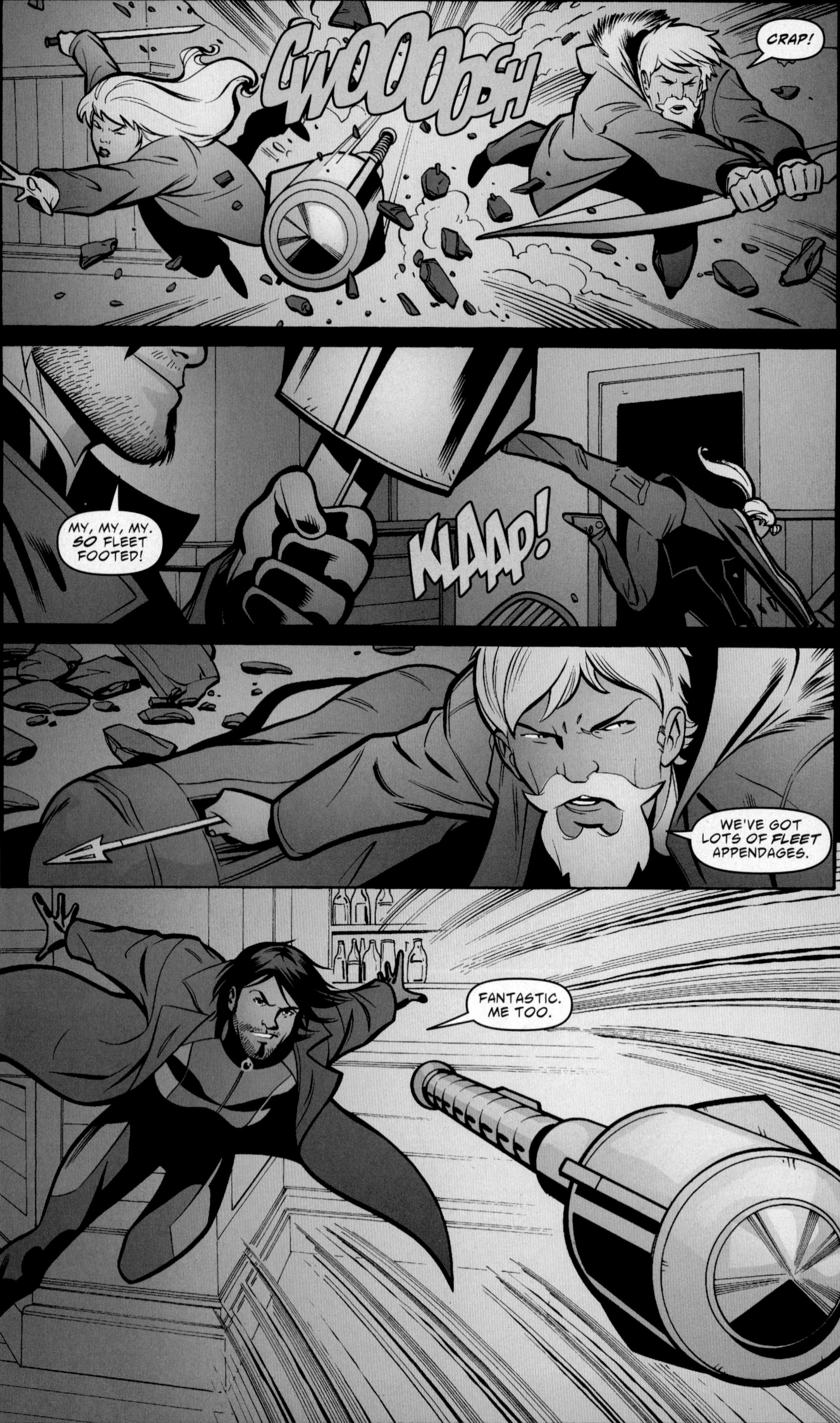
GWOOOOSH
CRAP!
MY, MY, MY. SO FLEET FOOTED!
KLAAP!
WE'VE GOT LOTS OF FLEET APPENDAGES.
FANTASTIC. ME TOO.

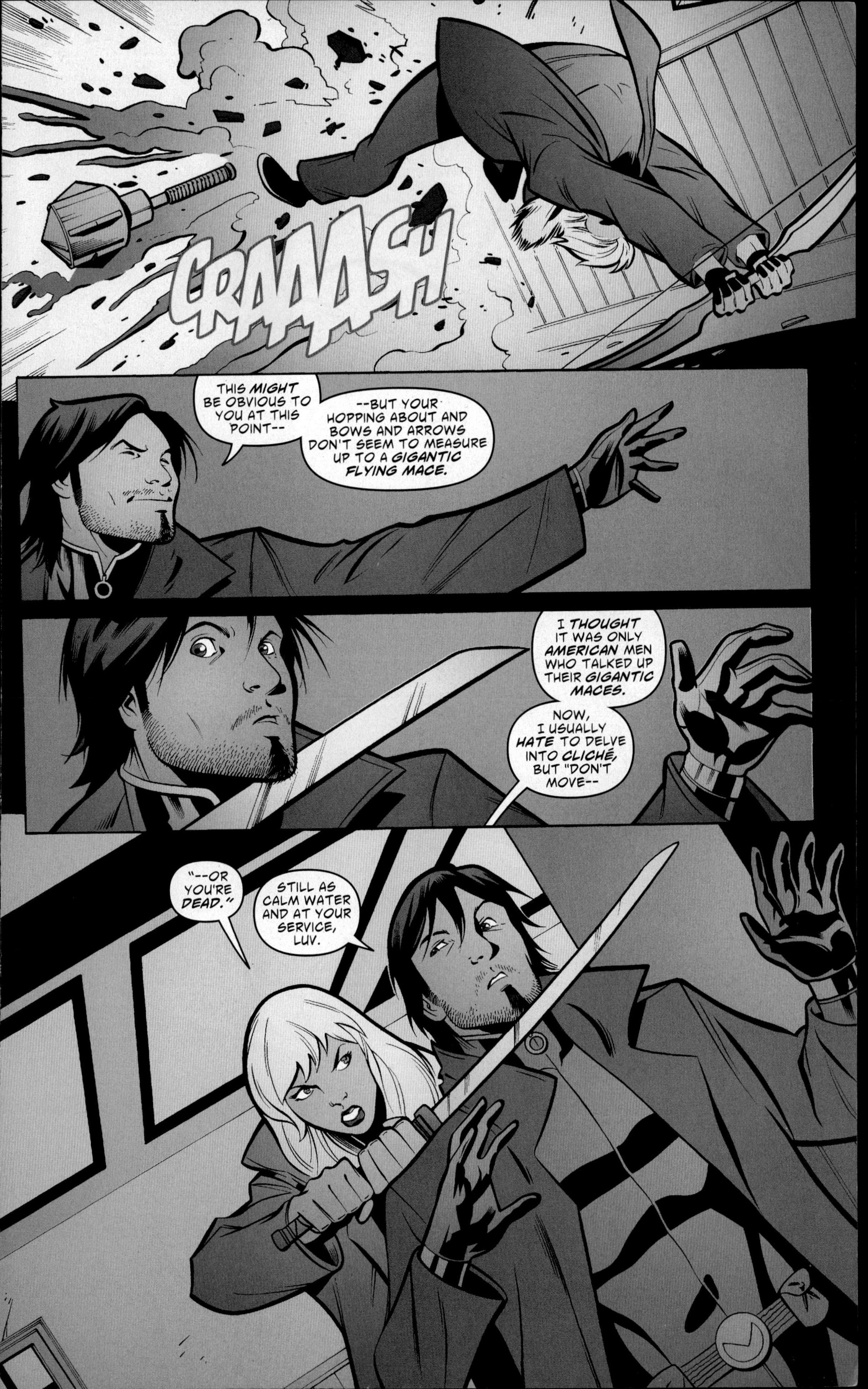
CRAAASH
THIS MIGHT BE OBVIOUS TO YOU AT THIS POINT--
--BUT YOUR HOPPING ABOUT AND BOWS AND ARROWS DON'T SEEM TO MEASURE UP TO A GIGANTIC FLYING MACE.
I THOUGHT IT WAS ONLY AMERICAN MEN WHO TALKED UP THEIR GIGANTIC MACES.
NOW, I USUALLY HATE TO DELVE INTO CLICHÉ, BUT "DON'T MOVE--
"--OR YOU'RE DEAD."
STILL AS CALM WATER AND AT YOUR SERVICE, LUV.

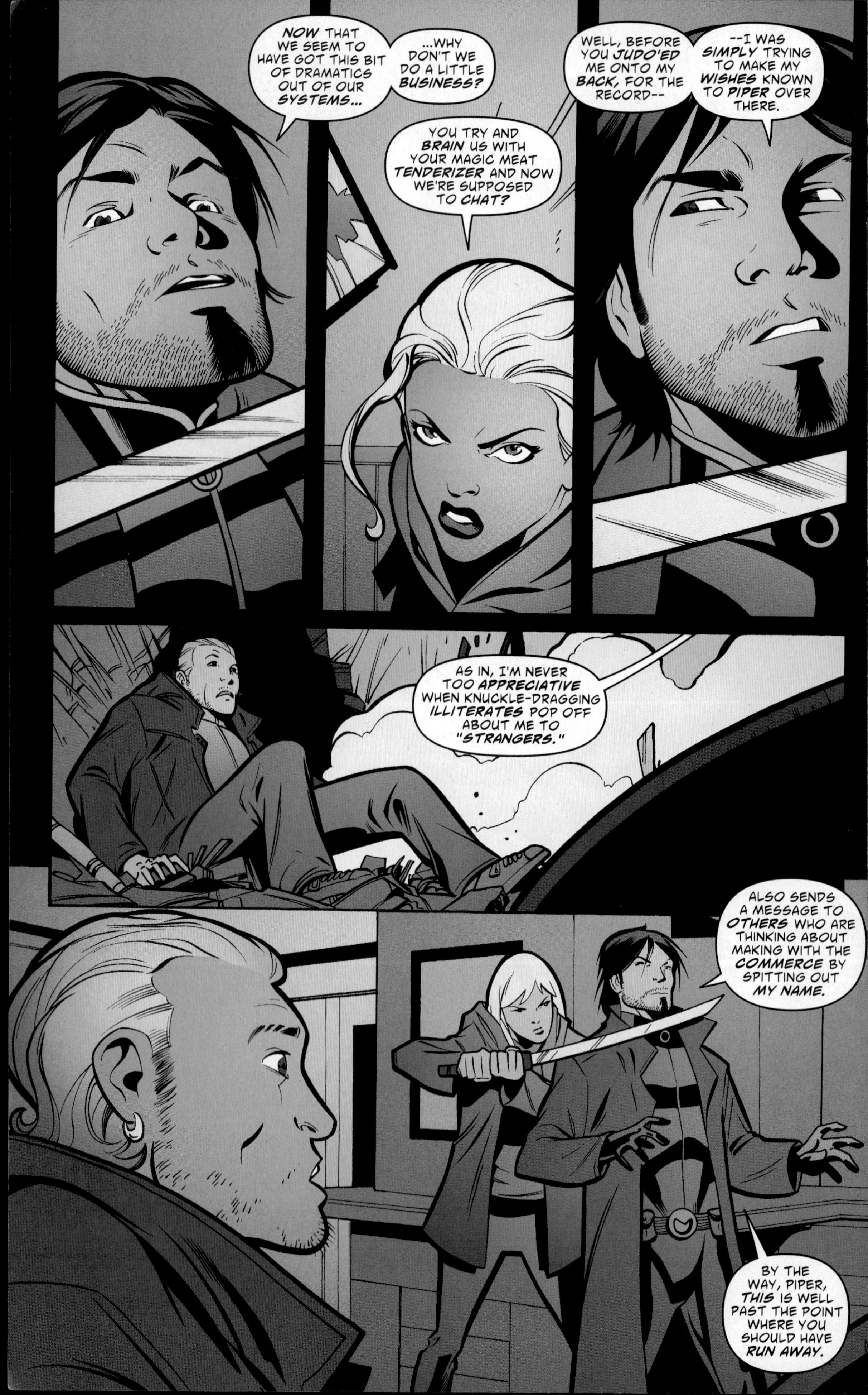
NOW THAT WE SEEM TO HAVE GOT THIS BIT OF DRAMATICS OUT OF OUR SYSTEMS...
...WHY DON'T WE DO A LITTLE BUSINESS?
YOU TRY AND BRAIN US WITH YOUR MAGIC MEAT TENDERIZER AND NOW WE'RE SUPPOSED TO CHAT?
WELL, BEFORE YOU JUDO'ED ME ONTO MY BACK, FOR THE RECORD--
--I WAS SIMPLY TRYING TO MAKE MY WISHES KNOWN TO PIPER OVER THERE.
AS IN, I'M NEVER TOO APPRECIATIVE WHEN KNUCKLE-DRAGGING ILLITERATES POP OFF ABOUT ME TO "STRANGERS."
ALSO SENDS A MESSAGE TO OTHERS WHO ARE THINKING ABOUT MAKING WITH THE COMMERCE BY SPITTING OUT MY NAME.
BY THE WAY, PIPER, THIS IS WELL PAST THE POINT WHERE YOU SHOULD HAVE RUN AWAY.

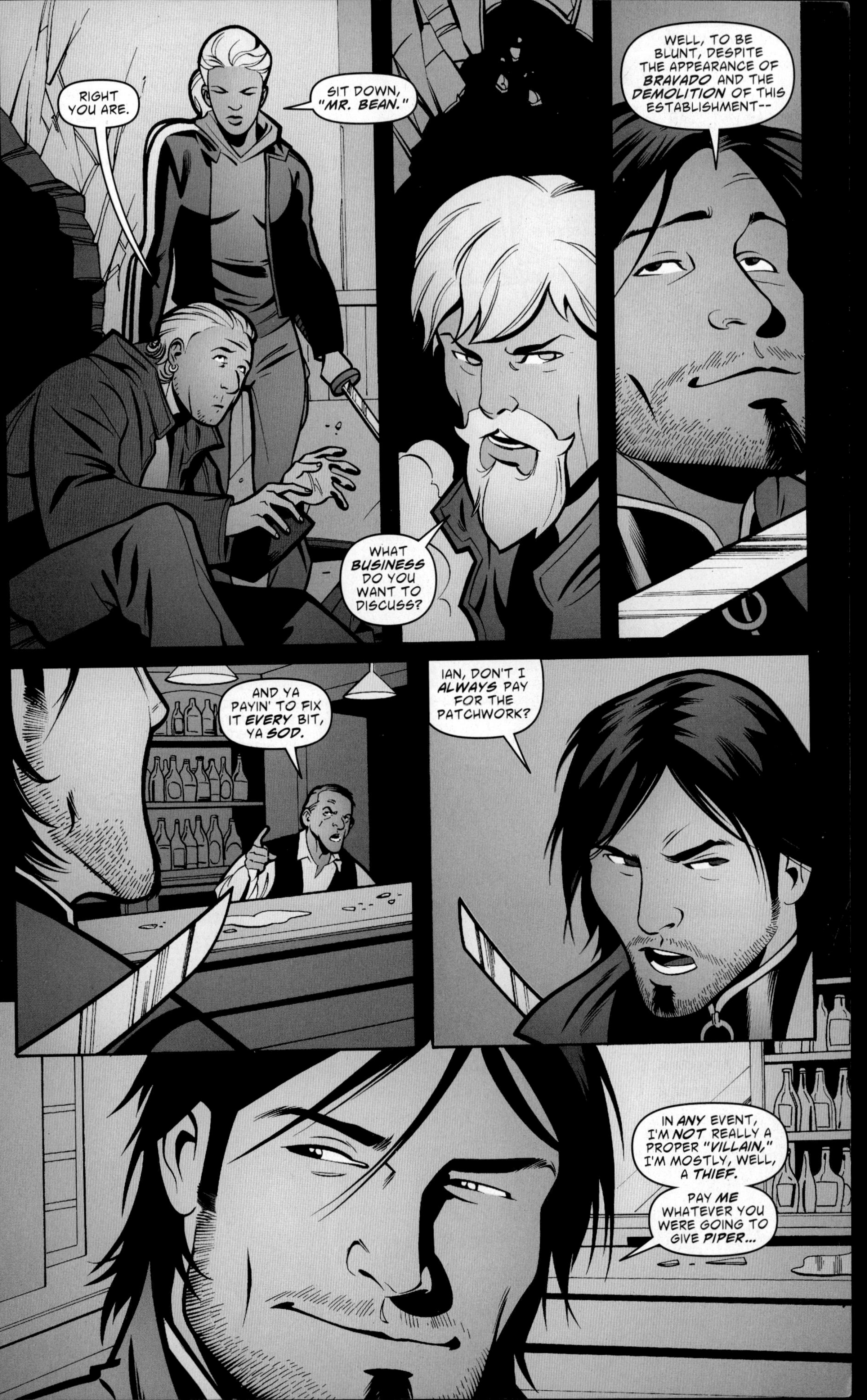
RIGHT YOU ARE.
SIT DOWN, "MR. BEAN."
WHAT BUSINESS DO YOU WANT TO DISCUSS?
WELL, TO BE BLUNT, DESPITE THE APPEARANCE OF BRAVADO AND THE DEMOLITION OF THIS ESTABLISHMENT--
AND YA PAYIN' TO FIX IT EVERY BIT, YA SOD.
IAN, DON'T I ALWAYS PAY FOR THE PATCHWORK?
IN ANY EVENT, I'M NOT REALLY A PROPER "VILLAIN," I'M MOSTLY, WELL, A THIEF.
PAY ME WHATEVER YOU WERE GOING TO GIVE PIPER...

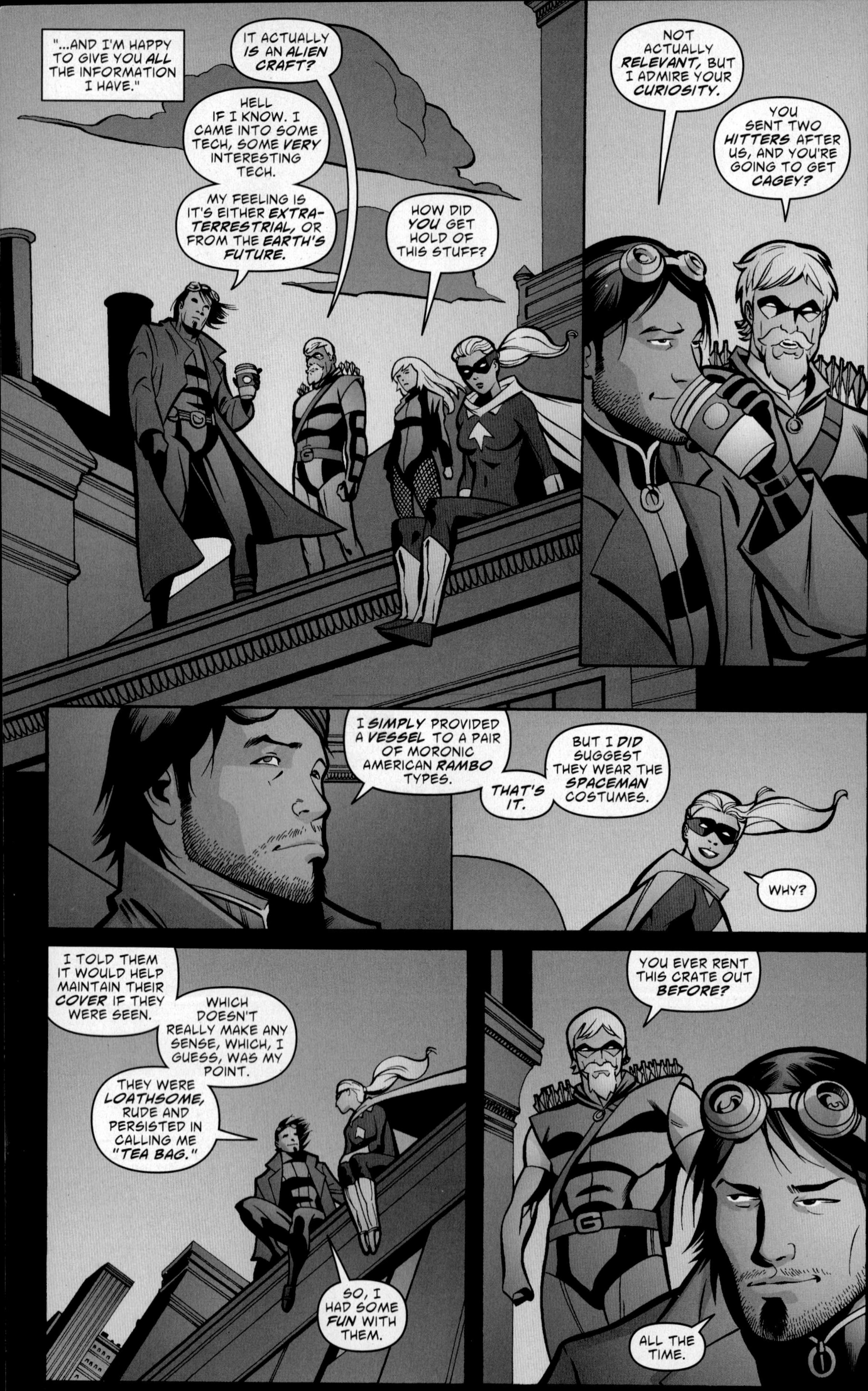
"...AND I'M HAPPY TO GIVE YOU ALL THE INFORMATION I HAVE."
IT ACTUALLY IS AN ALIEN CRAFT?
HELL IF I KNOW. I CAME INTO SOME TECH, SOME VERY INTERESTING TECH.
MY FEELING IS IT'S EITHER EXTRA-TERRESTRIAL, OR FROM THE EARTH'S FUTURE.
HOW DID YOU GET HOLD OF THIS STUFF?
NOT ACTUALLY RELEVANT, BUT I ADMIRE YOUR CURIOSITY.
YOU SENT TWO HITTERS AFTER US, AND YOU'RE GOING TO GET CAGEY?
I SIMPLY PROVIDED A VESSEL TO A PAIR OF MORONIC AMERICAN RAMBO TYPES.
THAT'S IT.
BUT I DID SUGGEST THEY WEAR THE SPACEMAN COSTUMES.
WHY?
I TOLD THEM IT WOULD HELP MAINTAIN THEIR COVER IF THEY WERE SEEN.
WHICH DOESN'T REALLY MAKE ANY SENSE, WHICH, I GUESS, WAS MY POINT.
THEY WERE LOATHSOME, RUDE AND PERSISTED IN CALLING ME "TEA BAG."
SO, I HAD SOME FUN WITH THEM.
YOU EVER RENT THIS CRATE OUT BEFORE?
ALL THE TIME.

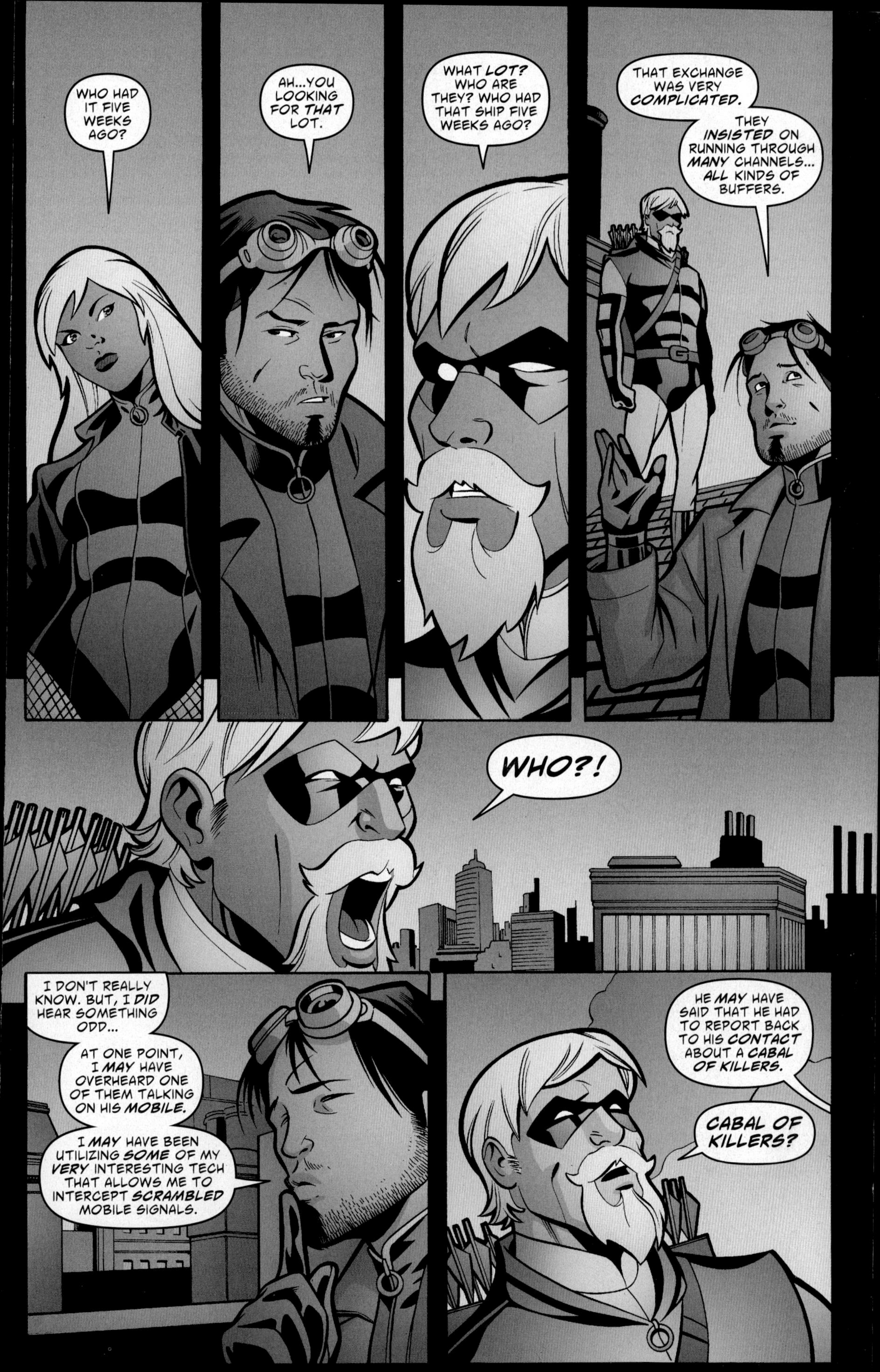
WHO HAD IT FIVE WEEKS AGO?
AH...YOU LOOKING FOR THAT LOT.
WHAT LOT? WHO ARE THEY? WHO HAD THAT SHIP FIVE WEEKS AGO?
THAT EXCHANGE WAS VERY COMPLICATED.
THEY INSISTED ON RUNNING THROUGH MANY CHANNELS... ALL KINDS OF BUFFERS.
WHO?!
I DON'T REALLY KNOW. BUT, I DID HEAR SOMETHING ODD...
AT ONE POINT, I MAY HAVE OVERHEARD ONE OF THEM TALKING ON HIS MOBILE.
I MAY HAVE BEEN UTILIZING SOME OF MY VERY INTERESTING TECH THAT ALLOWS ME TO INTERCEPT SCRAMBLED MOBILE SIGNALS.
HE MAY HAVE SAID THAT HE HAD TO REPORT BACK TO HIS CONTACT ABOUT A CABAL OF KILLERS.
CABAL OF KILLERS?

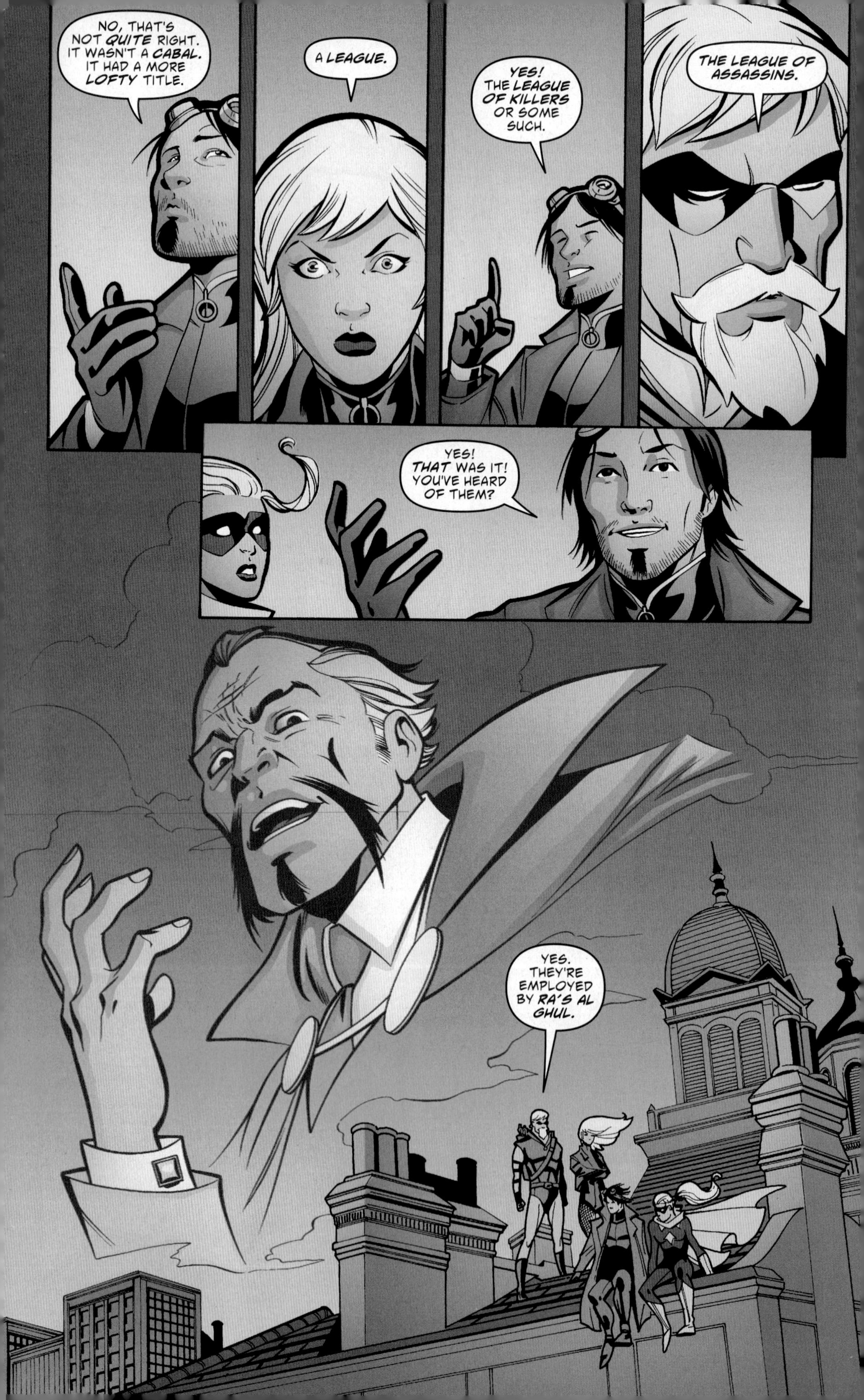

NO, THAT'S NOT QUITE RIGHT. IT WASN'T A CABAL. IT HAD A MORE LOFTY TITLE.
A LEAGUE.
YES! THE LEAGUE OF KILLERS OR SOME SUCH.
THE LEAGUE OF ASSASSINS.
YES! THAT WAS IT! YOU'VE HEARD OF THEM?
YES. THEY'RE EMPLOYED BY RA'S AL GHUL.

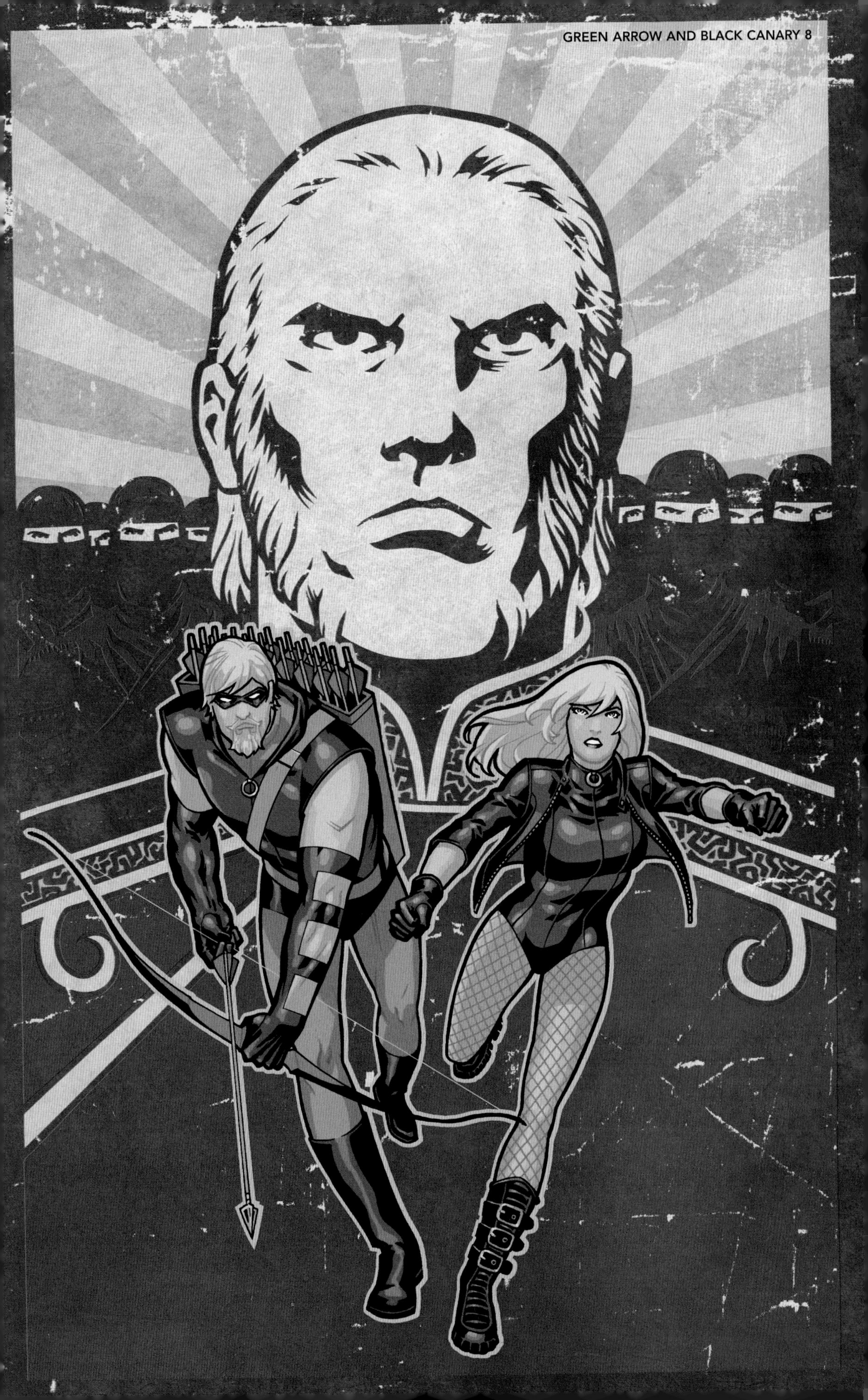
GREEN ARROW AND BLACK CANARY 8

HAYSTACK

PART 3: THE NEEDLE

JUDD WINICK
STORY

MIKE NORTON / RODNEY RAMOS
ART

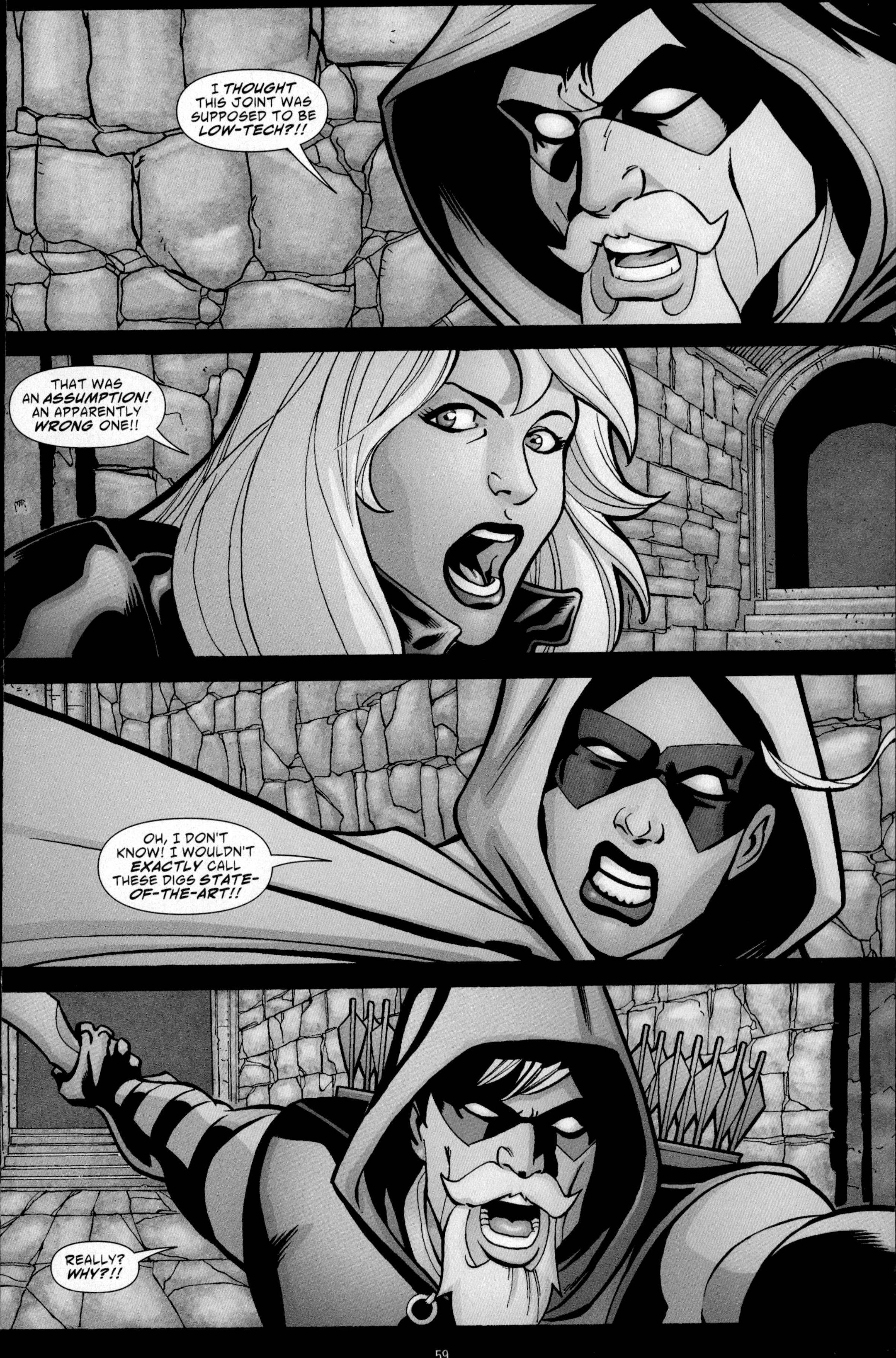
I *THOUGHT* THIS JOINT WAS SUPPOSED TO BE *LOW-TECH?!!*
THAT WAS AN *ASSUMPTION!* AN APPARENTLY *WRONG* ONE!!
OH, I DON'T KNOW! I WOULDN'T *EXACTLY* CALL THESE DIGS *STATE-OF-THE-ART!!*
REALLY? *WHY?!!*

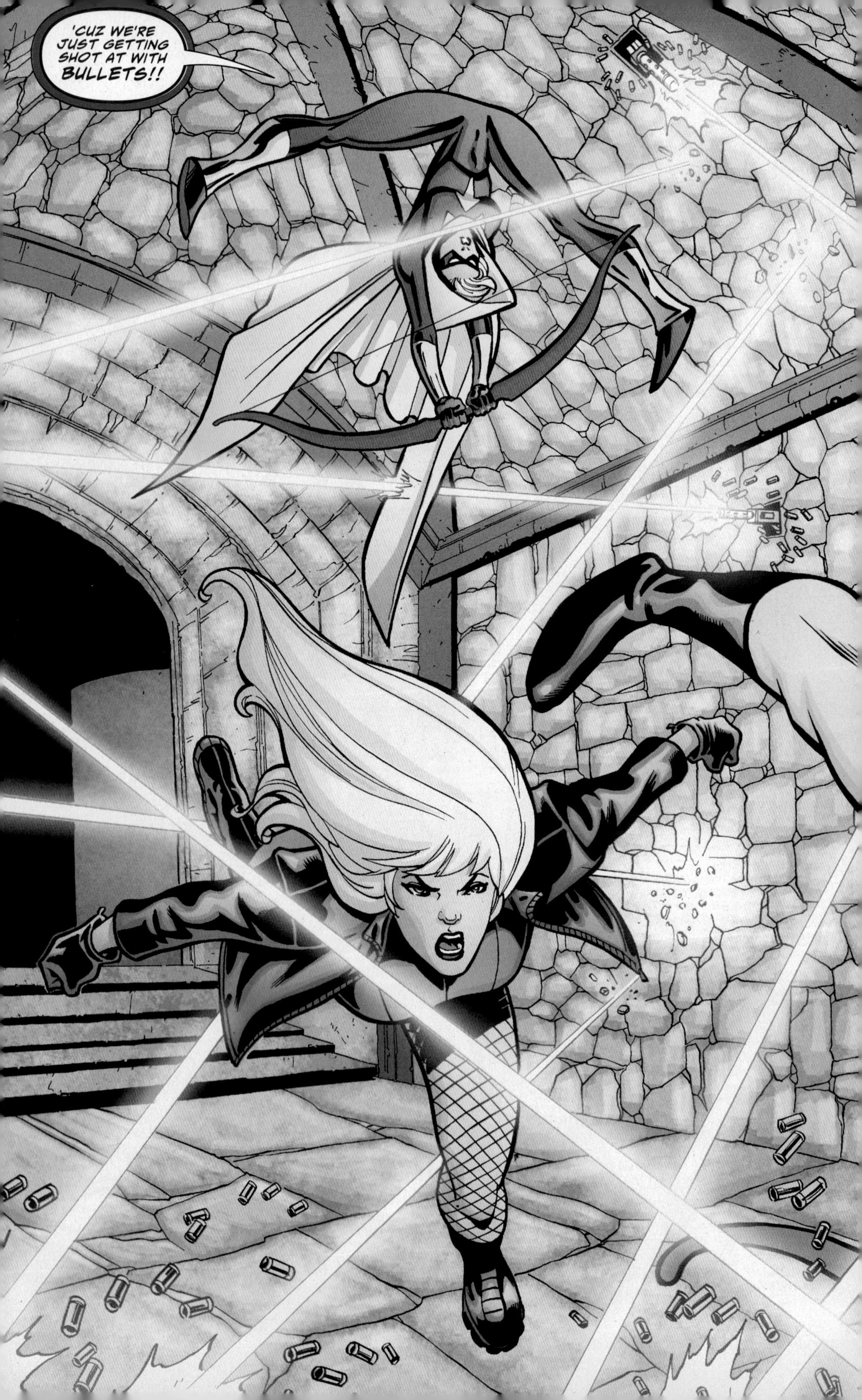
'CUZ WE'RE JUST GETTING SHOT AT WITH BULLETS!!

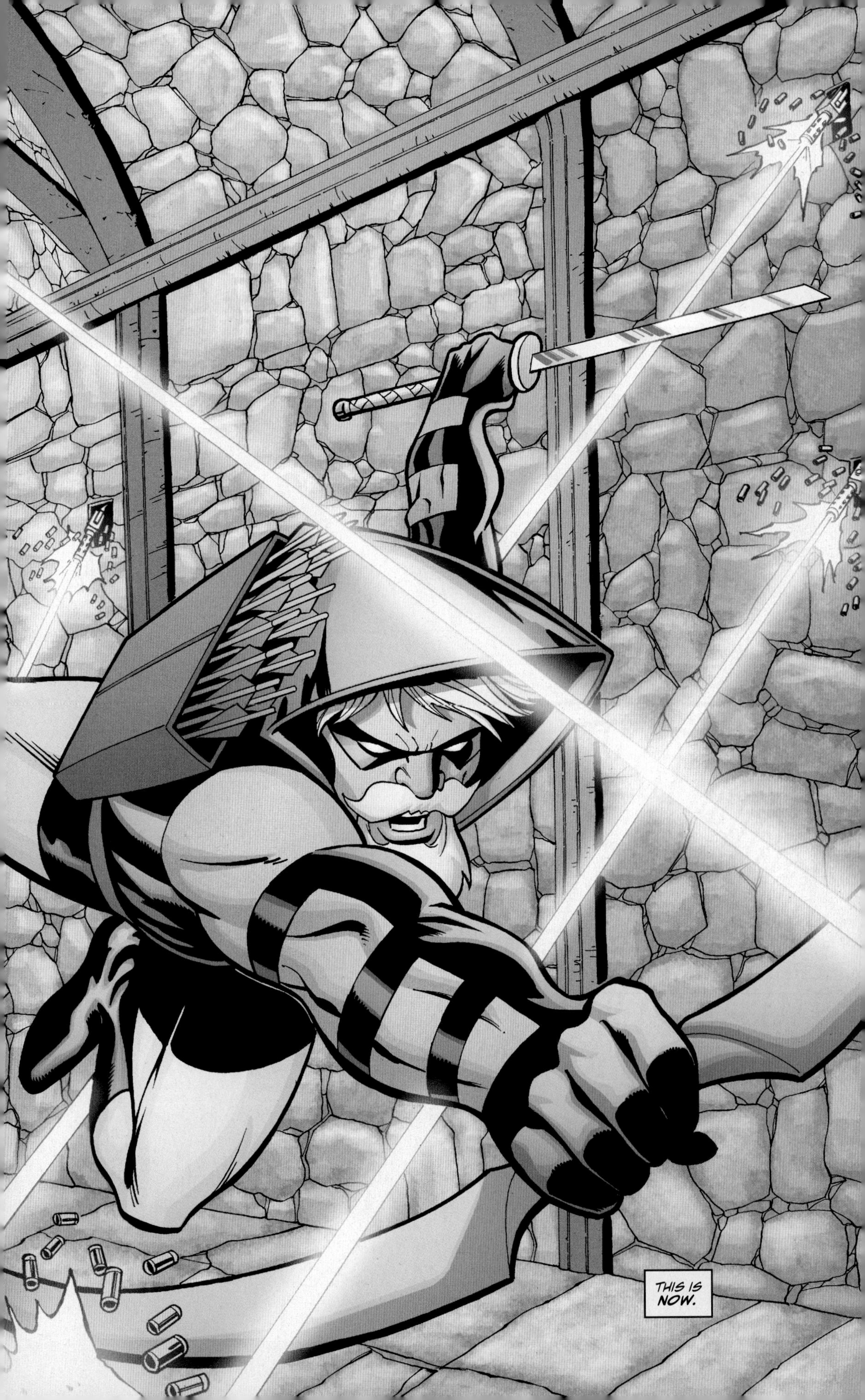
THIS IS NOW.

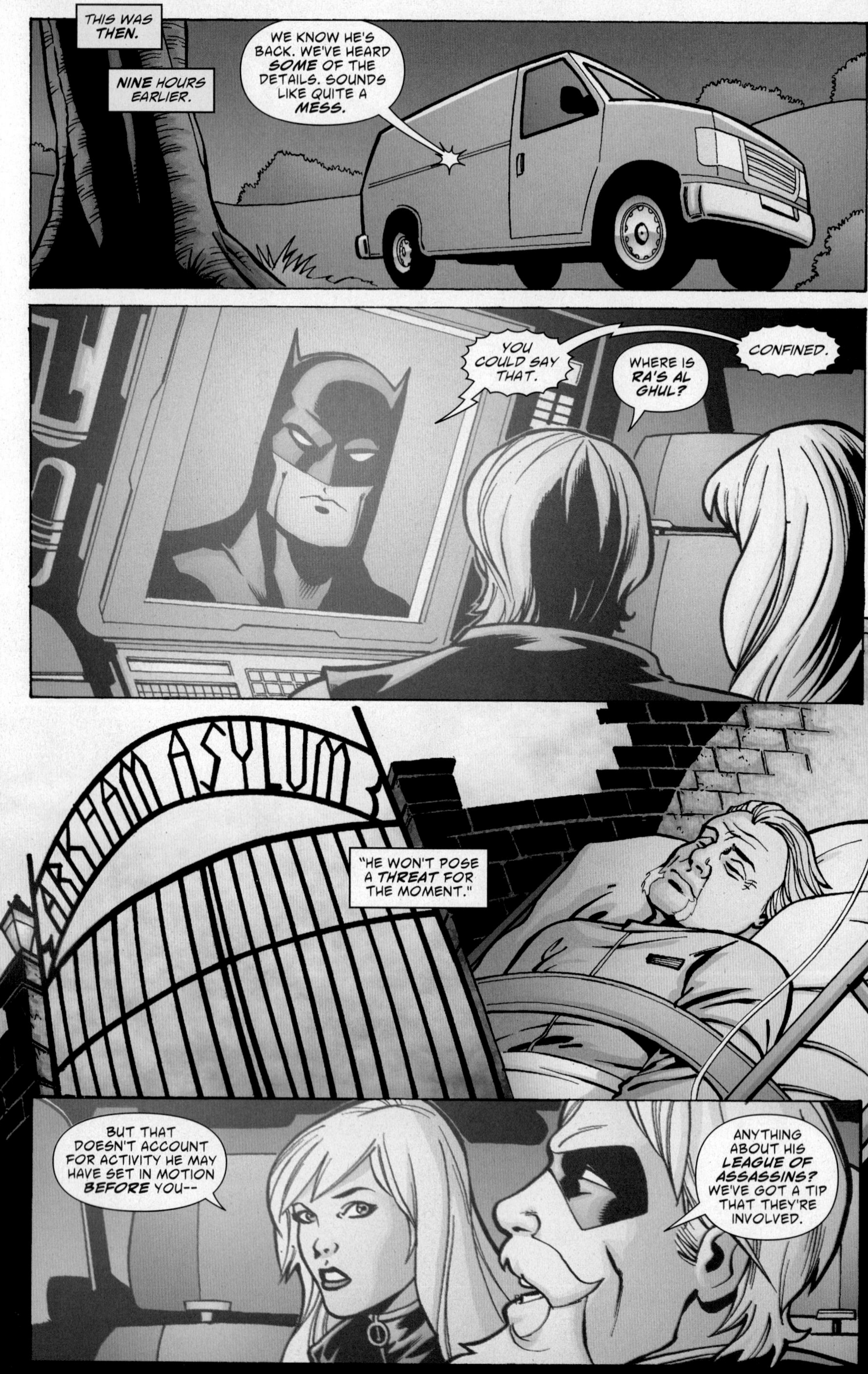
THIS WAS THEN.
NINE HOURS EARLIER.
WE KNOW HE'S BACK. WE'VE HEARD SOME OF THE DETAILS. SOUNDS LIKE QUITE A MESS.
YOU COULD SAY THAT.
WHERE IS RA'S AL GHUL?
CONFINED.
ARKHAM ASYLUM
"HE WON'T POSE A THREAT FOR THE MOMENT."
BUT THAT DOESN'T ACCOUNT FOR ACTIVITY HE MAY HAVE SET IN MOTION BEFORE YOU--
ANYTHING ABOUT HIS LEAGUE OF ASSASSINS? WE'VE GOT A TIP THAT THEY'RE INVOLVED.

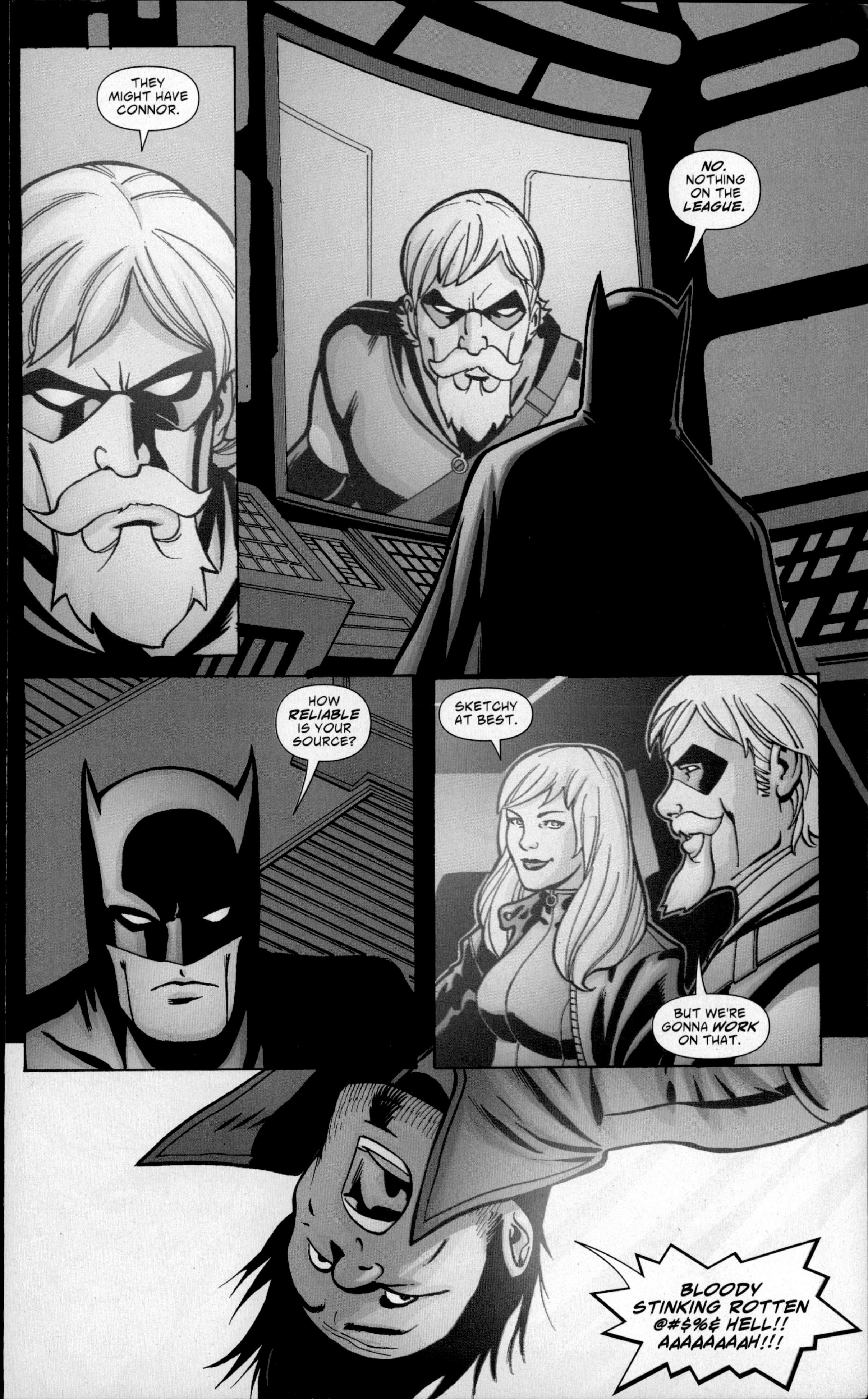
THEY MIGHT HAVE CONNOR.
NO. NOTHING ON THE *LEAGUE.*
HOW *RELIABLE* IS YOUR SOURCE?
SKETCHY AT BEST.
BUT WE'RE GONNA *WORK* ON THAT.
BLOODY STINKING ROTTEN @#$%& HELL!! AAAAAAAAH!!!

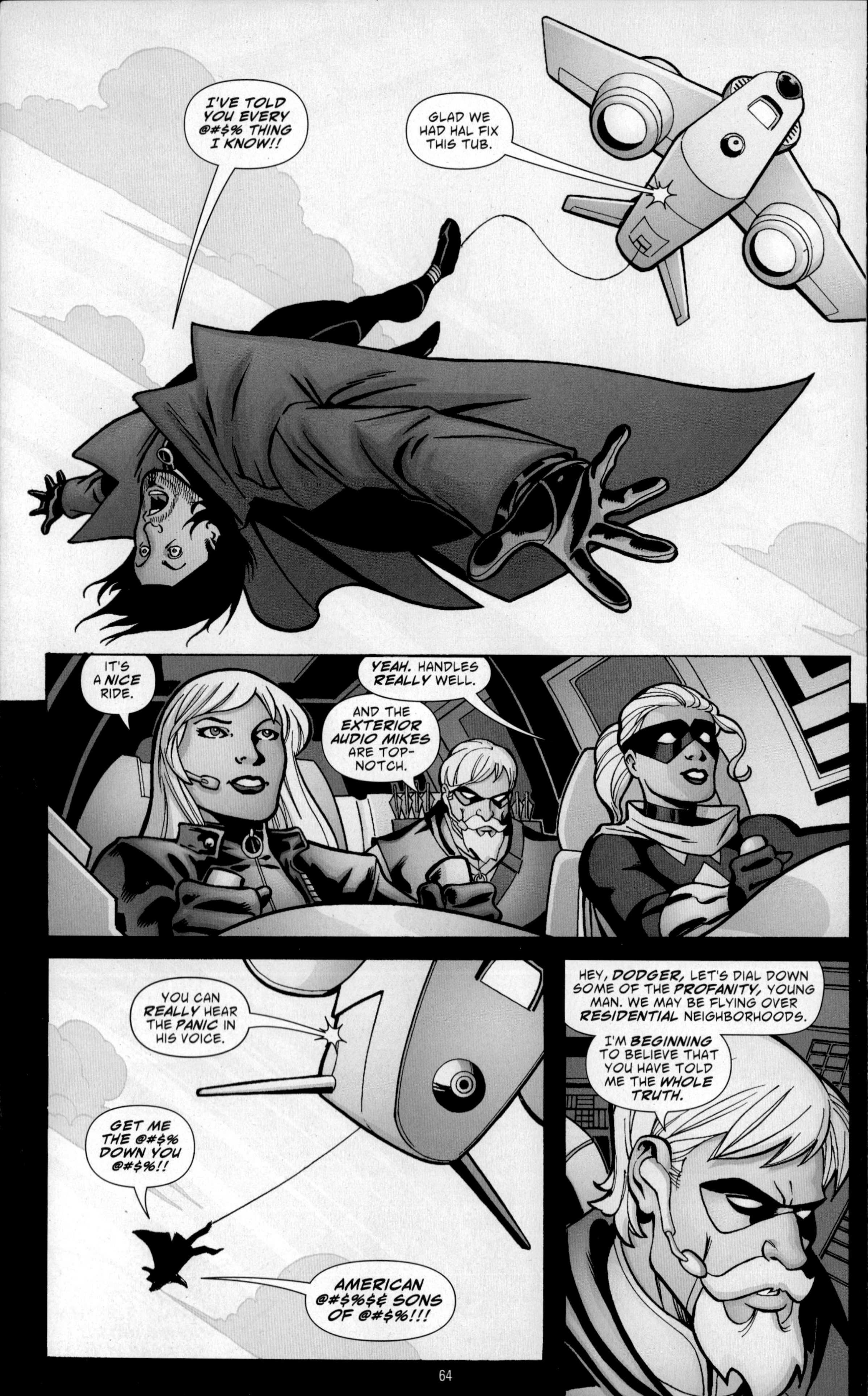
I'VE TOLD YOU EVERY @#$% THING I KNOW!!
GLAD WE HAD HAL FIX THIS TUB.
IT'S A NICE RIDE.
YEAH. HANDLES REALLY WELL.
AND THE EXTERIOR AUDIO MIKES ARE TOP-NOTCH.
YOU CAN REALLY HEAR THE PANIC IN HIS VOICE.
GET ME THE @#$% DOWN YOU @#$%!!
AMERICAN @#$%$& SONS OF @#$%!!!
HEY, DODGER, LET'S DIAL DOWN SOME OF THE PROFANITY, YOUNG MAN. WE MAY BE FLYING OVER RESIDENTIAL NEIGHBORHOODS.
I'M BEGINNING TO BELIEVE THAT YOU HAVE TOLD ME THE WHOLE TRUTH.

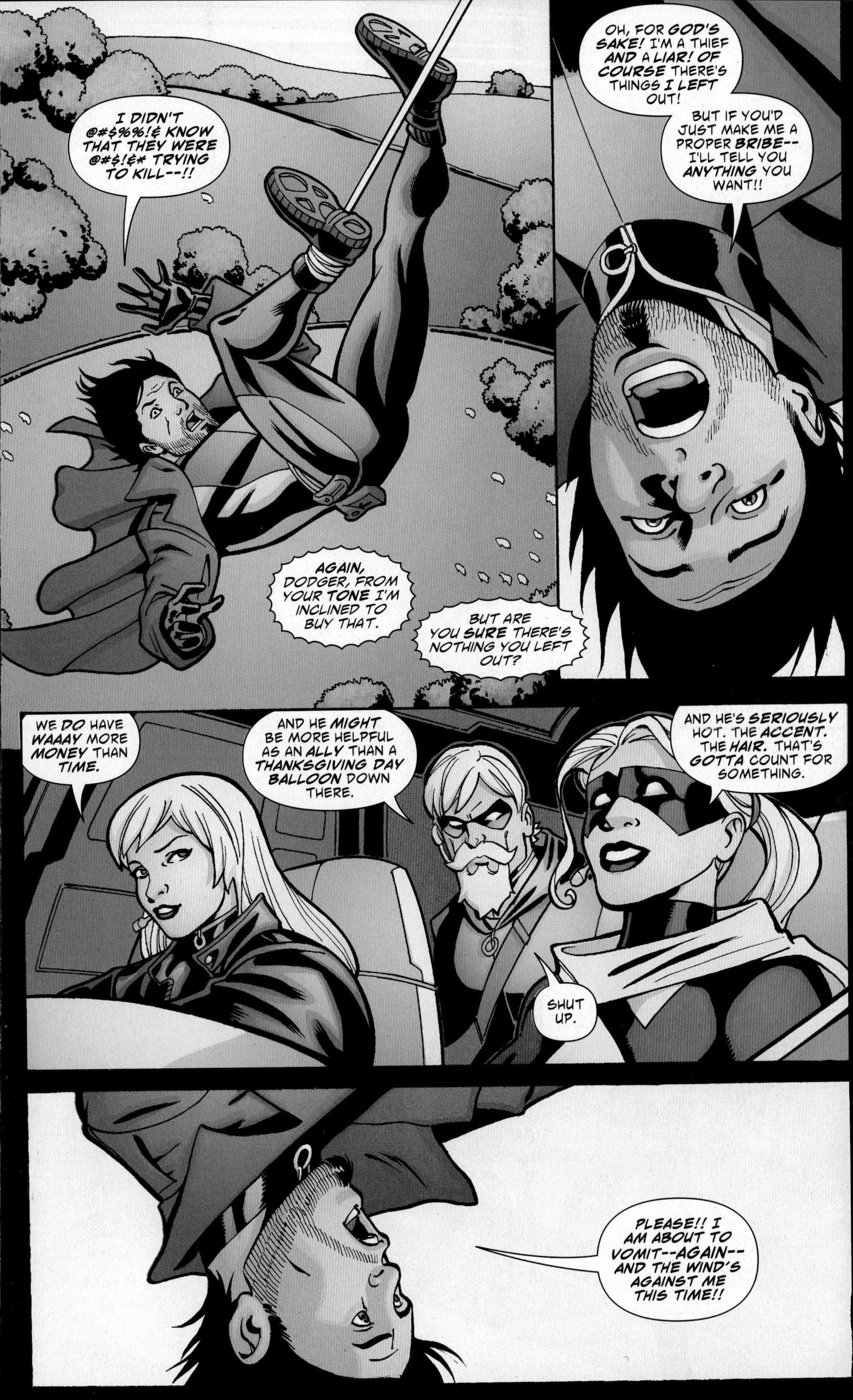

I DIDN'T @#$%%!& KNOW THAT THEY WERE @#$!&* TRYING TO KILL--!!
OH, FOR GOD'S SAKE! I'M A THIEF AND A LIAR! OF COURSE THERE'S THINGS I LEFT OUT!
BUT IF YOU'D JUST MAKE ME A PROPER BRIBE-- I'LL TELL YOU ANYTHING YOU WANT!!
AGAIN, DODGER, FROM YOUR TONE I'M INCLINED TO BUY THAT.
BUT ARE YOU SURE THERE'S NOTHING YOU LEFT OUT?
WE DO HAVE WAAAY MORE MONEY THAN TIME.
AND HE MIGHT BE MORE HELPFUL AS AN ALLY THAN A THANKSGIVING DAY BALLOON DOWN THERE.
AND HE'S SERIOUSLY HOT. THE ACCENT. THE HAIR. THAT'S GOTTA COUNT FOR SOMETHING.
SHUT UP.
PLEASE!! I AM ABOUT TO VOMIT--AGAIN-- AND THE WIND'S AGAINST ME THIS TIME!!

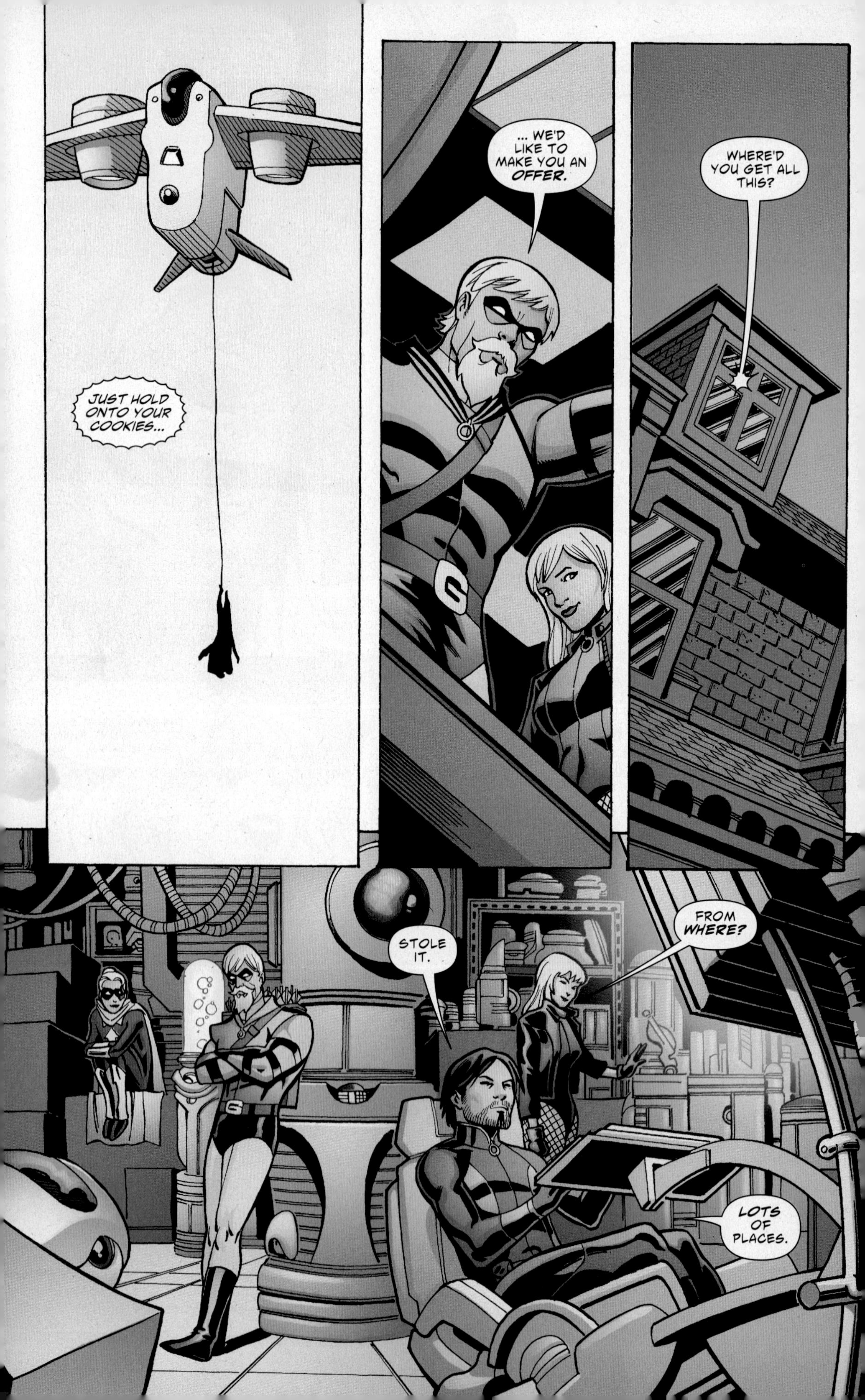
JUST HOLD ONTO YOUR COOKIES...
... WE'D LIKE TO MAKE YOU AN OFFER.
WHERE'D YOU GET ALL THIS?
STOLE IT.
FROM WHERE?
LOTS OF PLACES.

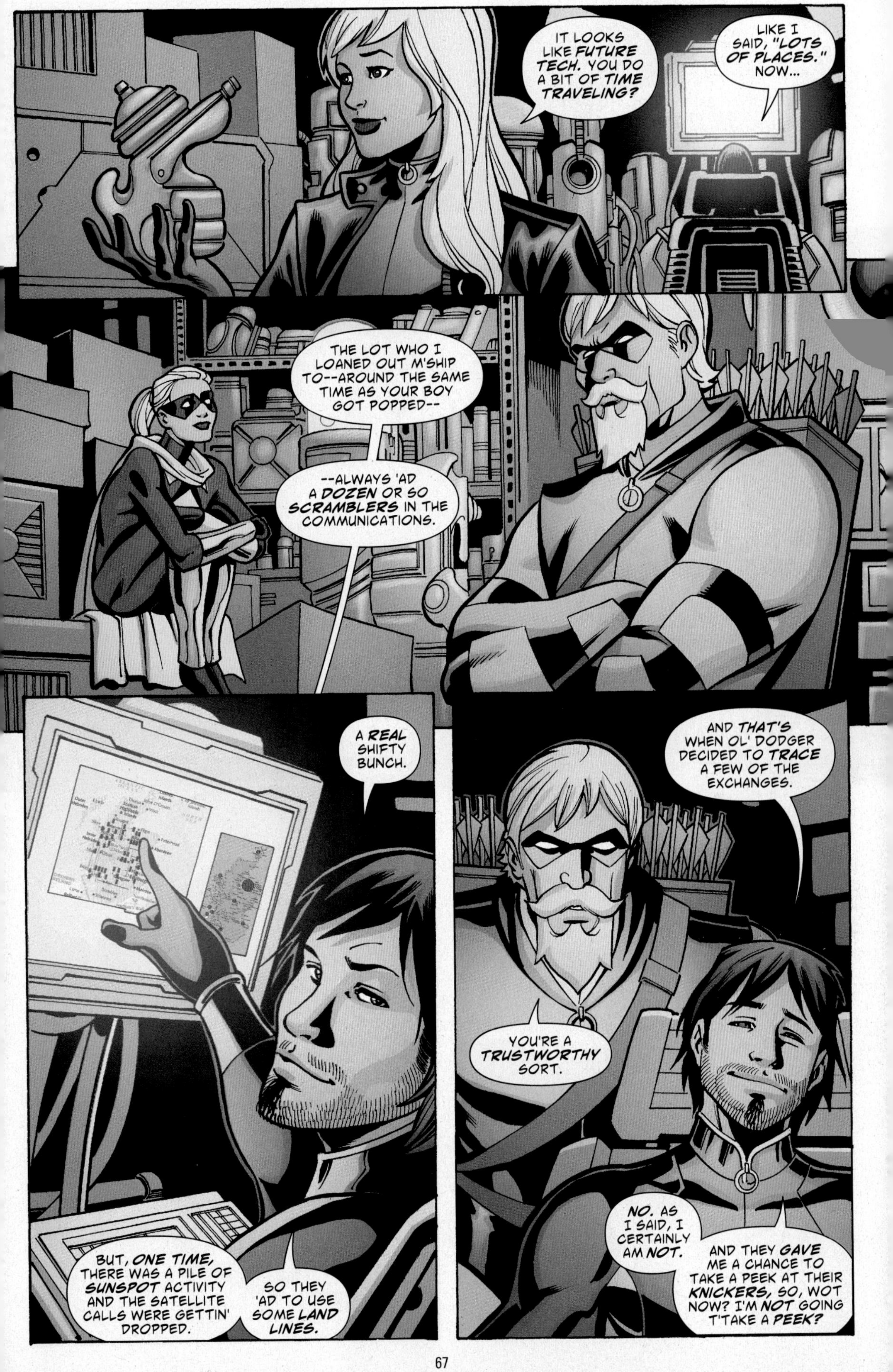
IT LOOKS LIKE FUTURE TECH. YOU DO A BIT OF TIME TRAVELING?
LIKE I SAID, "LOTS OF PLACES." NOW...
THE LOT WHO I LOANED OUT M'SHIP TO--AROUND THE SAME TIME AS YOUR BOY GOT POPPED--
--ALWAYS 'AD A DOZEN OR SO SCRAMBLERS IN THE COMMUNICATIONS.
A REAL SHIFTY BUNCH.
BUT, ONE TIME, THERE WAS A PILE OF SUNSPOT ACTIVITY AND THE SATELLITE CALLS WERE GETTIN' DROPPED.
SO THEY 'AD TO USE SOME LAND LINES.
AND THAT'S WHEN OL' DODGER DECIDED TO TRACE A FEW OF THE EXCHANGES.
YOU'RE A TRUSTWORTHY SORT.
NO. AS I SAID, I CERTAINLY AM NOT.
AND THEY GAVE ME A CHANCE TO TAKE A PEEK AT THEIR KNICKERS, SO, WOT NOW? I'M NOT GOING T'TAKE A PEEK?

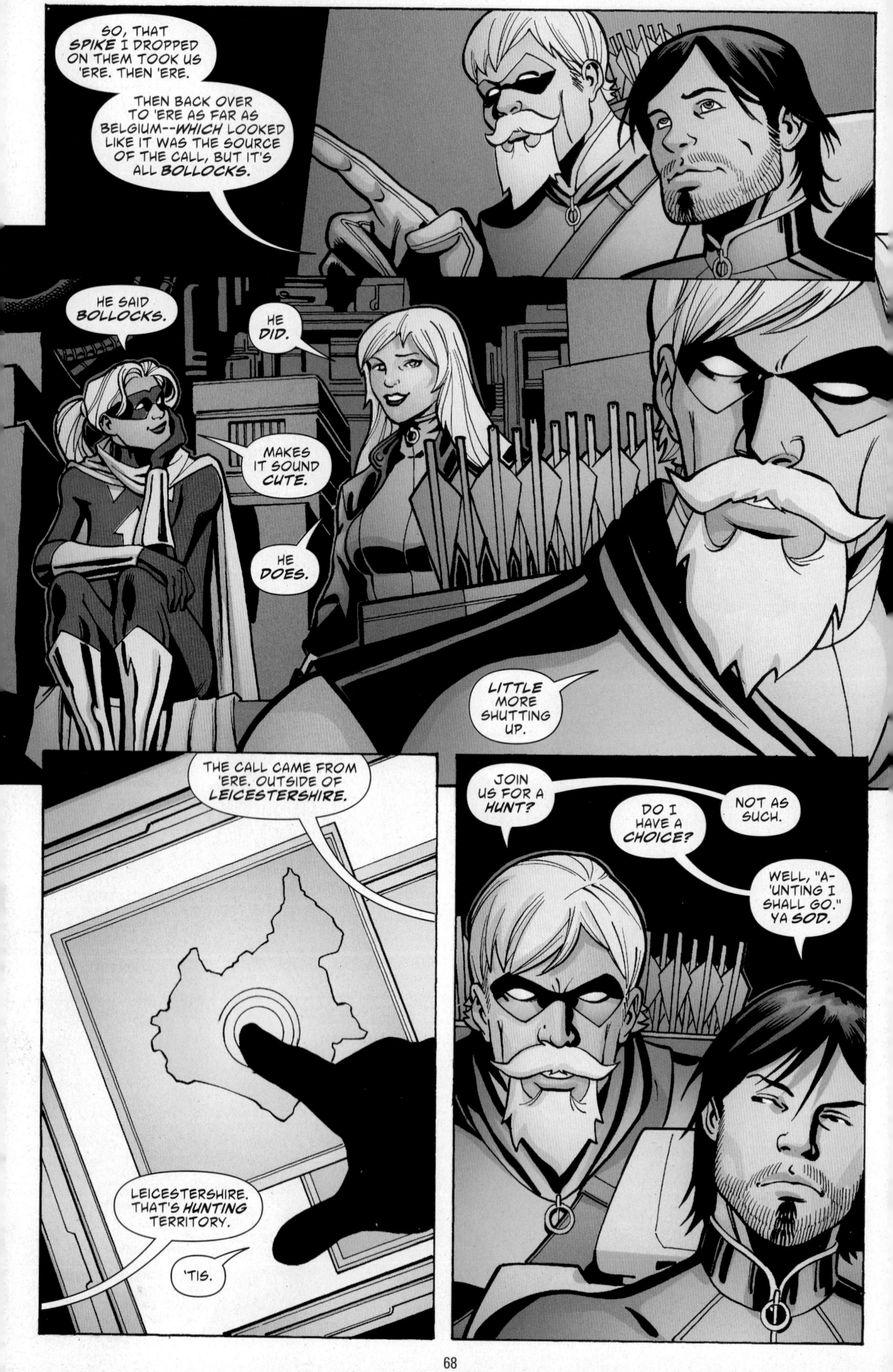
SO, THAT SPIKE I DROPPED ON THEM TOOK US 'ERE. THEN 'ERE.
THEN BACK OVER TO 'ERE AS FAR AS BELGIUM--WHICH LOOKED LIKE IT WAS THE SOURCE OF THE CALL, BUT IT'S ALL BOLLOCKS.
HE SAID BOLLOCKS.
HE DID.
MAKES IT SOUND CUTE.
HE DOES.
LITTLE MORE SHUTTING UP.
THE CALL CAME FROM 'ERE. OUTSIDE OF LEICESTERSHIRE.
LEICESTERSHIRE. THAT'S HUNTING TERRITORY.
'TIS.
JOIN US FOR A HUNT?
NOT AS SUCH.
DO I HAVE A CHOICE?
WELL, "A-'UNTING I SHALL GO." YA SOD.

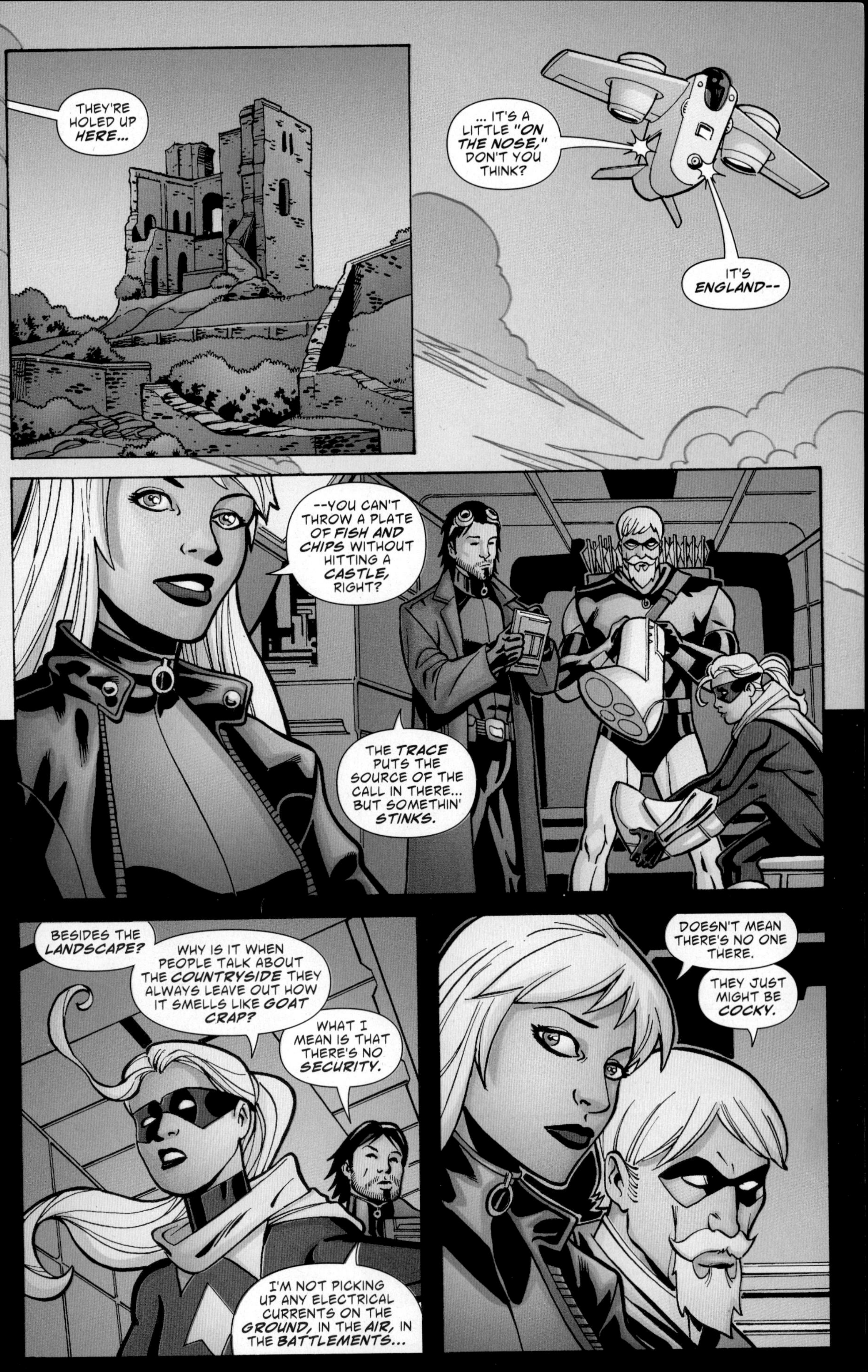
THEY'RE HOLED UP HERE...
... IT'S A LITTLE "ON THE NOSE," DON'T YOU THINK?
IT'S ENGLAND--
--YOU CAN'T THROW A PLATE OF FISH AND CHIPS WITHOUT HITTING A CASTLE, RIGHT?
THE TRACE PUTS THE SOURCE OF THE CALL IN THERE... BUT SOMETHIN' STINKS.
BESIDES THE LANDSCAPE?
WHY IS IT WHEN PEOPLE TALK ABOUT THE COUNTRYSIDE THEY ALWAYS LEAVE OUT HOW IT SMELLS LIKE GOAT CRAP?
WHAT I MEAN IS THAT THERE'S NO SECURITY.
I'M NOT PICKING UP ANY ELECTRICAL CURRENTS ON THE GROUND, IN THE AIR, IN THE BATTLEMENTS...
DOESN'T MEAN THERE'S NO ONE THERE.
THEY JUST MIGHT BE COCKY.

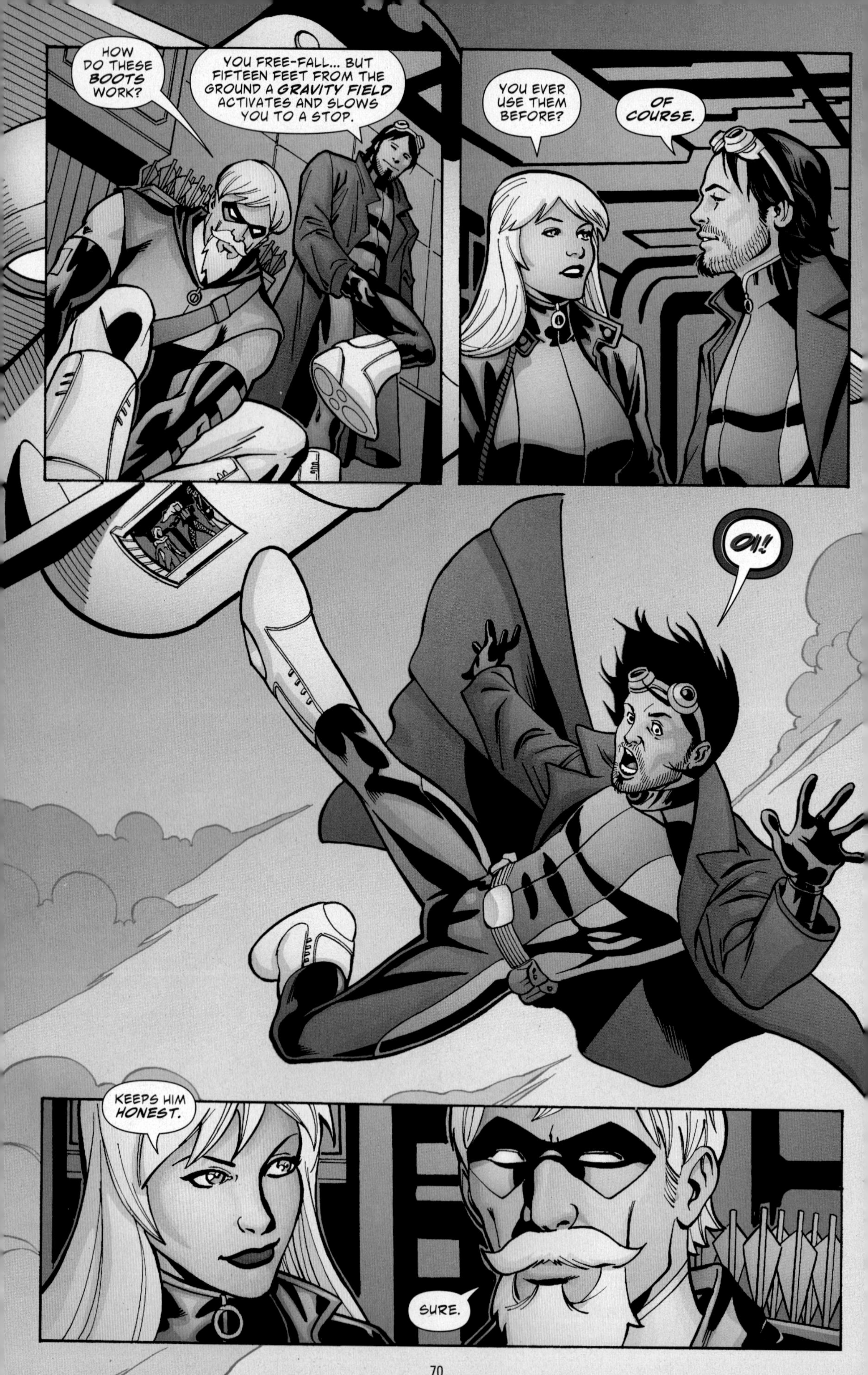
HOW DO THESE BOOTS WORK?
YOU FREE-FALL... BUT FIFTEEN FEET FROM THE GROUND A GRAVITY FIELD ACTIVATES AND SLOWS YOU TO A STOP.
YOU EVER USE THEM BEFORE?
OF COURSE.
OI!!
KEEPS HIM HONEST.
SURE.

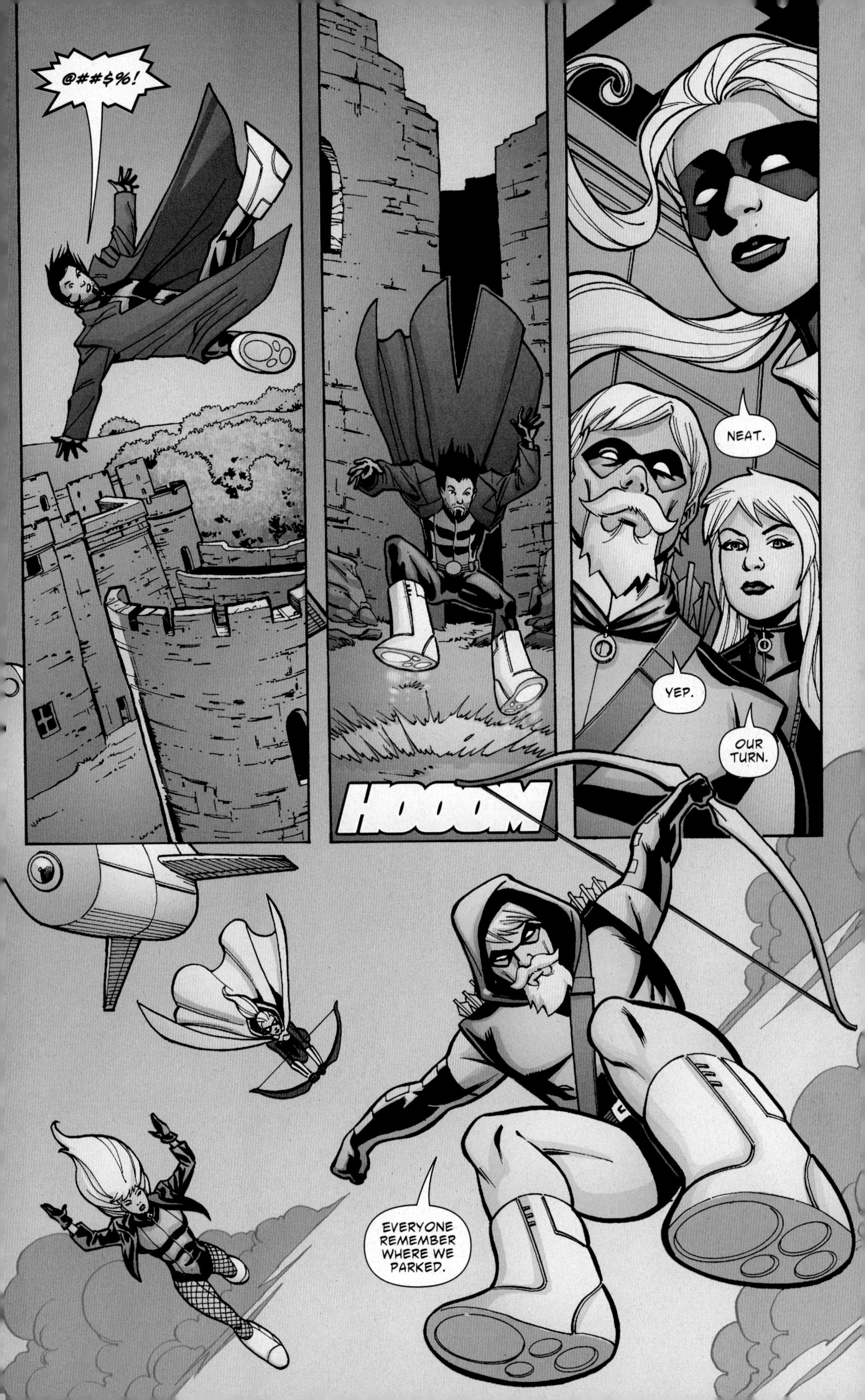

@##$%!
HOOOM
NEAT.
YEP.
OUR TURN.
EVERYONE REMEMBER WHERE WE PARKED.

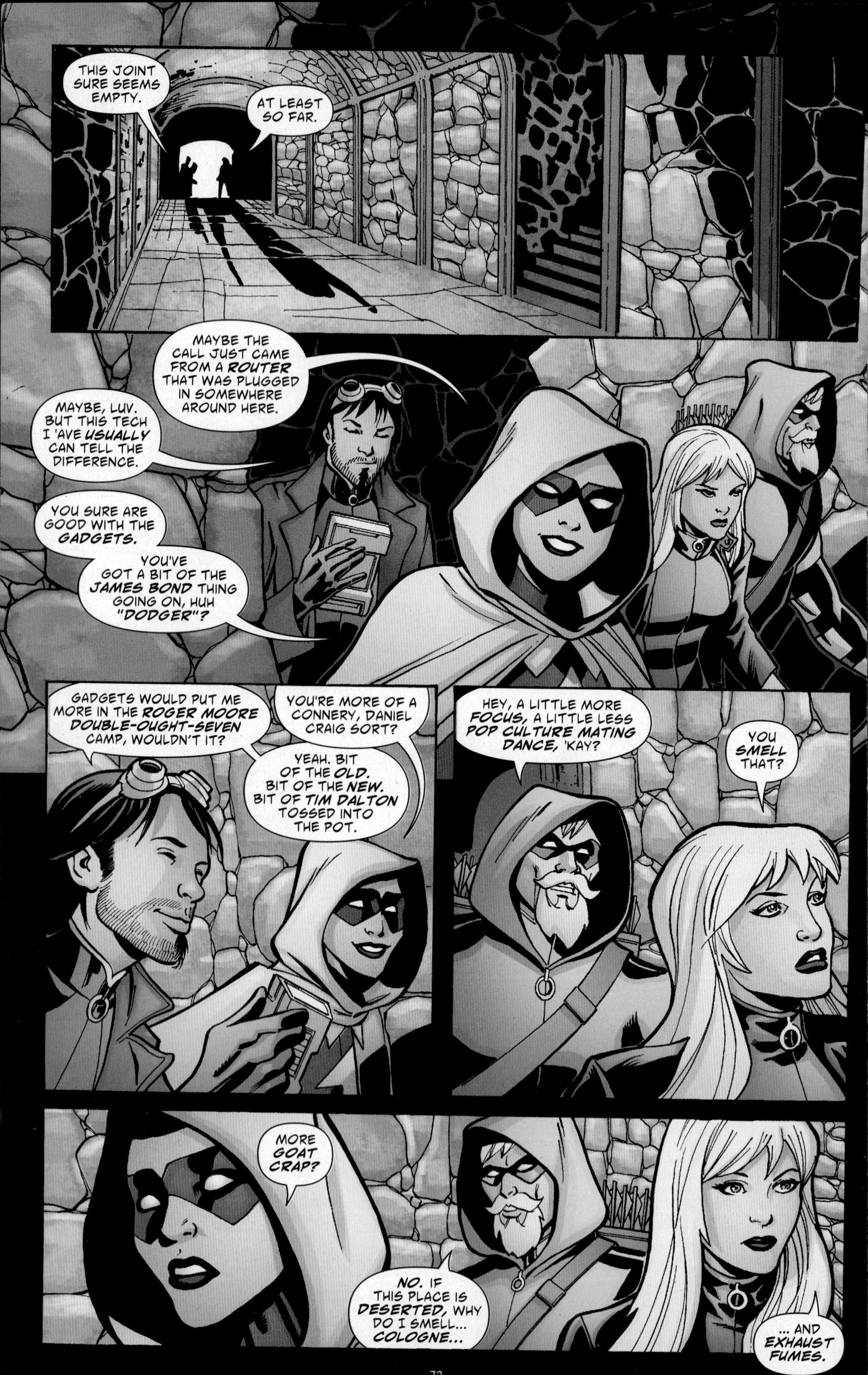
THIS JOINT SURE SEEMS EMPTY.
AT LEAST SO FAR.
MAYBE THE CALL JUST CAME FROM A ROUTER THAT WAS PLUGGED IN SOMEWHERE AROUND HERE.
MAYBE, LUV. BUT THIS TECH I 'AVE USUALLY CAN TELL THE DIFFERENCE.
YOU SURE ARE GOOD WITH THE GADGETS.
YOU'VE GOT A BIT OF THE JAMES BOND THING GOING ON, HUH "DODGER"?
GADGETS WOULD PUT ME MORE IN THE ROGER MOORE DOUBLE-OUGHT-SEVEN CAMP, WOULDN'T IT?
YOU'RE MORE OF A CONNERY, DANIEL CRAIG SORT?
YEAH. BIT OF THE OLD. BIT OF THE NEW. BIT OF TIM DALTON TOSSED INTO THE POT.
HEY, A LITTLE MORE FOCUS, A LITTLE LESS POP CULTURE MATING DANCE, 'KAY?
YOU SMELL THAT?
MORE GOAT CRAP?
NO. IF THIS PLACE IS DESERTED, WHY DO I SMELL... COLOGNE...
... AND EXHAUST FUMES.

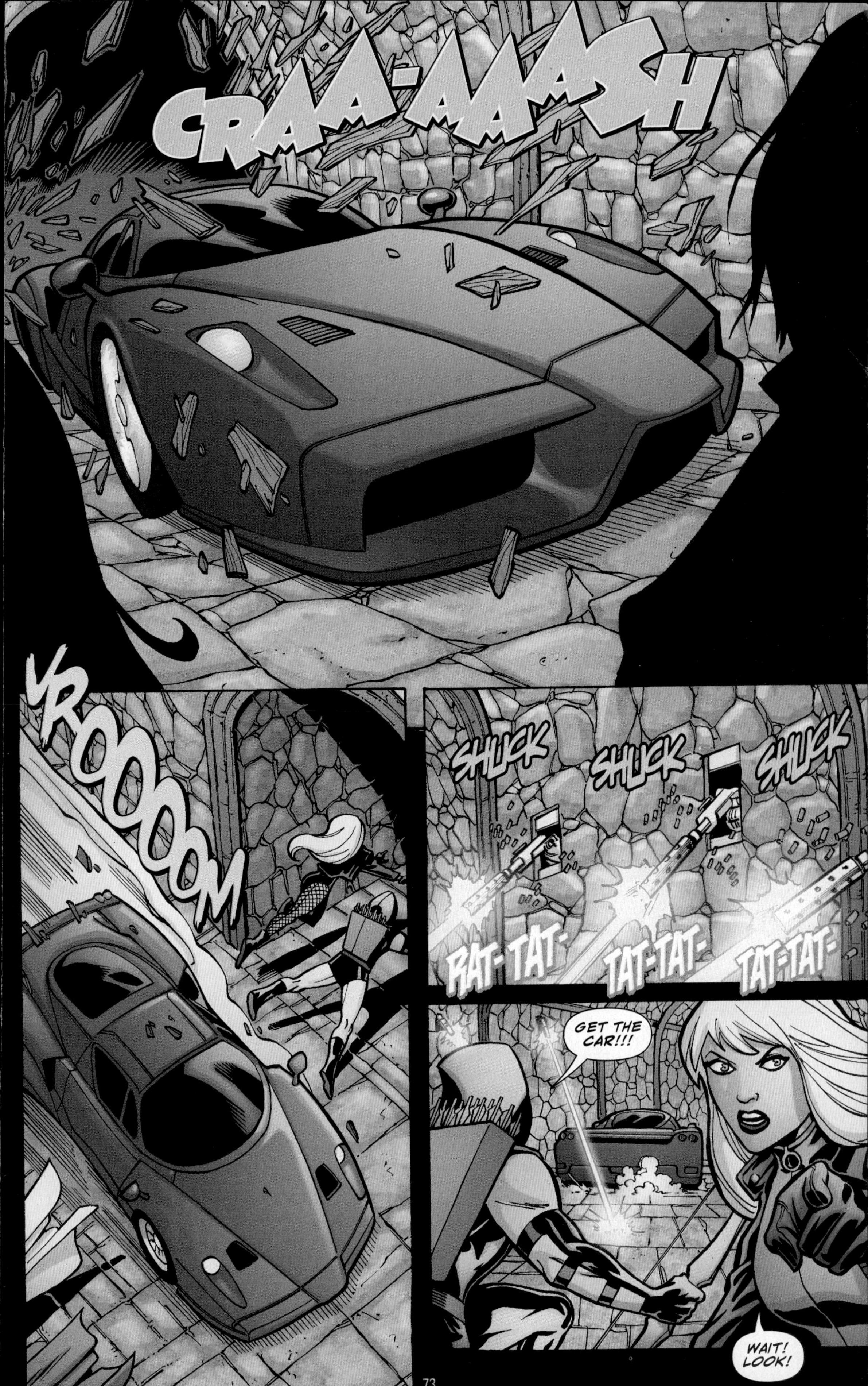
CRAA-AAASH
VROOOOOM
SHUCK
SHUCK
SHUCK
RAT-TAT-
TAT-TAT-
TAT-TAT-
GET THE CAR!!!
WAIT! LOOK!

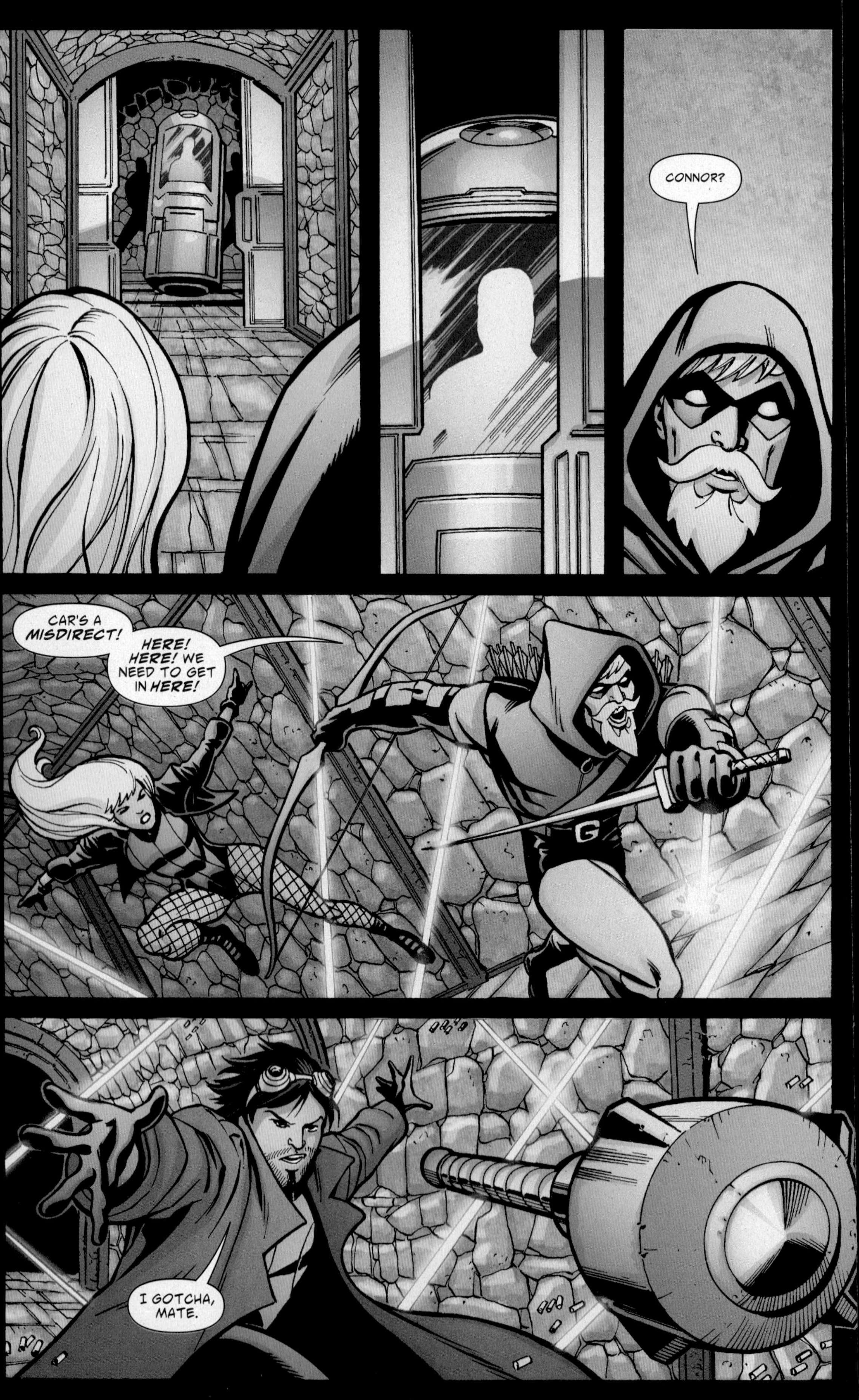
CONNOR?
CAR'S A MISDIRECT!
HERE! HERE! WE NEED TO GET IN HERE!
I GOTCHA, MATE.

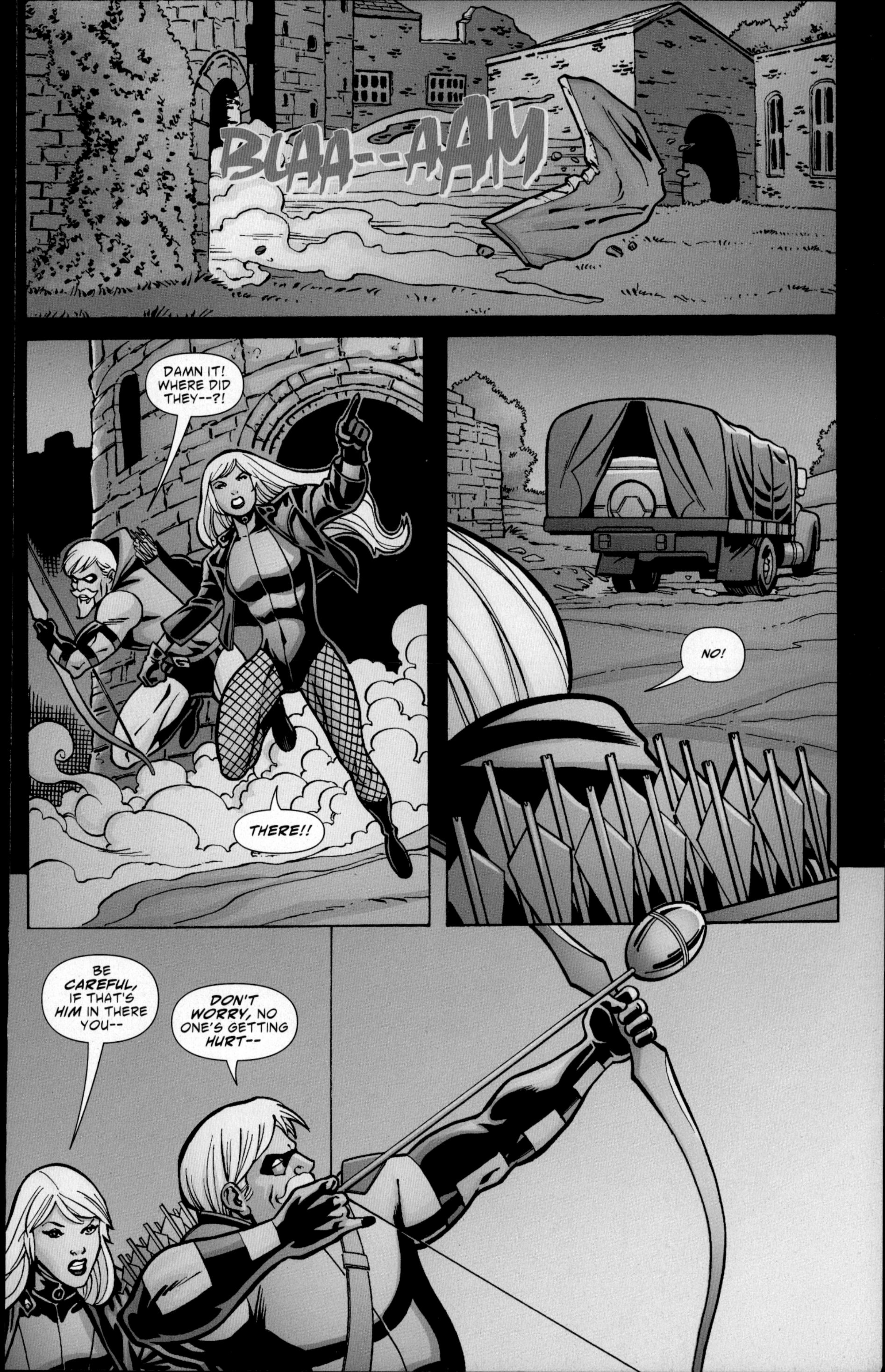
BLAA--AAM
DAMN IT! WHERE DID THEY--?!
THERE!!
NO!
BE CAREFUL, IF THAT'S HIM IN THERE YOU--
DON'T WORRY, NO ONE'S GETTING HURT--

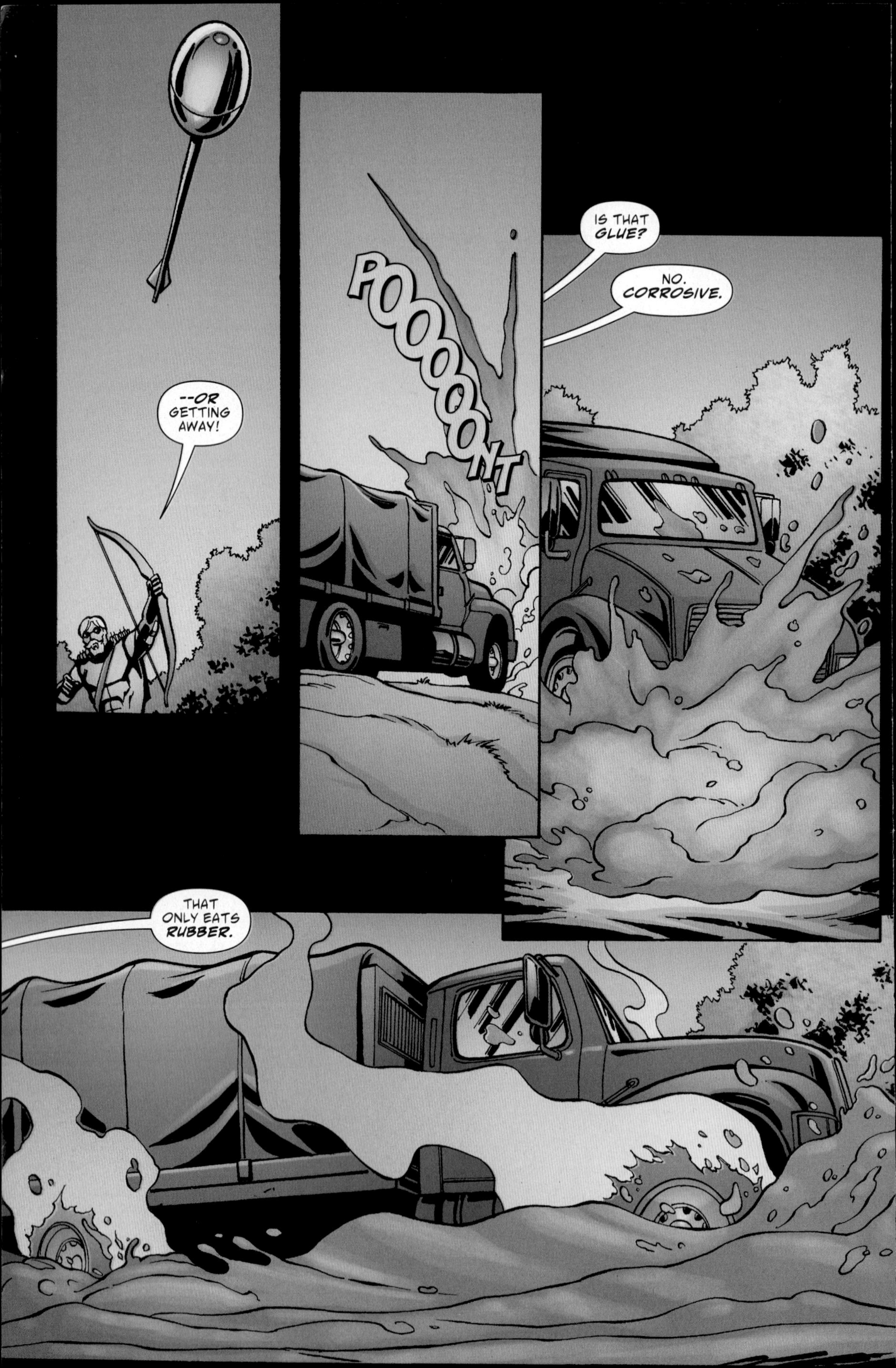
--OR GETTING AWAY!
POOOOOONT
IS THAT GLUE?
NO. CORROSIVE.
THAT ONLY EATS RUBBER.

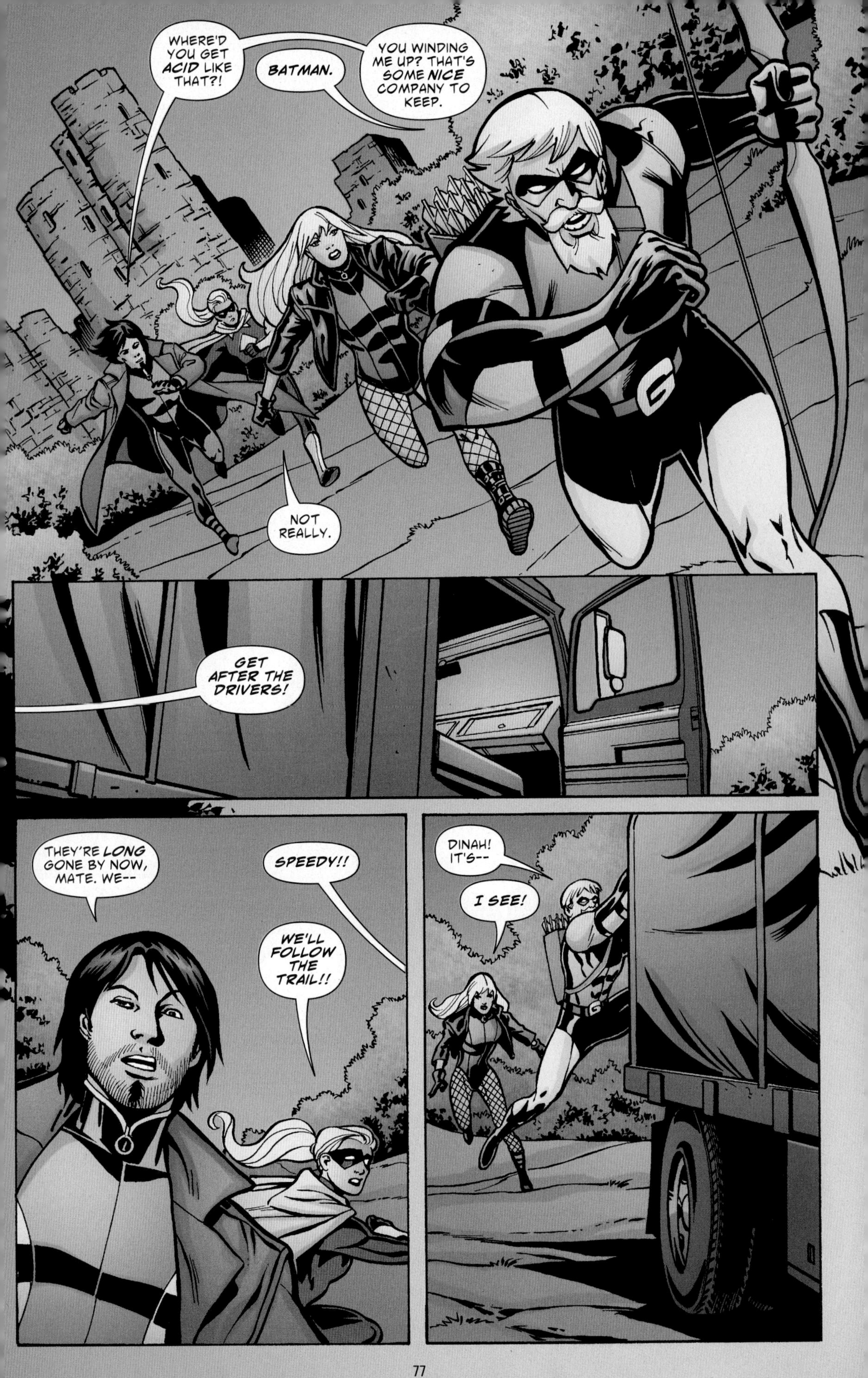
WHERE'D YOU GET ACID LIKE THAT?!
BATMAN.
YOU WINDING ME UP? THAT'S SOME NICE COMPANY TO KEEP.
NOT REALLY.
GET AFTER THE DRIVERS!
THEY'RE LONG GONE BY NOW, MATE. WE--
SPEEDY!!
WE'LL FOLLOW THE TRAIL!!
DINAH! IT'S--
I SEE!

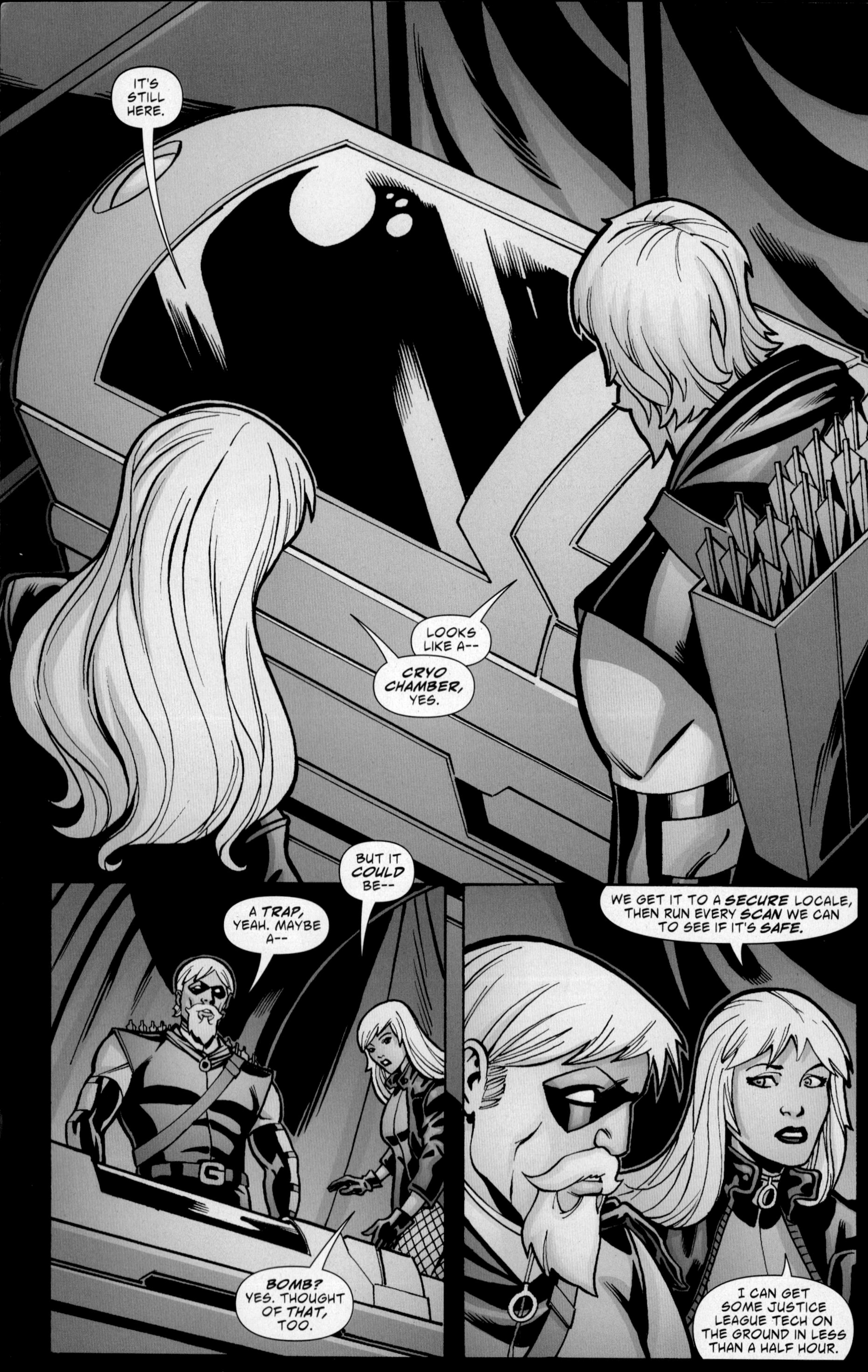
IT'S STILL HERE.
LOOKS LIKE A--
CRYO CHAMBER, YES.
A TRAP, YEAH. MAYBE A--
BUT IT COULD BE--
BOMB? YES. THOUGHT OF THAT, TOO.
WE GET IT TO A SECURE LOCALE, THEN RUN EVERY SCAN WE CAN TO SEE IF IT'S SAFE.
I CAN GET SOME JUSTICE LEAGUE TECH ON THE GROUND IN LESS THAN A HALF HOUR.

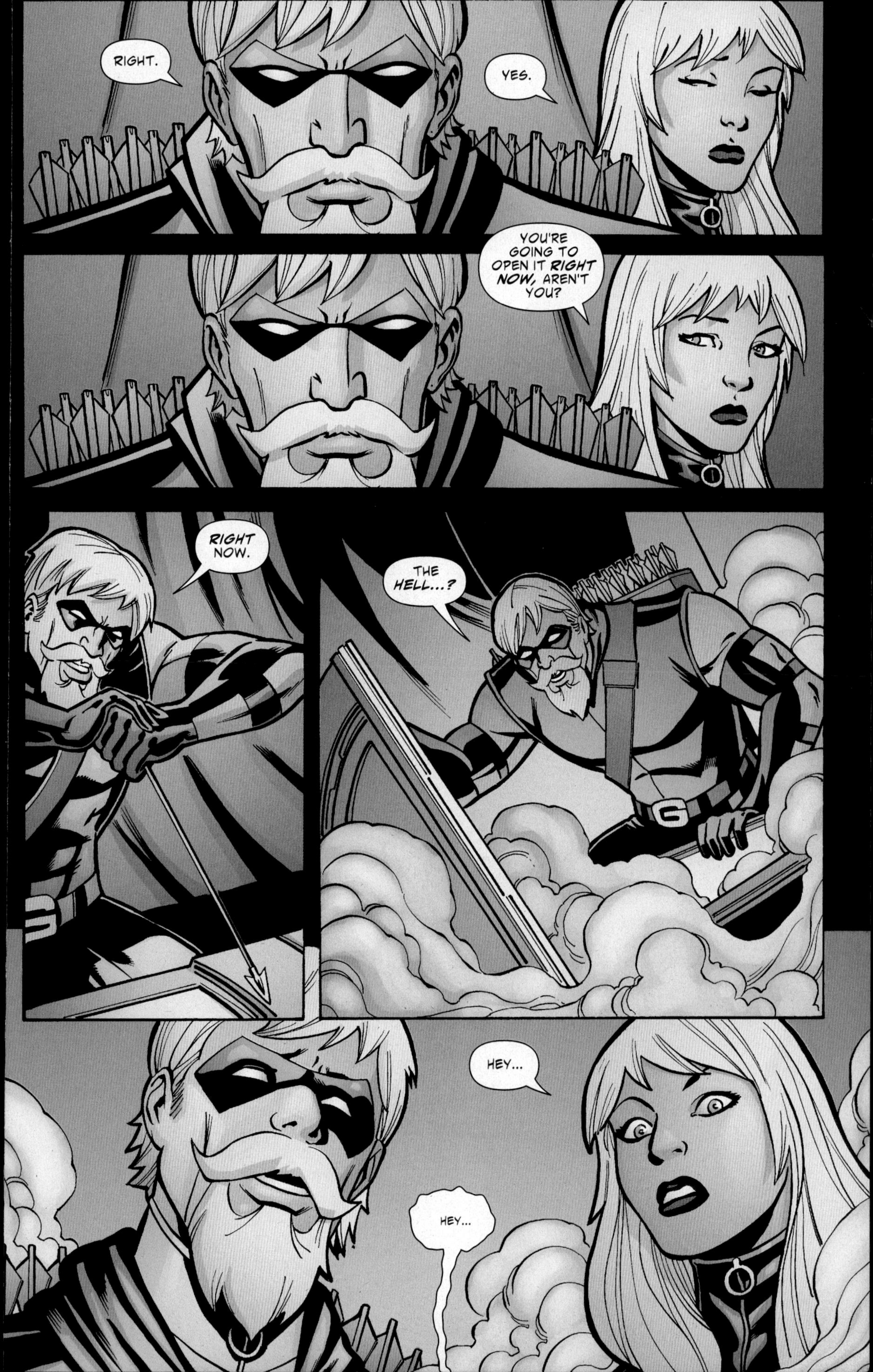
RIGHT.
YES.
YOU'RE GOING TO OPEN IT *RIGHT NOW,* AREN'T YOU?
RIGHT NOW.
THE *HELL...?*
HEY...
HEY...

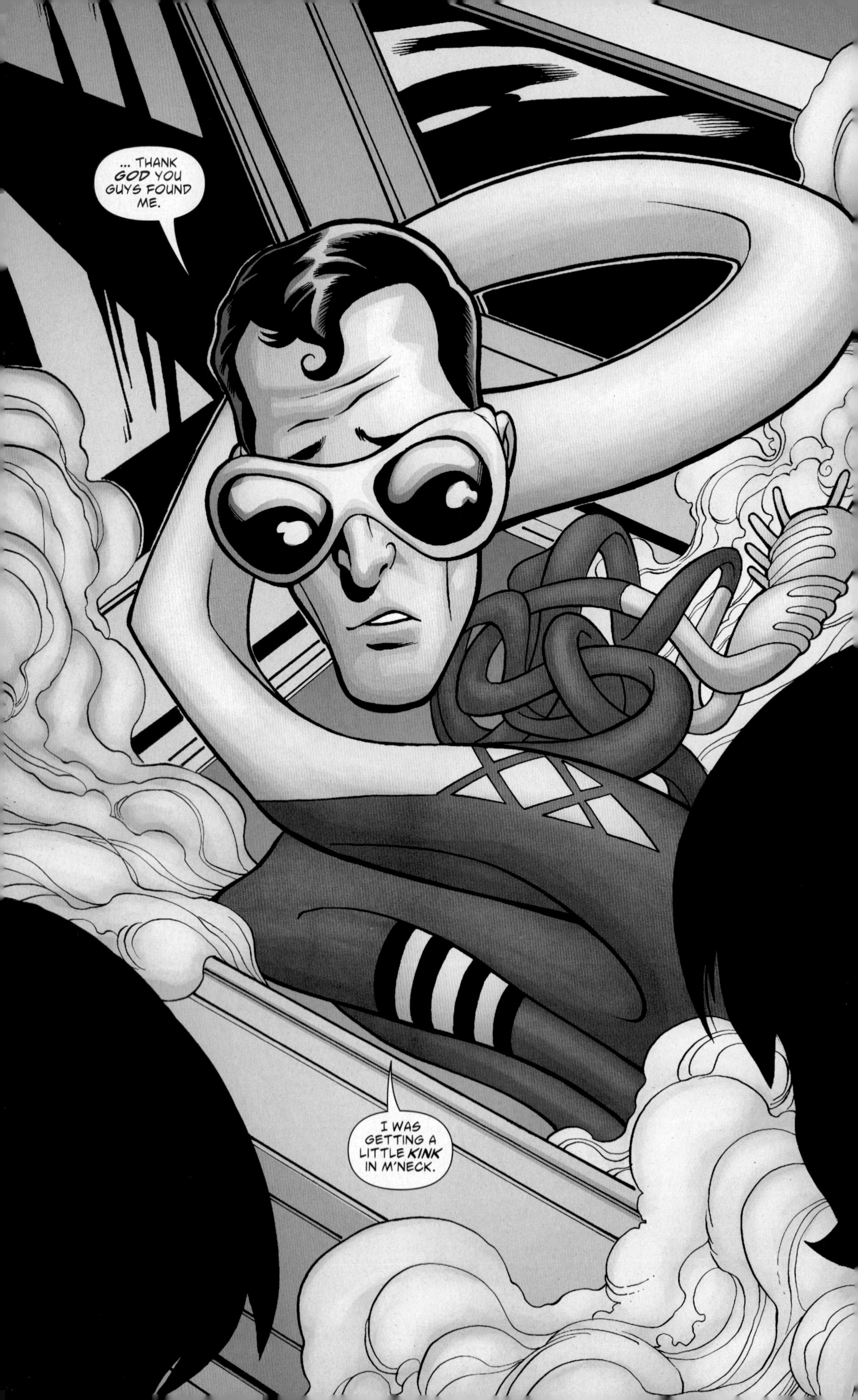
... THANK GOD YOU GUYS FOUND ME.
I WAS GETTING A LITTLE KINK IN M'NECK.

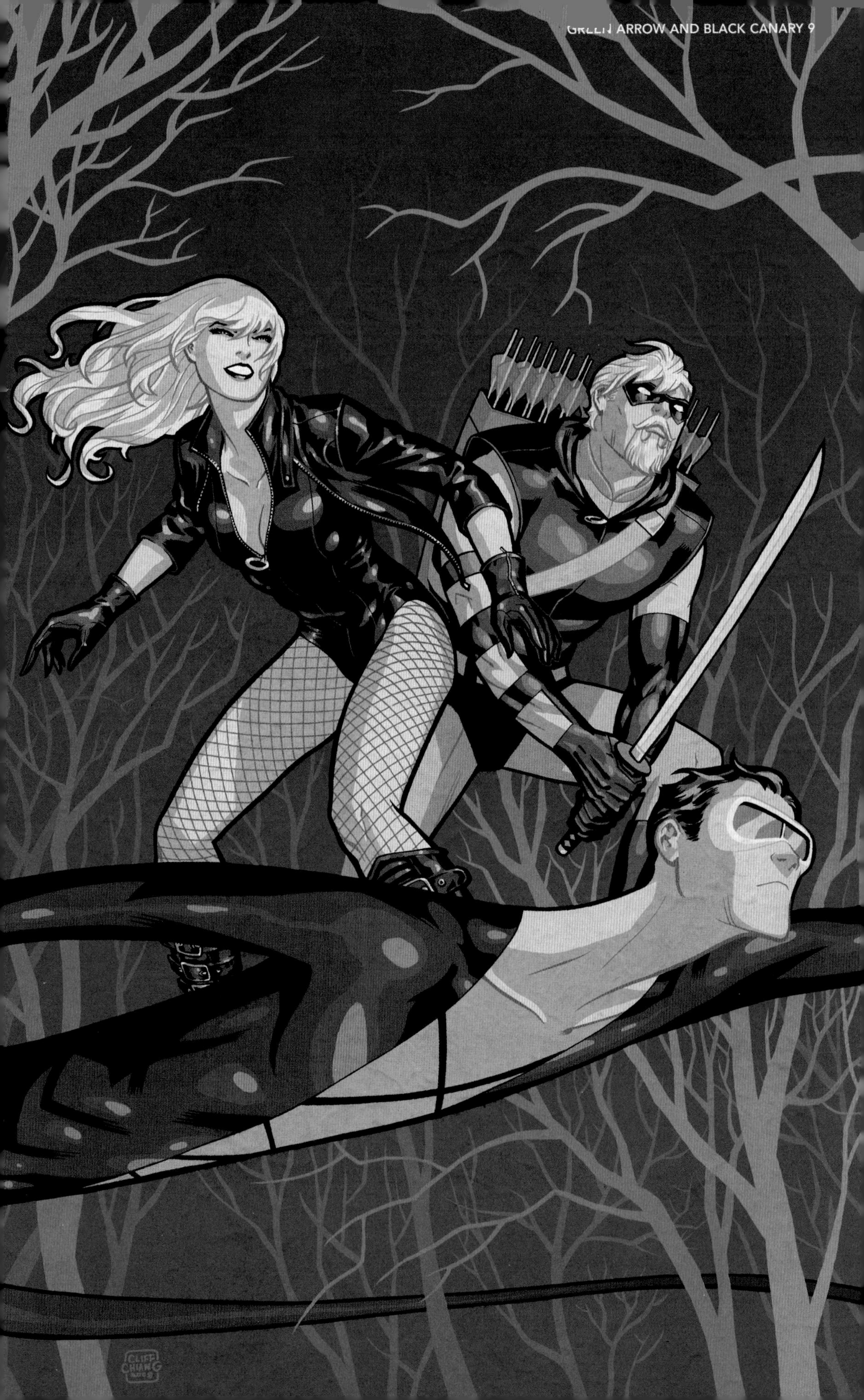
CLIFF CHIANG

A LEAGUE OF THEIR OWN

PART 1: RUBBER AND GLUE

JUDD WINICK
STORY

MIKE NORTON / WAYNE FAUCHER
ART

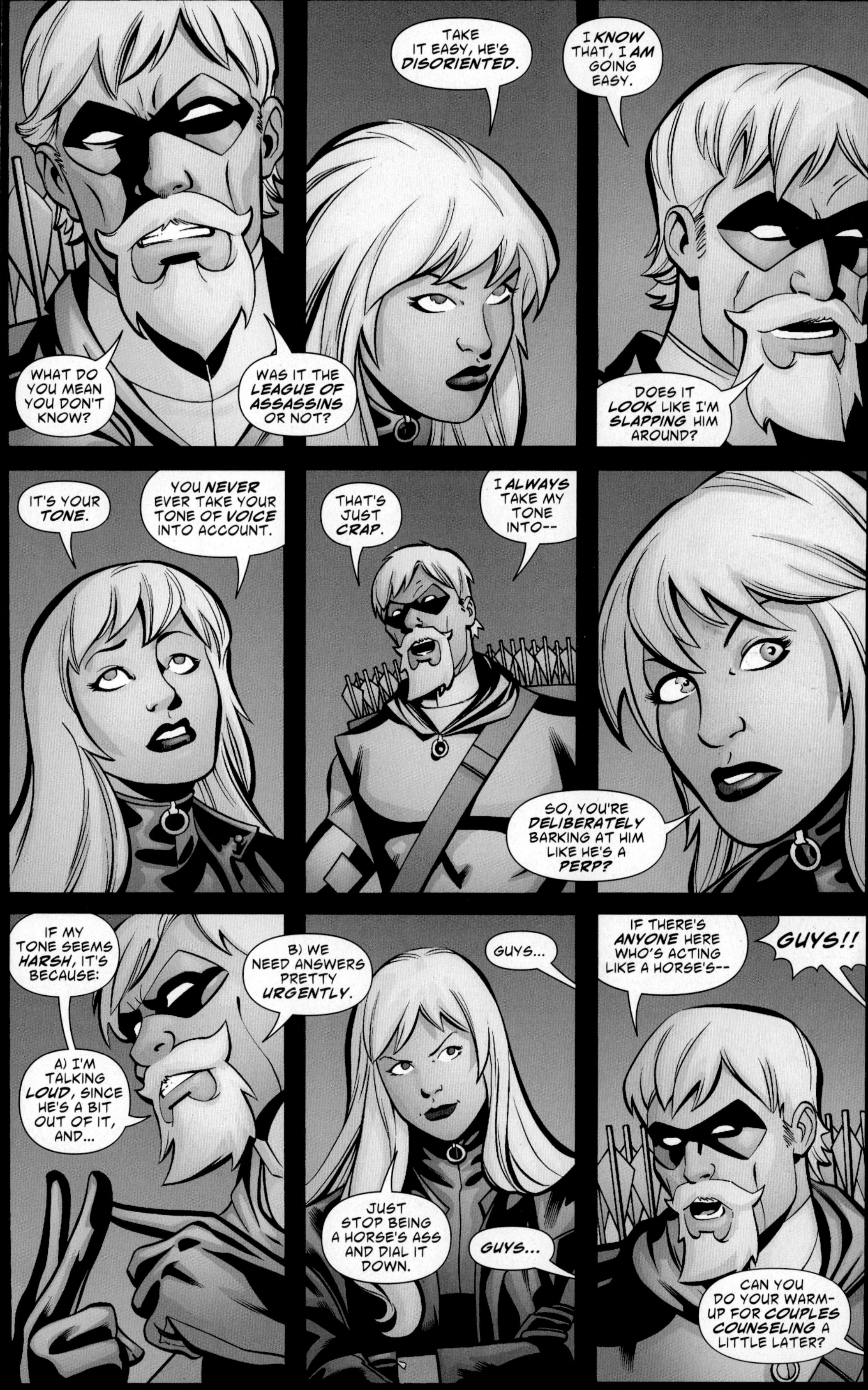
WHAT DO YOU MEAN YOU DON'T KNOW?
WAS IT THE LEAGUE OF ASSASSINS OR NOT?
TAKE IT EASY, HE'S DISORIENTED.
I KNOW THAT, I AM GOING EASY.
DOES IT LOOK LIKE I'M SLAPPING HIM AROUND?
IT'S YOUR TONE.
YOU NEVER EVER TAKE YOUR TONE OF VOICE INTO ACCOUNT.
THAT'S JUST CRAP.
I ALWAYS TAKE MY TONE INTO--
SO, YOU'RE DELIBERATELY BARKING AT HIM LIKE HE'S A PERP?
IF MY TONE SEEMS HARSH, IT'S BECAUSE:
A) I'M TALKING LOUD, SINCE HE'S A BIT OUT OF IT, AND...
B) WE NEED ANSWERS PRETTY URGENTLY.
GUYS...
JUST STOP BEING A HORSE'S ASS AND DIAL IT DOWN.
GUYS...
IF THERE'S ANYONE HERE WHO'S ACTING LIKE A HORSE'S--
GUYS!!
CAN YOU DO YOUR WARM-UP FOR COUPLES COUNSELING A LITTLE LATER?

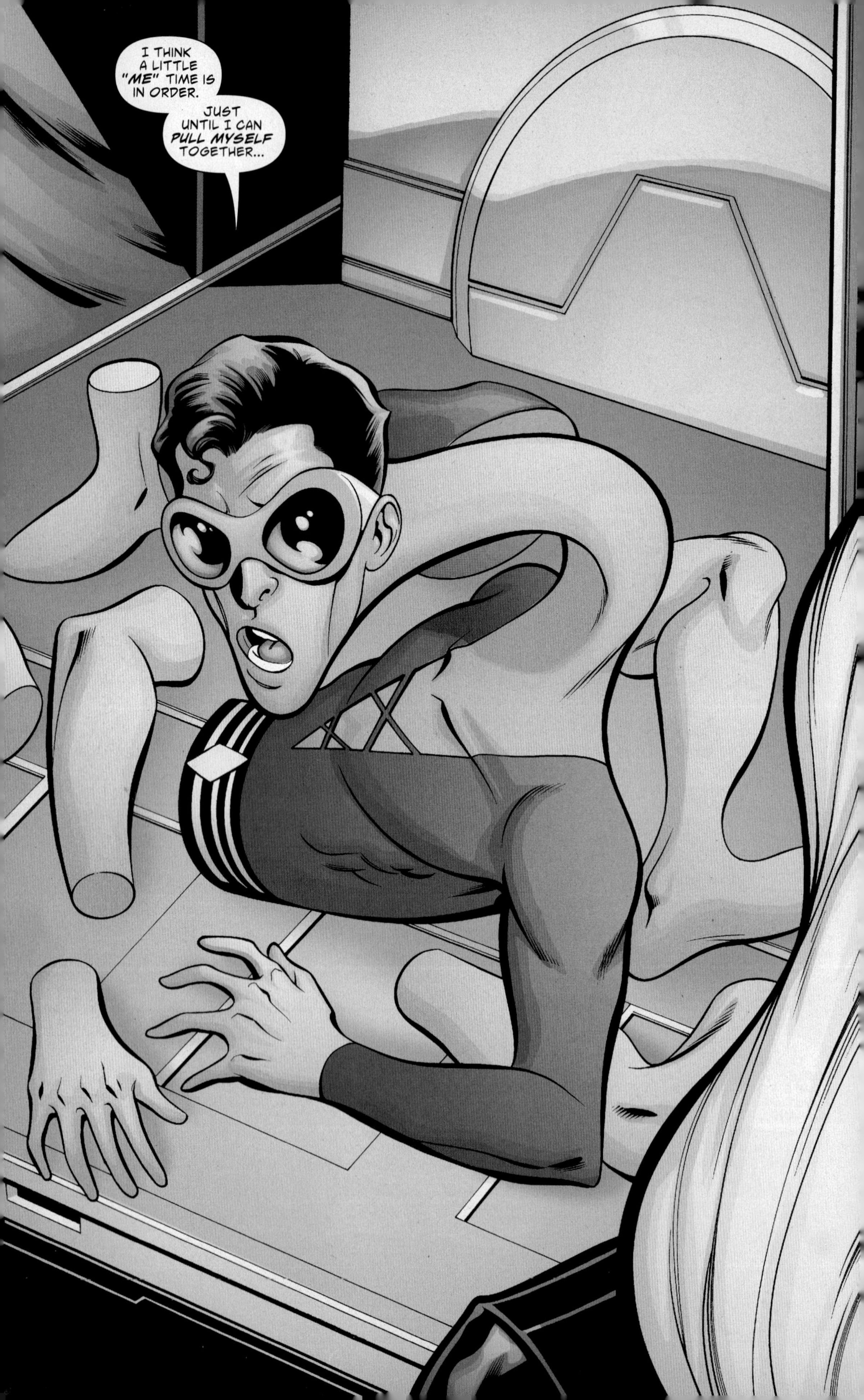

I THINK A LITTLE "ME" TIME IS IN ORDER.
JUST UNTIL I CAN PULL MYSELF TOGETHER...

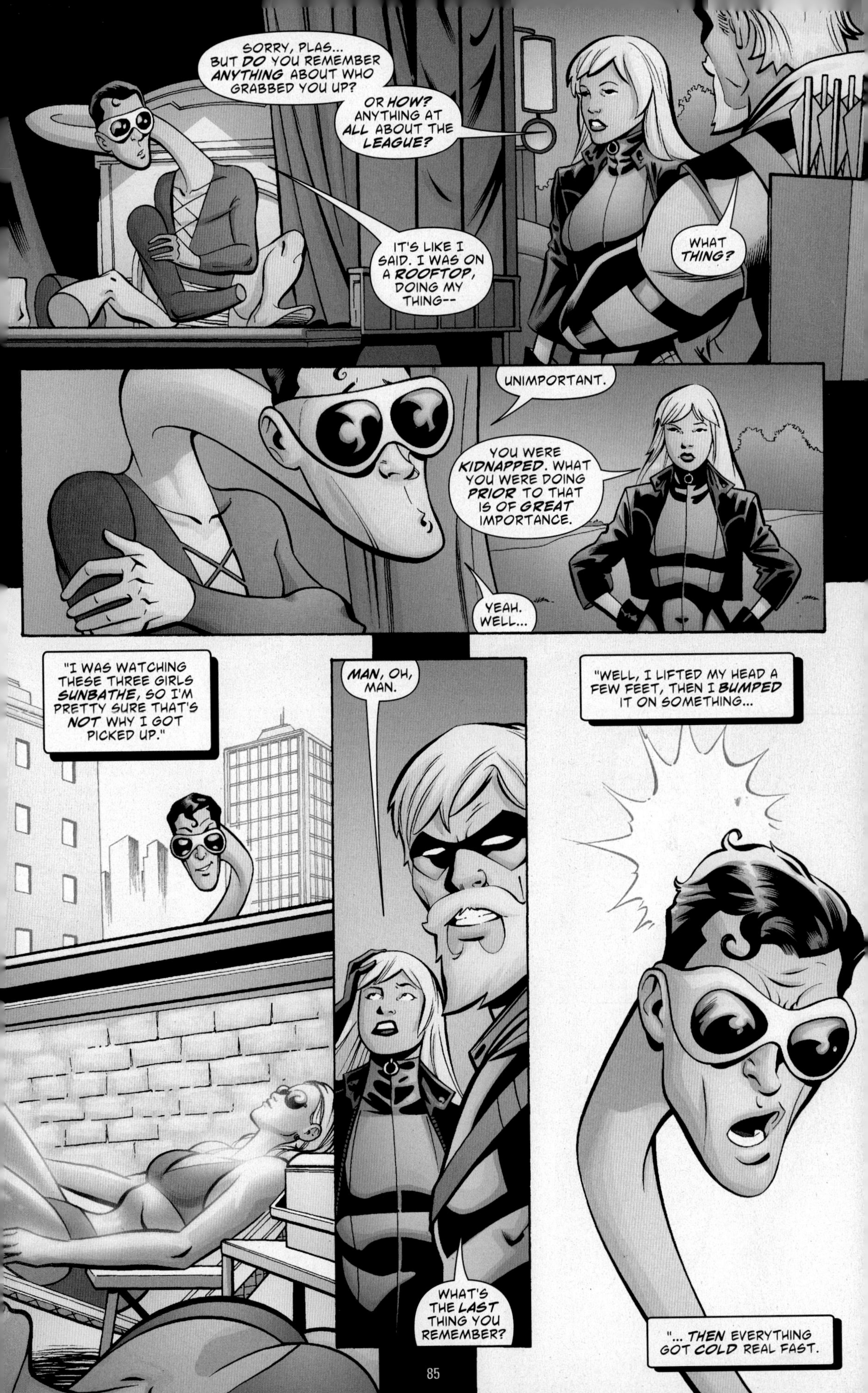
SORRY, PLAS... BUT DO YOU REMEMBER ANYTHING ABOUT WHO GRABBED YOU UP?
OR HOW? ANYTHING AT ALL ABOUT THE LEAGUE?
IT'S LIKE I SAID. I WAS ON A ROOFTOP, DOING MY THING--
WHAT THING?
UNIMPORTANT.
YOU WERE KIDNAPPED. WHAT YOU WERE DOING PRIOR TO THAT IS OF GREAT IMPORTANCE.
YEAH. WELL...
"I WAS WATCHING THESE THREE GIRLS SUNBATHE, SO I'M PRETTY SURE THAT'S NOT WHY I GOT PICKED UP."
MAN, OH, MAN.
WHAT'S THE LAST THING YOU REMEMBER?
"WELL, I LIFTED MY HEAD A FEW FEET, THEN I BUMPED IT ON SOMETHING...
"... THEN EVERYTHING GOT COLD REAL FAST.

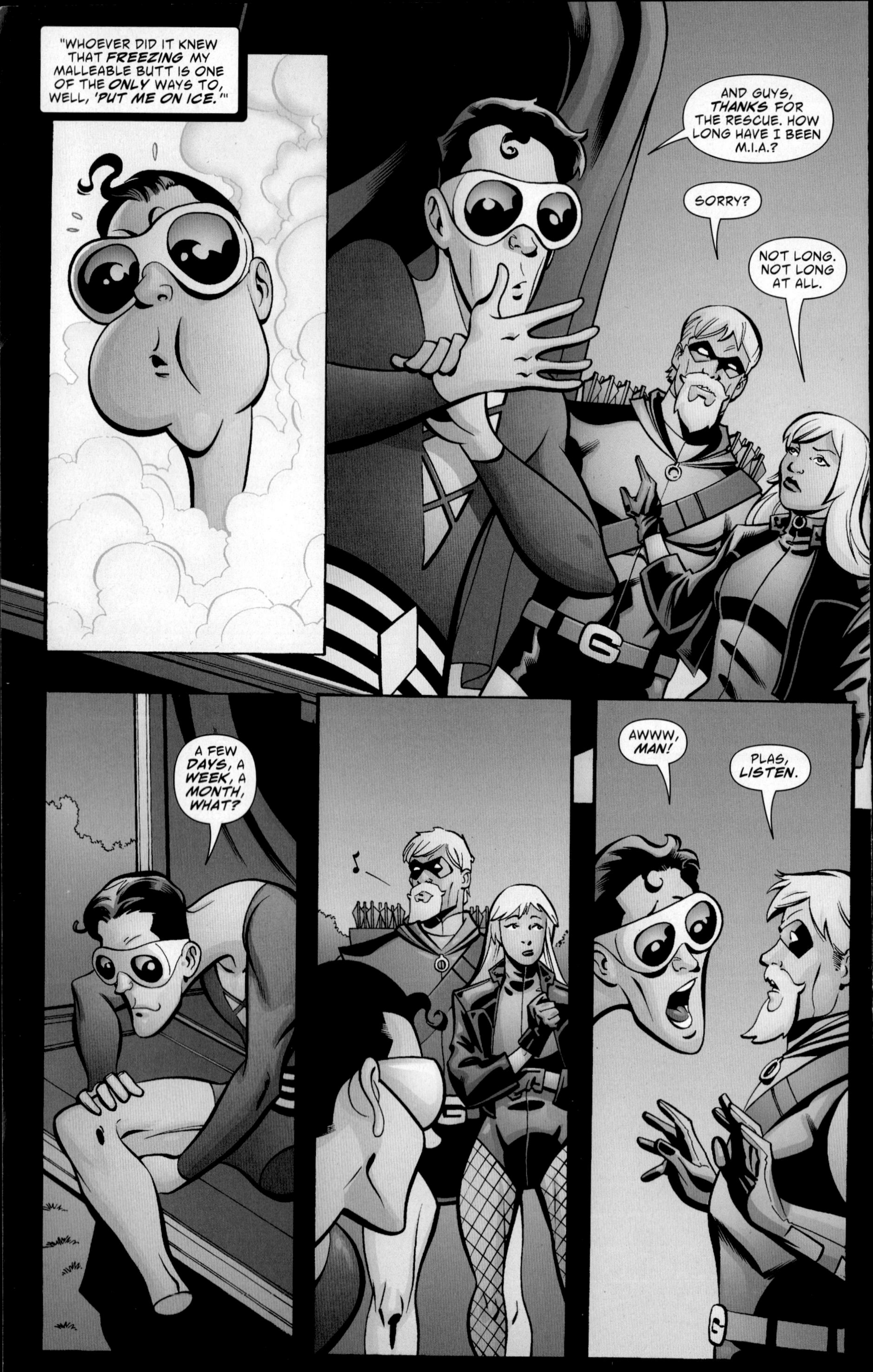
"WHOEVER DID IT KNEW THAT FREEZING MY MALLEABLE BUTT IS ONE OF THE ONLY WAYS TO, WELL, 'PUT ME ON ICE.'"
AND GUYS, THANKS FOR THE RESCUE. HOW LONG HAVE I BEEN M.I.A.?
SORRY?
NOT LONG. NOT LONG AT ALL.
A FEW DAYS, A WEEK, A MONTH, WHAT?
AWWW, MAN!
PLAS, LISTEN.

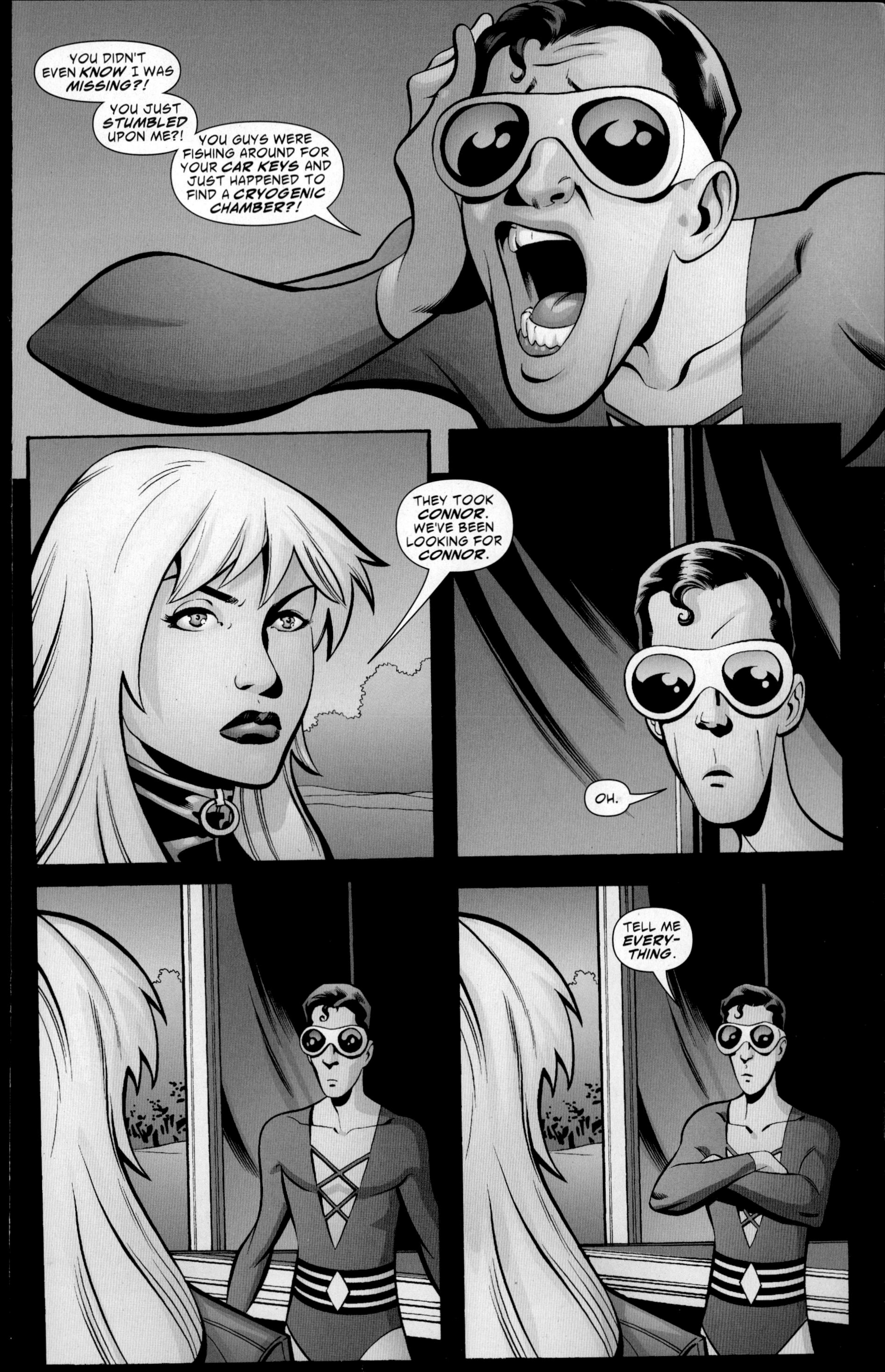
YOU DIDN'T EVEN KNOW I WAS MISSING?!
YOU JUST STUMBLED UPON ME?!
YOU GUYS WERE FISHING AROUND FOR YOUR CAR KEYS AND JUST HAPPENED TO FIND A CRYOGENIC CHAMBER?!
THEY TOOK CONNOR. WE'VE BEEN LOOKING FOR CONNOR.
OH.
TELL ME EVERY-THING.

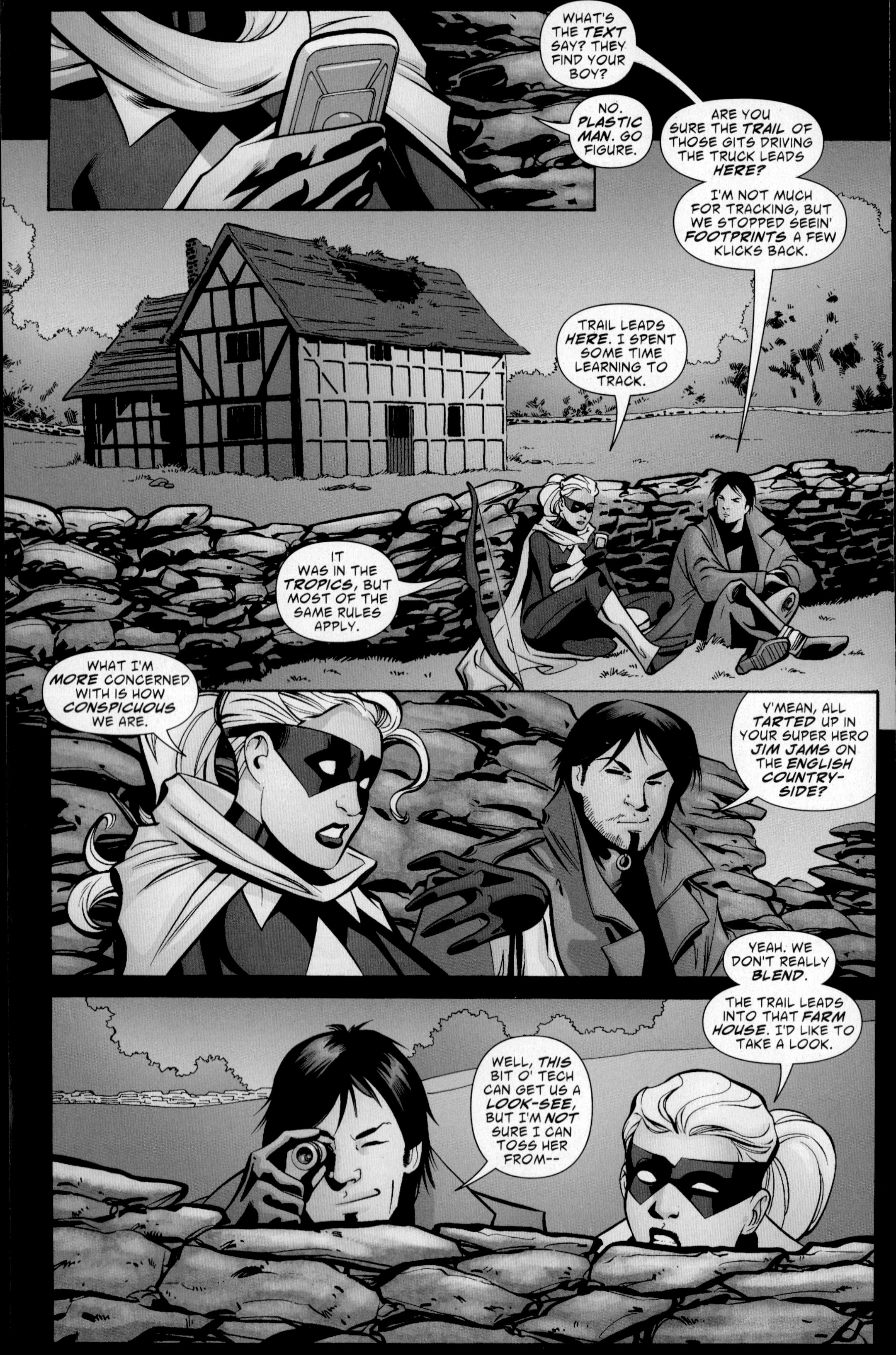

WHAT'S THE TEXT SAY? THEY FIND YOUR BOY?
NO. PLASTIC MAN. GO FIGURE.
ARE YOU SURE THE TRAIL OF THOSE GITS DRIVING THE TRUCK LEADS HERE?
I'M NOT MUCH FOR TRACKING, BUT WE STOPPED SEEIN' FOOTPRINTS A FEW KLICKS BACK.
TRAIL LEADS HERE. I SPENT SOME TIME LEARNING TO TRACK.
IT WAS IN THE TROPICS, BUT MOST OF THE SAME RULES APPLY.
WHAT I'M MORE CONCERNED WITH IS HOW CONSPICUOUS WE ARE.
Y'MEAN, ALL TARTED UP IN YOUR SUPER HERO JIM JAMS ON THE ENGLISH COUNTRY-SIDE?
YEAH. WE DON'T REALLY BLEND.
THE TRAIL LEADS INTO THAT FARM HOUSE. I'D LIKE TO TAKE A LOOK.
WELL, THIS BIT O' TECH CAN GET US A LOOK-SEE, BUT I'M NOT SURE I CAN TOSS HER FROM--

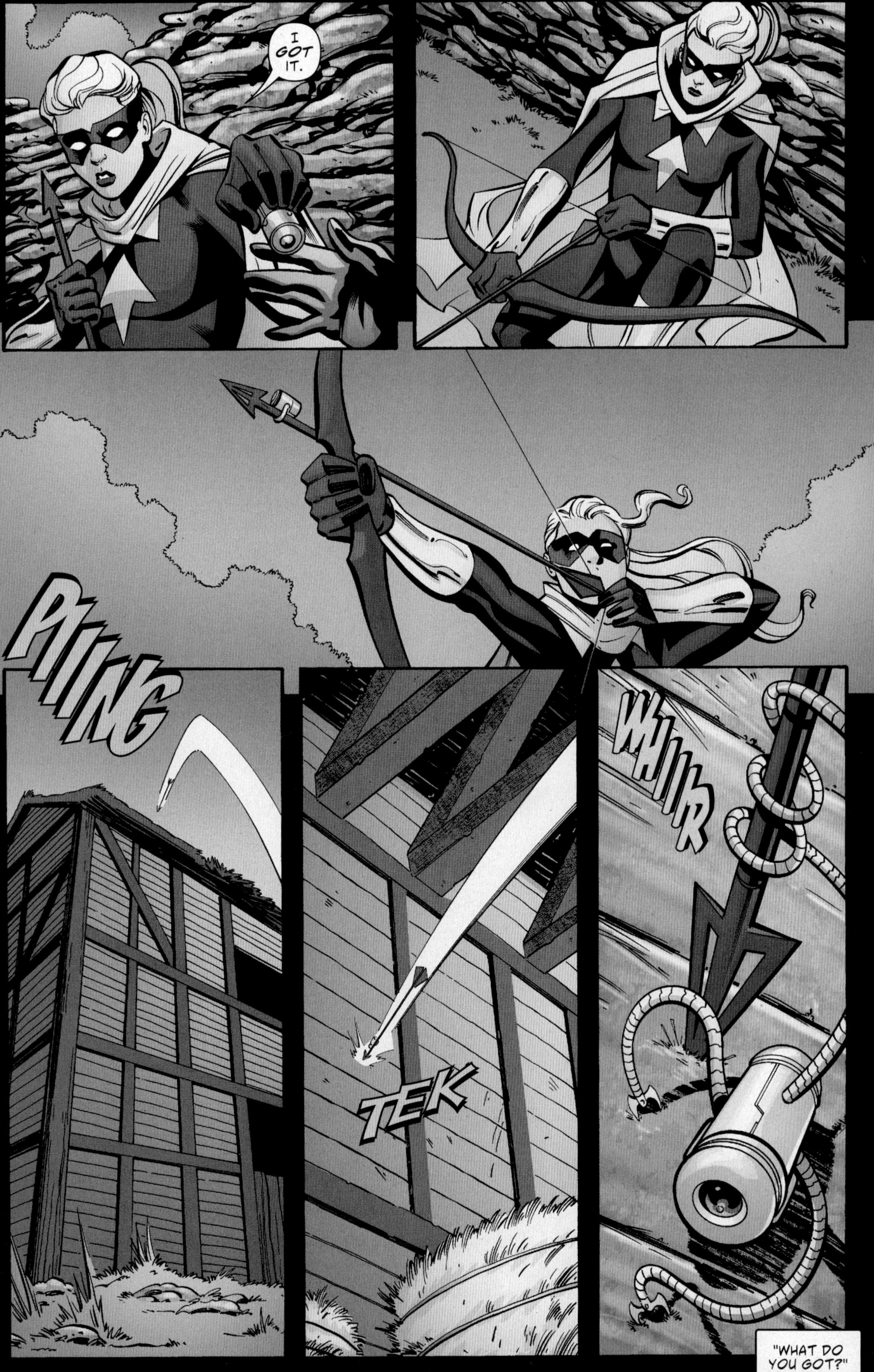

I GOT IT.
PTING
TEK
WHIR
"WHAT DO YOU GOT?"

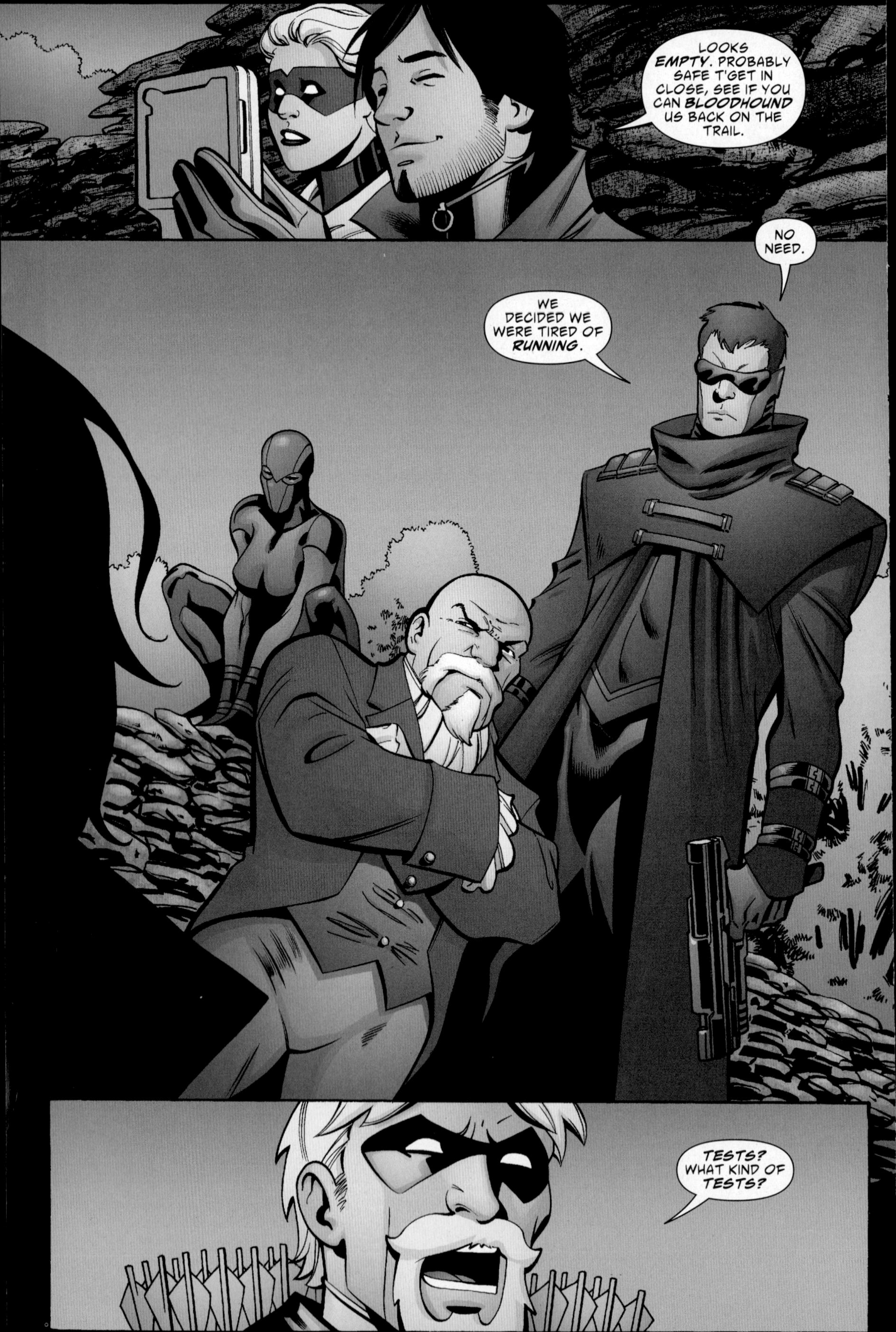
LOOKS EMPTY. PROBABLY SAFE T'GET IN CLOSE, SEE IF YOU CAN BLOODHOUND US BACK ON THE TRAIL.
NO NEED.
WE DECIDED WE WERE TIRED OF RUNNING.
TESTS? WHAT KIND OF TESTS?

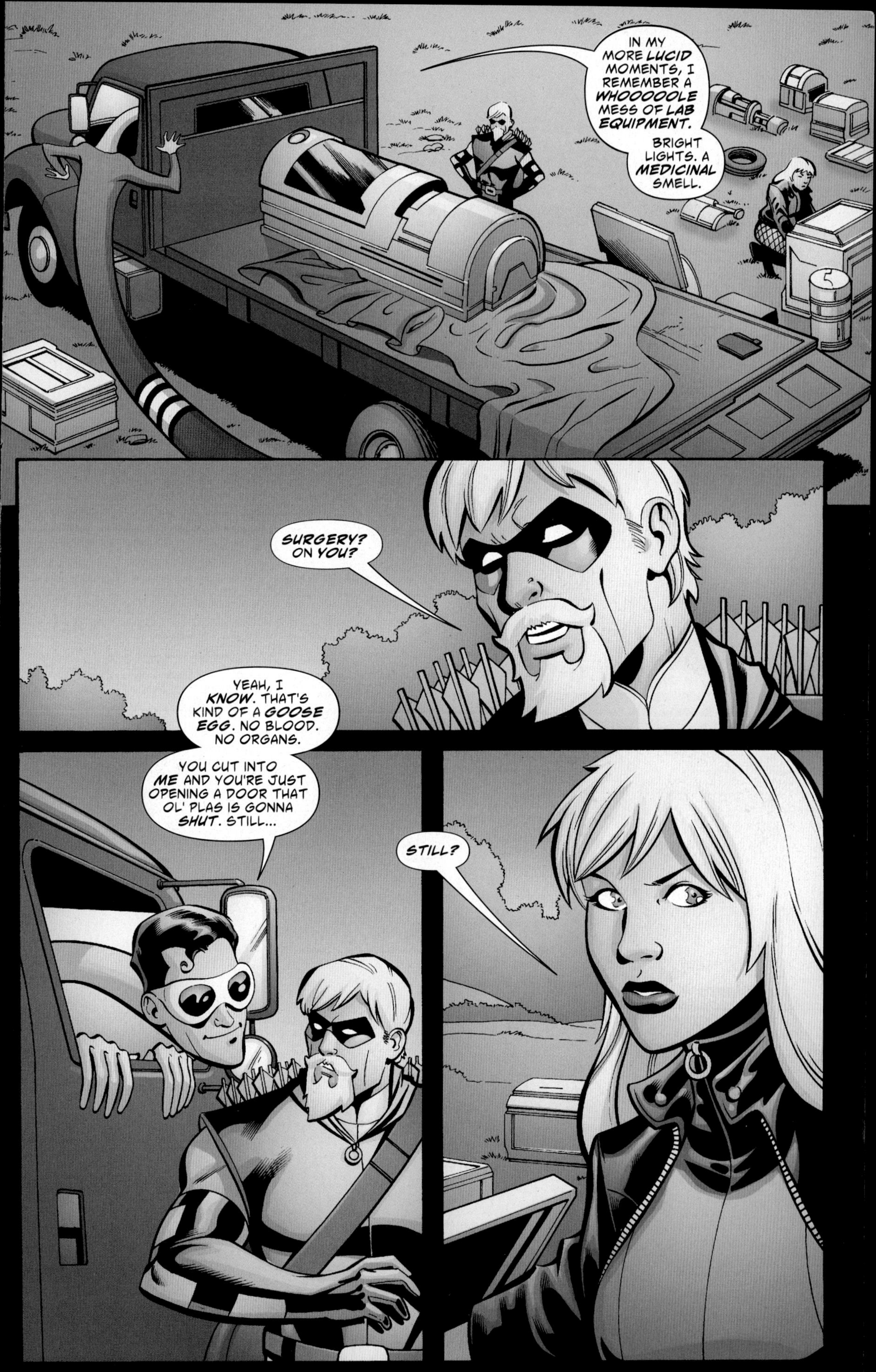
IN MY MORE LUCID MOMENTS, I REMEMBER A WHOOOOOLE MESS OF LAB EQUIPMENT.
BRIGHT LIGHTS. A MEDICINAL SMELL.
SURGERY? ON YOU?
YEAH, I KNOW. THAT'S KIND OF A GOOSE EGG. NO BLOOD. NO ORGANS.
YOU CUT INTO ME AND YOU'RE JUST OPENING A DOOR THAT OL' PLAS IS GONNA SHUT. STILL...
STILL?

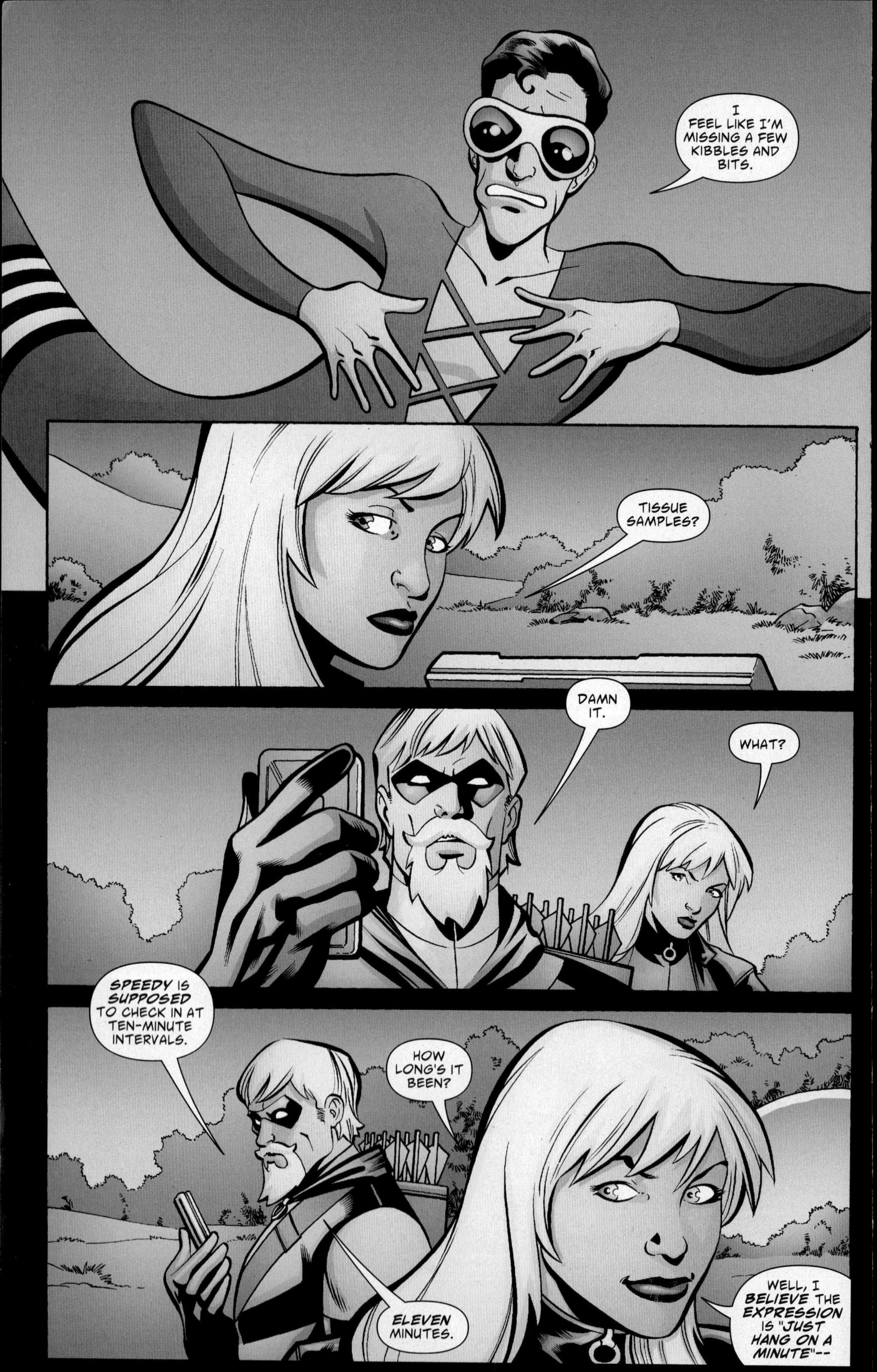
I FEEL LIKE I'M MISSING A FEW KIBBLES AND BITS.
TISSUE SAMPLES?
DAMN IT.
WHAT?
SPEEDY IS SUPPOSED TO CHECK IN AT TEN-MINUTE INTERVALS.
HOW LONG'S IT BEEN?
ELEVEN MINUTES.
WELL, I BELIEVE THE EXPRESSION IS "JUST HANG ON A MINUTE"--

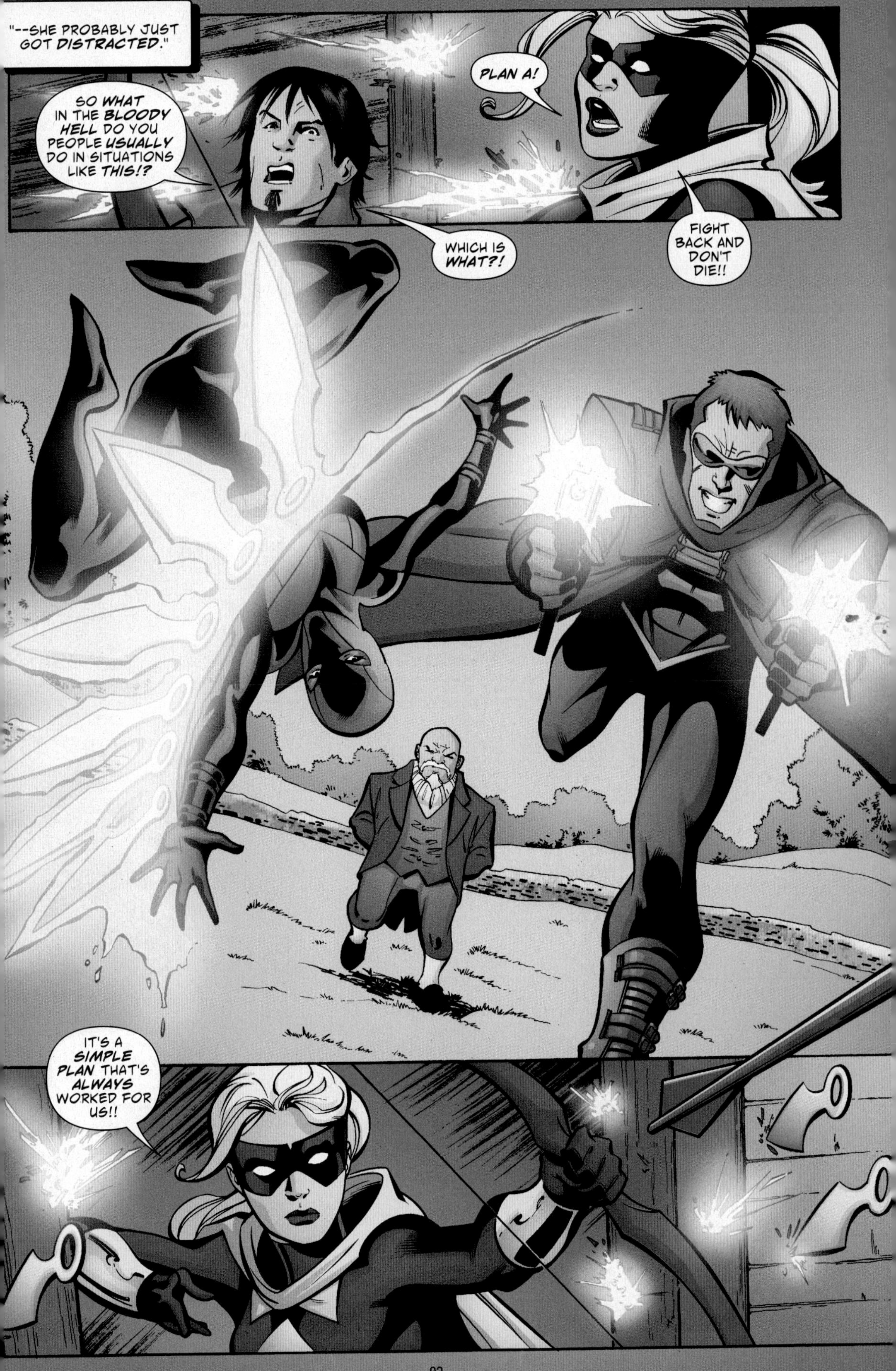
"--SHE PROBABLY JUST GOT DISTRACTED."
SO WHAT IN THE BLOODY HELL DO YOU PEOPLE USUALLY DO IN SITUATIONS LIKE THIS!?
PLAN A!
WHICH IS WHAT?!
FIGHT BACK AND DON'T DIE!!
IT'S A SIMPLE PLAN THAT'S ALWAYS WORKED FOR US!!

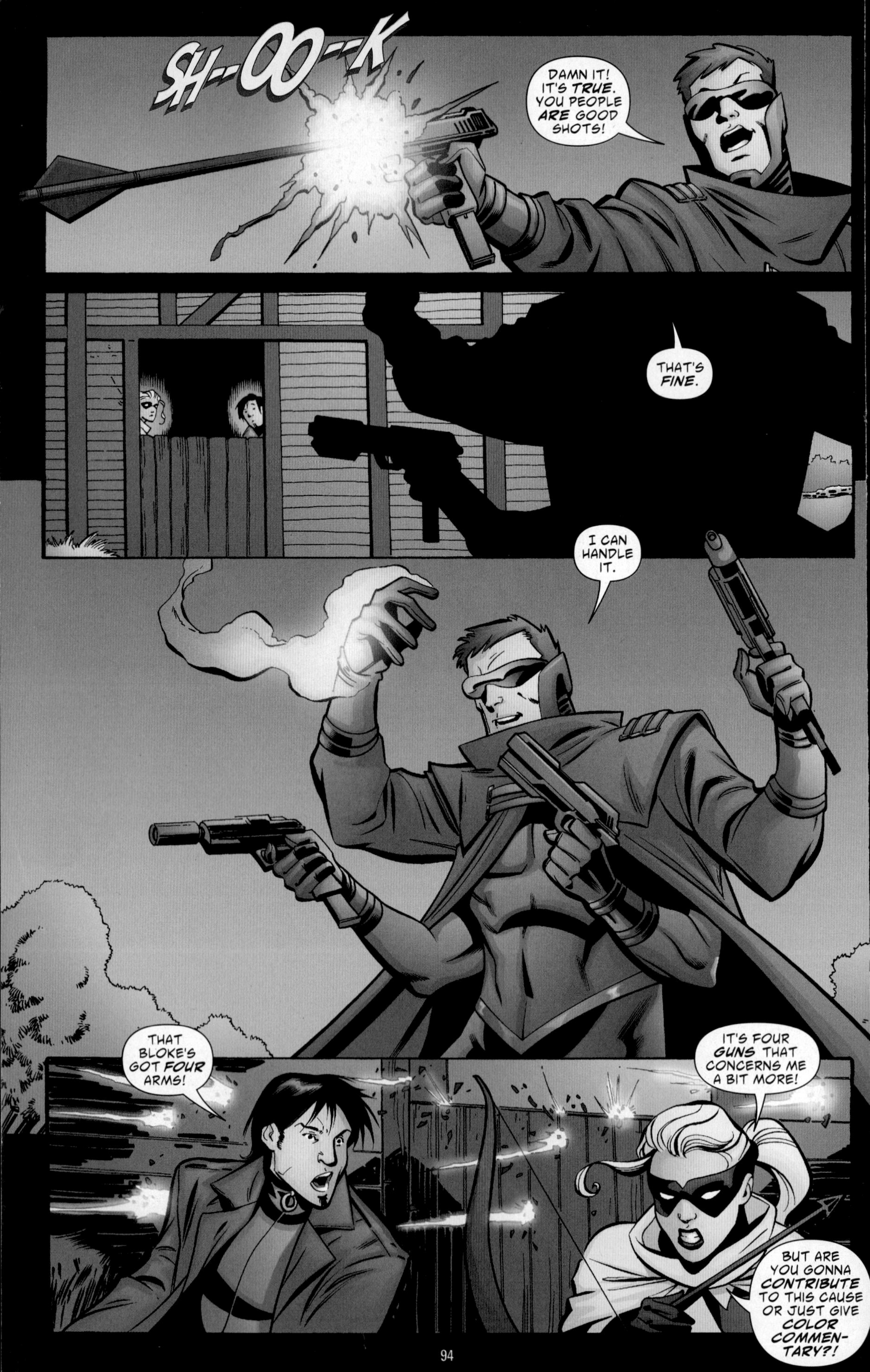
SH--OO--K
DAMN IT! IT'S TRUE. YOU PEOPLE ARE GOOD SHOTS!
THAT'S FINE.
I CAN HANDLE IT.
THAT BLOKE'S GOT FOUR ARMS!
IT'S FOUR GUNS THAT CONCERNS ME A BIT MORE!
BUT ARE YOU GONNA CONTRIBUTE TO THIS CAUSE OR JUST GIVE COLOR COMMENTARY?!

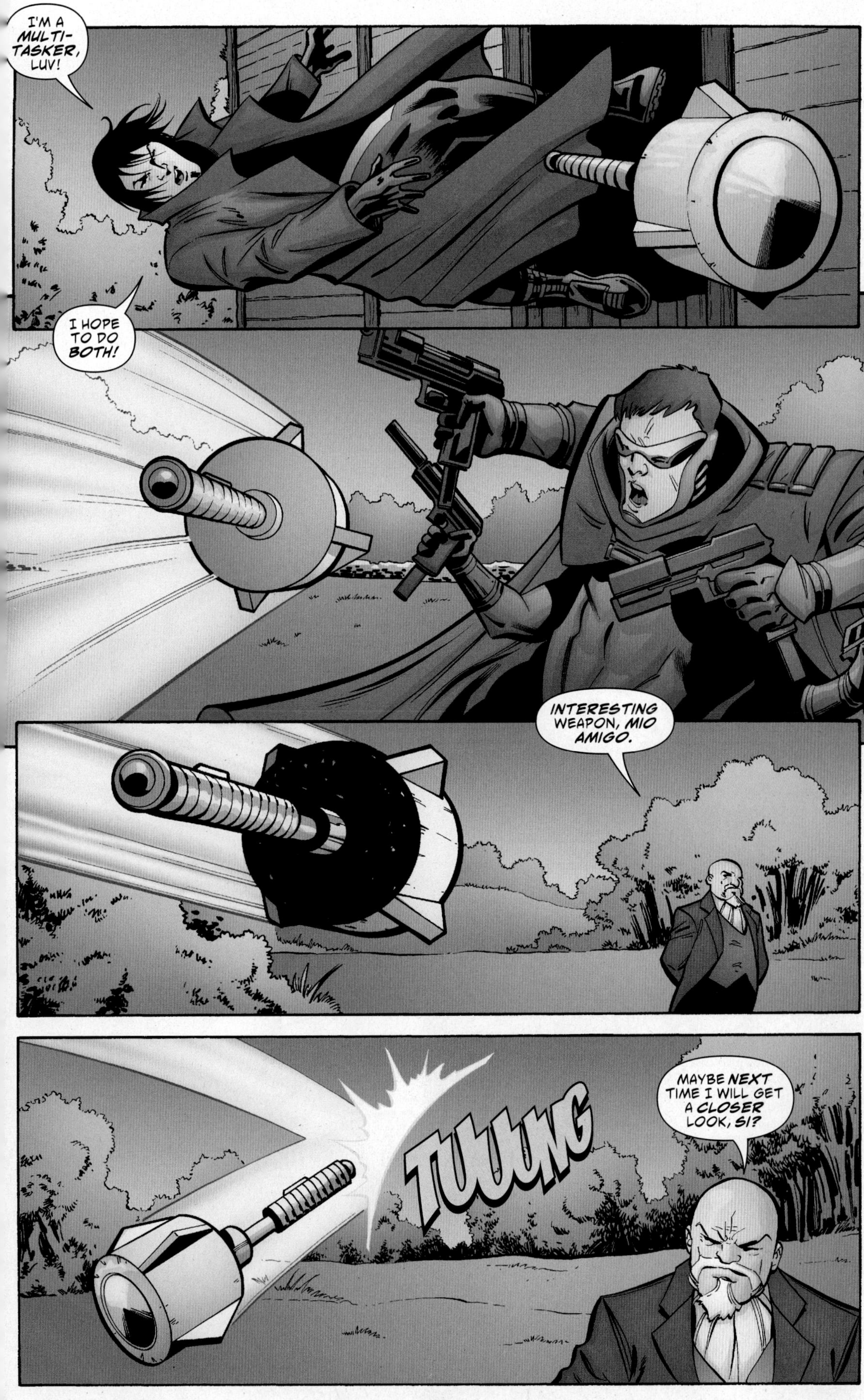
I'M A MULTI-TASKER, LUV!
I HOPE TO DO BOTH!
INTERESTING WEAPON, MIO AMIGO.
TUUUNG
MAYBE NEXT TIME I WILL GET A CLOSER LOOK, SI?

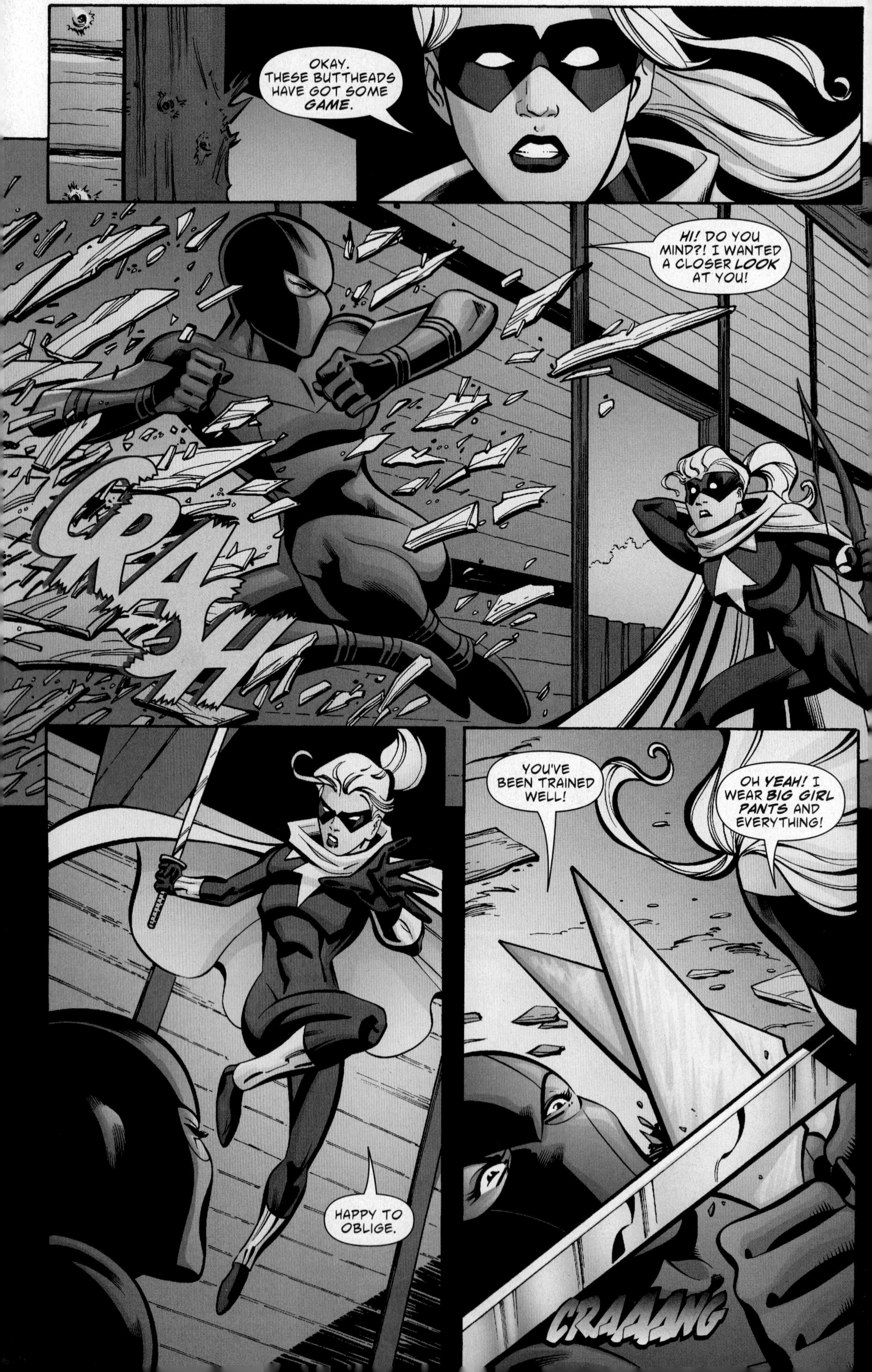
OKAY. THESE BUTTHEADS HAVE GOT SOME GAME.
HI! DO YOU MIND?! I WANTED A CLOSER LOOK AT YOU!
CRASH
HAPPY TO OBLIGE.
YOU'VE BEEN TRAINED WELL!
OH YEAH! I WEAR BIG GIRL PANTS AND EVERYTHING!
CRAAANG

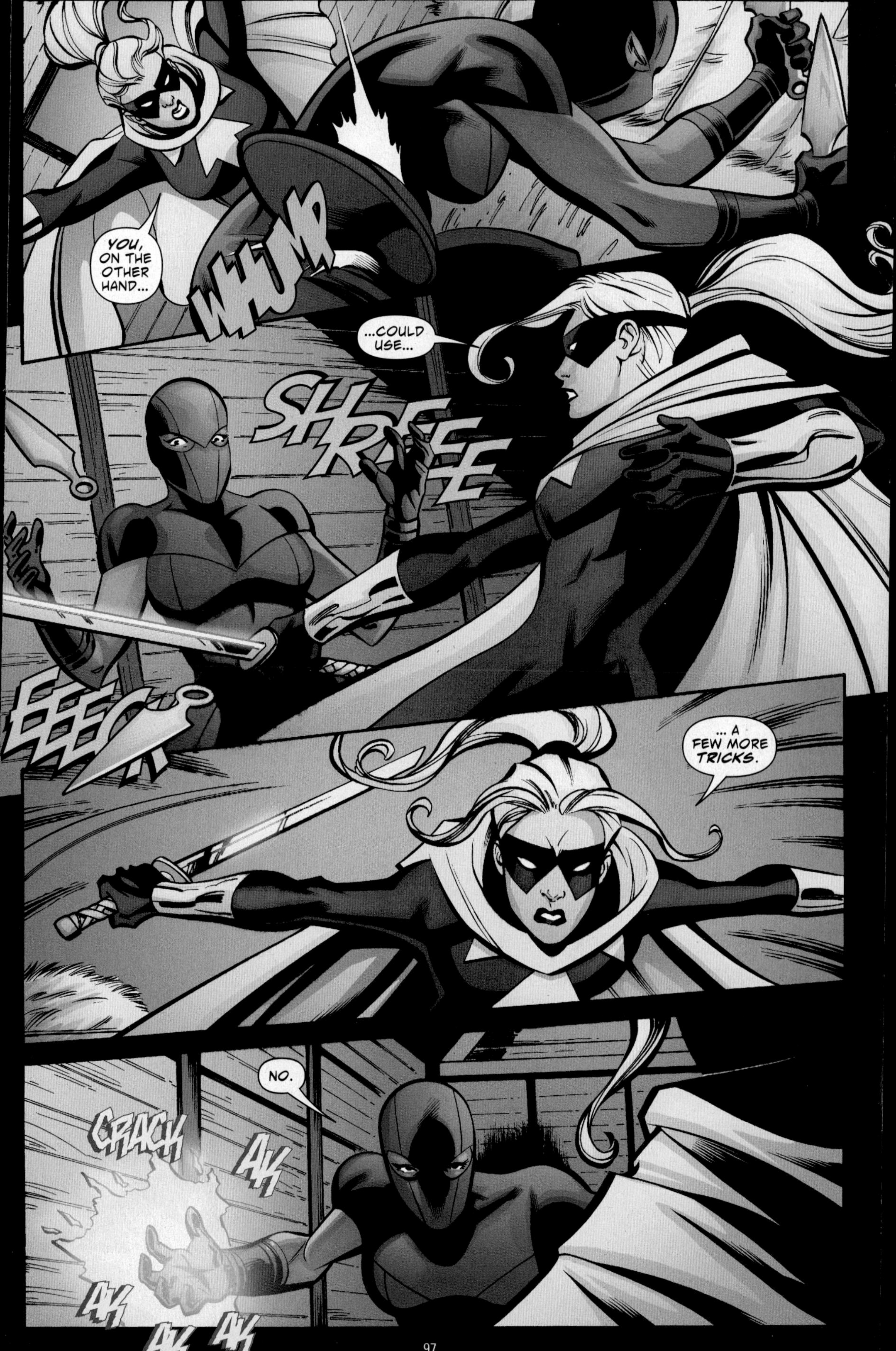

YOU, ON THE OTHER HAND...
WHUMP
...COULD USE...
SHREEEEEE
... A FEW MORE TRICKS.
NO.
CRACK
AK
AK
AK AK

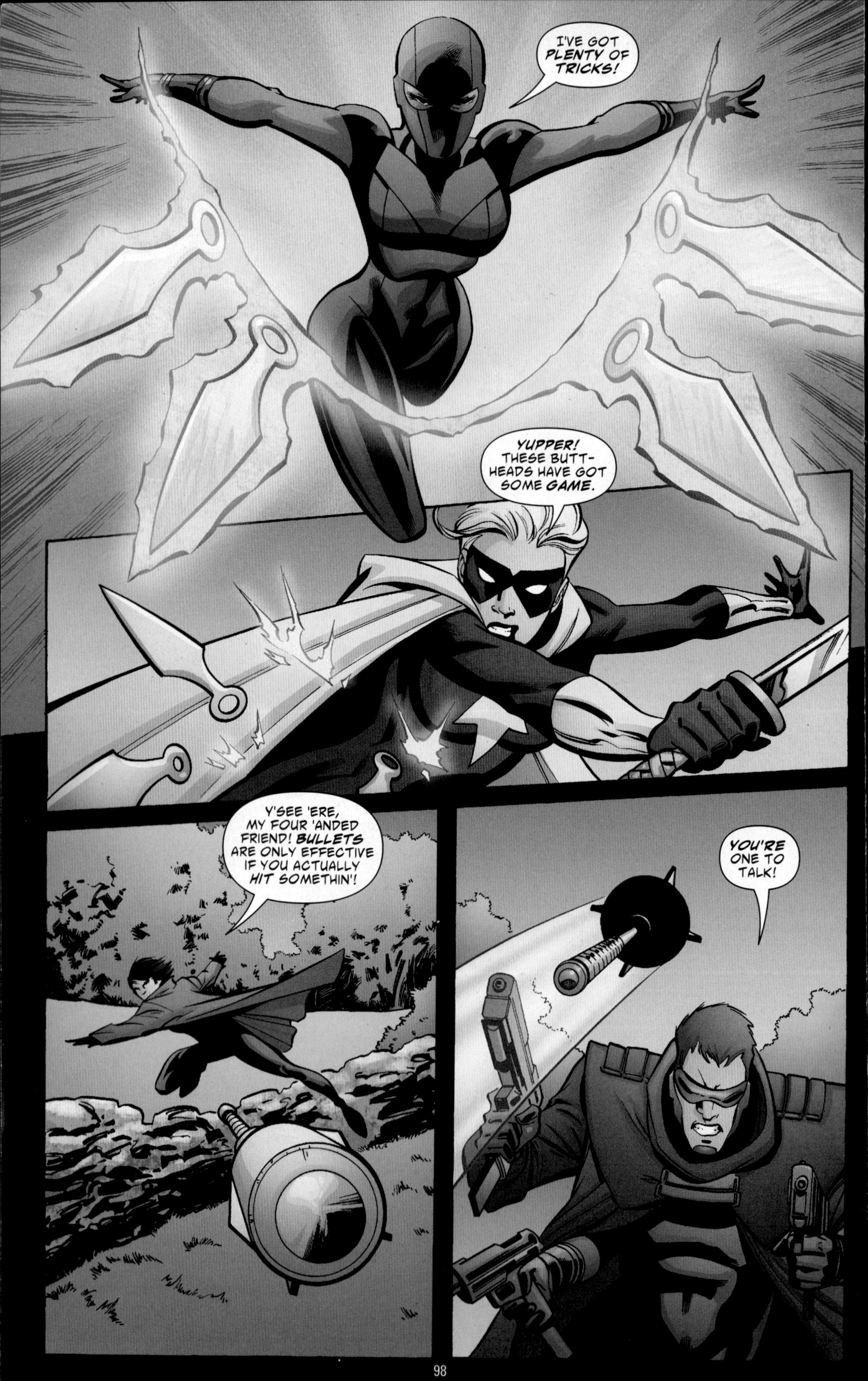
I'VE GOT PLENTY OF TRICKS!
YUPPER! THESE BUTT-HEADS HAVE GOT SOME GAME.
Y'SEE 'ERE, MY FOUR 'ANDED FRIEND! BULLETS ARE ONLY EFFECTIVE IF YOU ACTUALLY HIT SOMETHIN'!
YOU'RE ONE TO TALK!

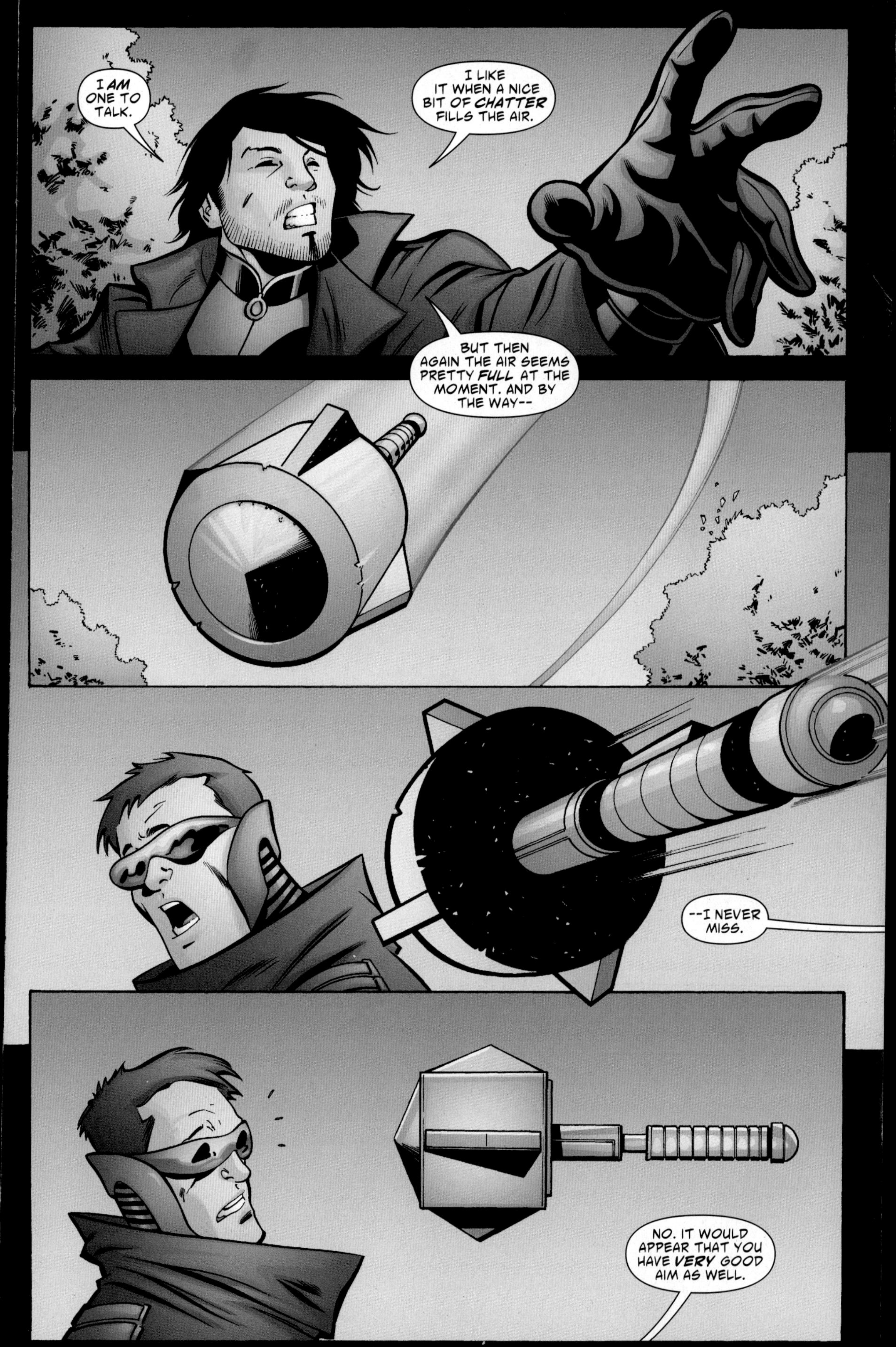
I AM ONE TO TALK.
I LIKE IT WHEN A NICE BIT OF CHATTER FILLS THE AIR.
BUT THEN AGAIN THE AIR SEEMS PRETTY FULL AT THE MOMENT. AND BY THE WAY--
--I NEVER MISS.
NO. IT WOULD APPEAR THAT YOU HAVE VERY GOOD AIM AS WELL.

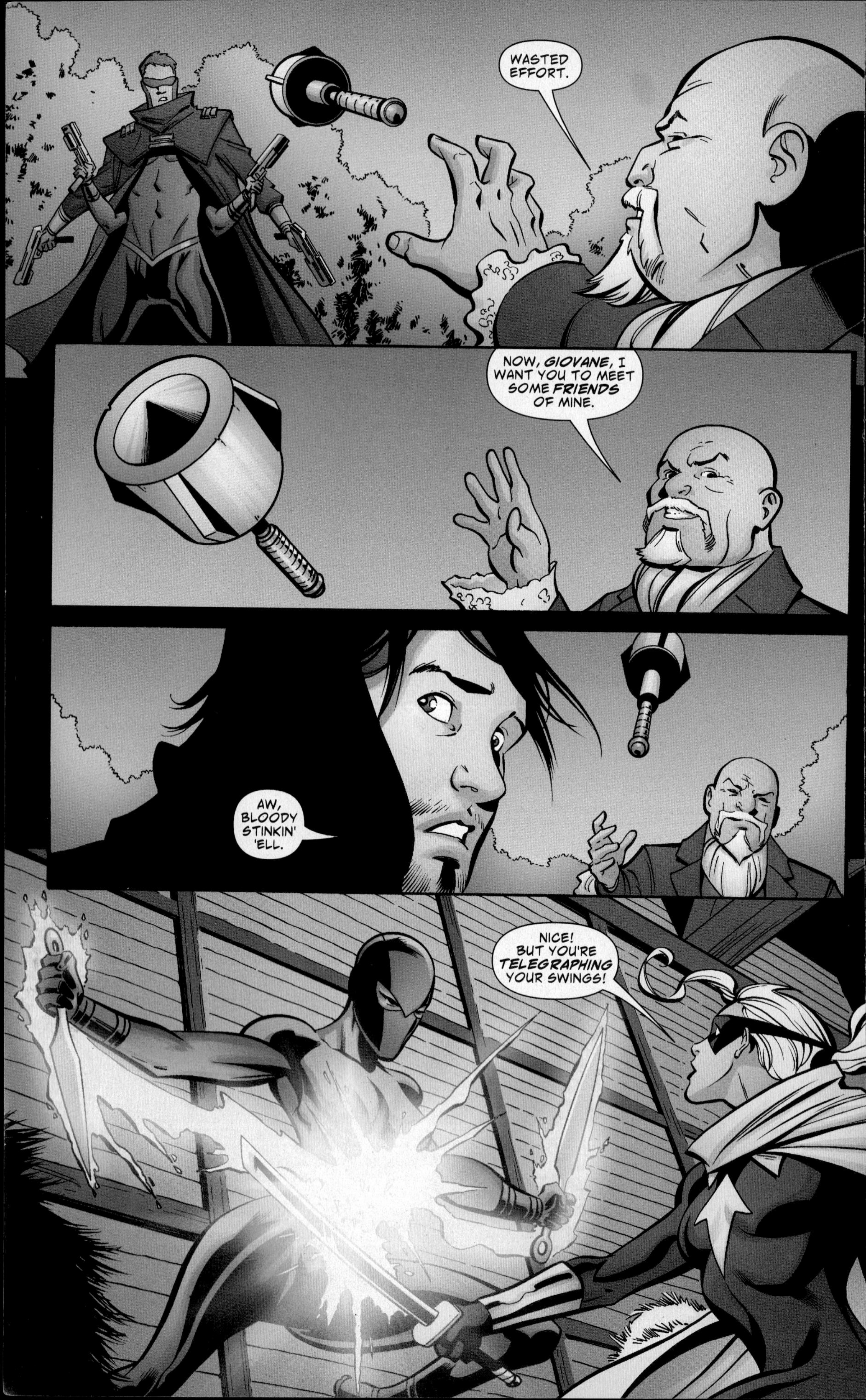

WASTED EFFORT.
NOW, GIOVANE, I WANT YOU TO MEET SOME FRIENDS OF MINE.
AW, BLOODY STINKIN' 'ELL.
NICE! BUT YOU'RE TELEGRAPHING YOUR SWINGS!

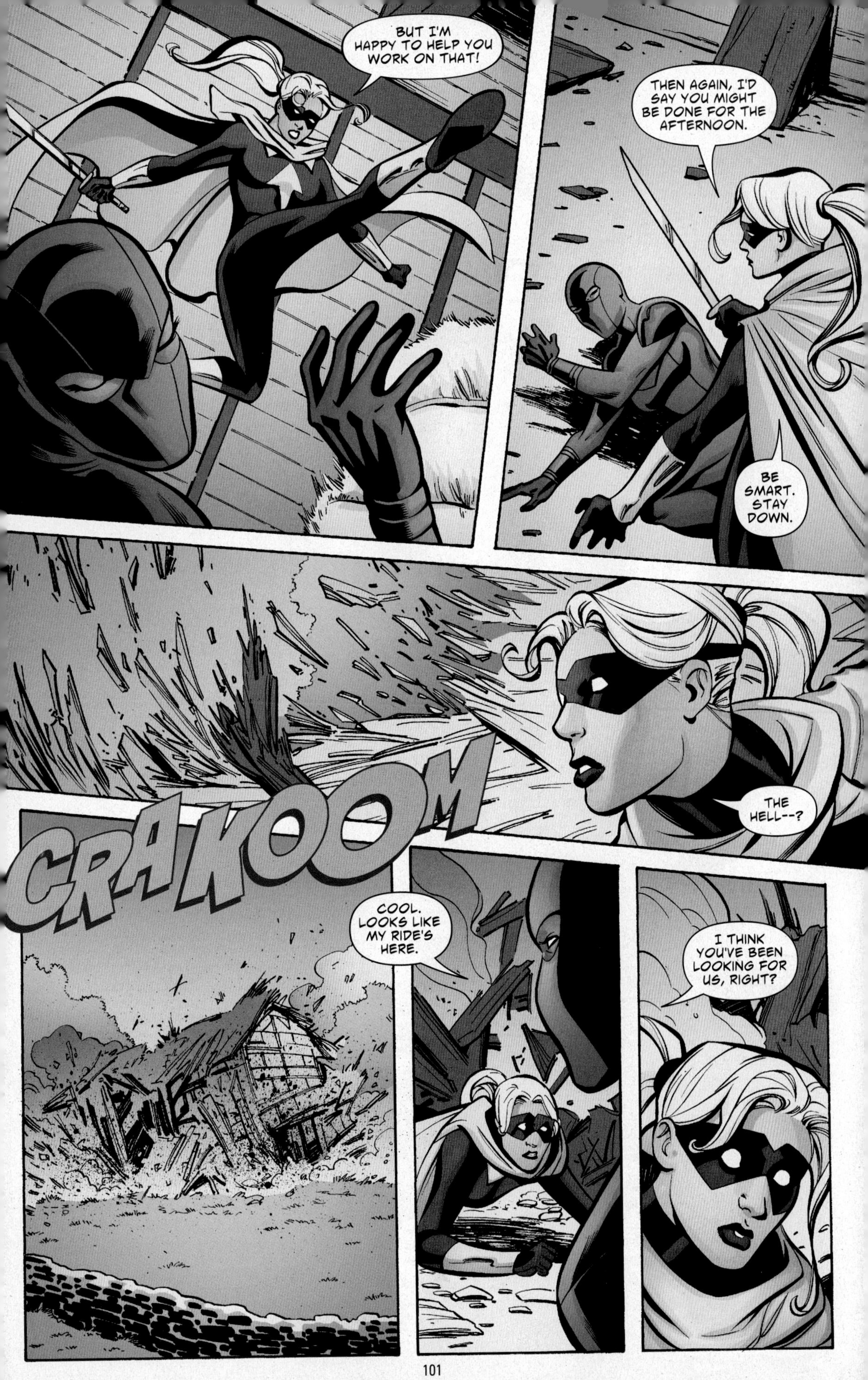
BUT I'M HAPPY TO HELP YOU WORK ON THAT!
THEN AGAIN, I'D SAY YOU MIGHT BE DONE FOR THE AFTERNOON.
BE SMART. STAY DOWN.
THE HELL--?
CRAKOOM
COOL. LOOKS LIKE MY RIDE'S HERE.
I THINK YOU'VE BEEN LOOKING FOR US, RIGHT?

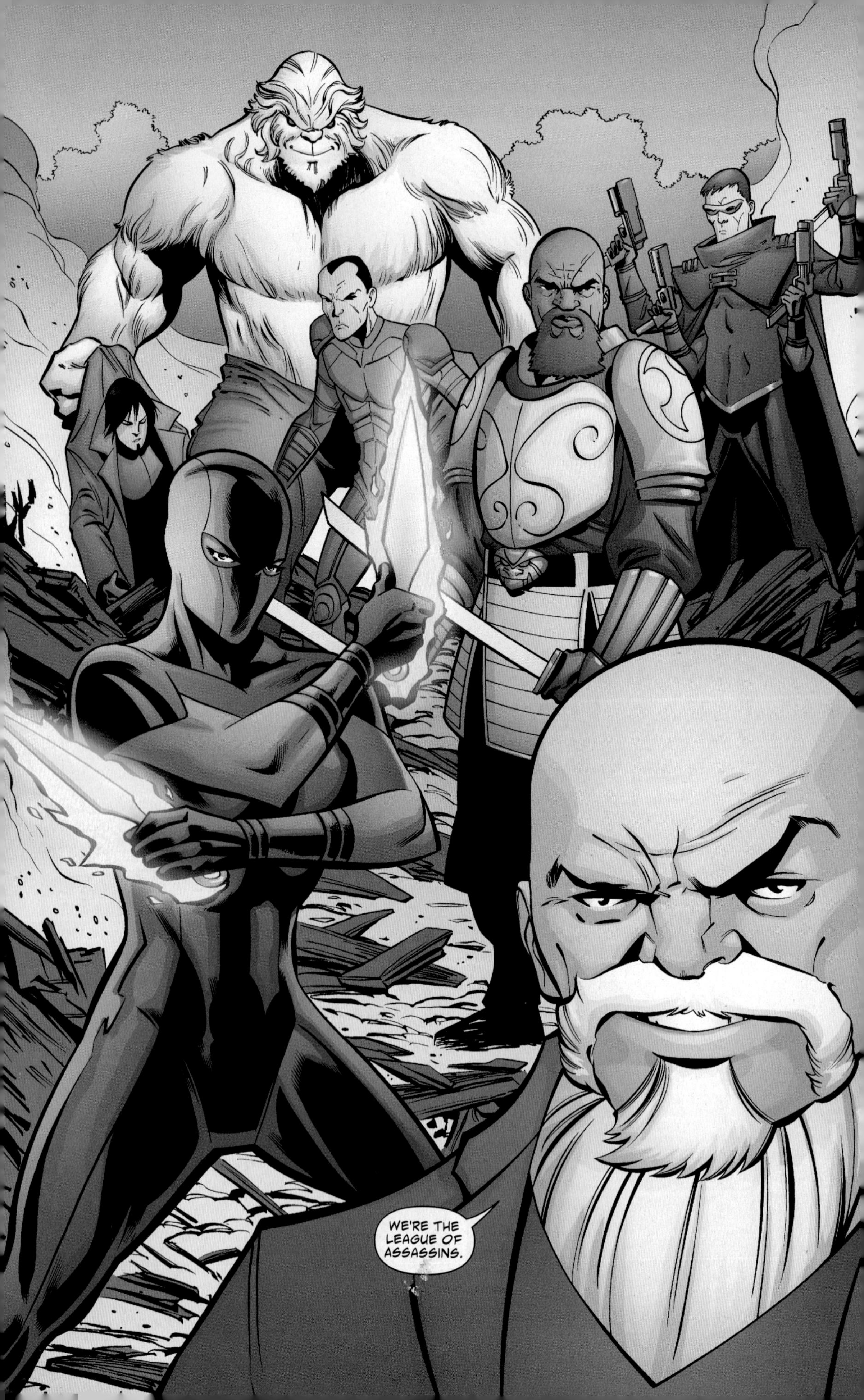
WE'RE THE LEAGUE OF ASSASSINS.

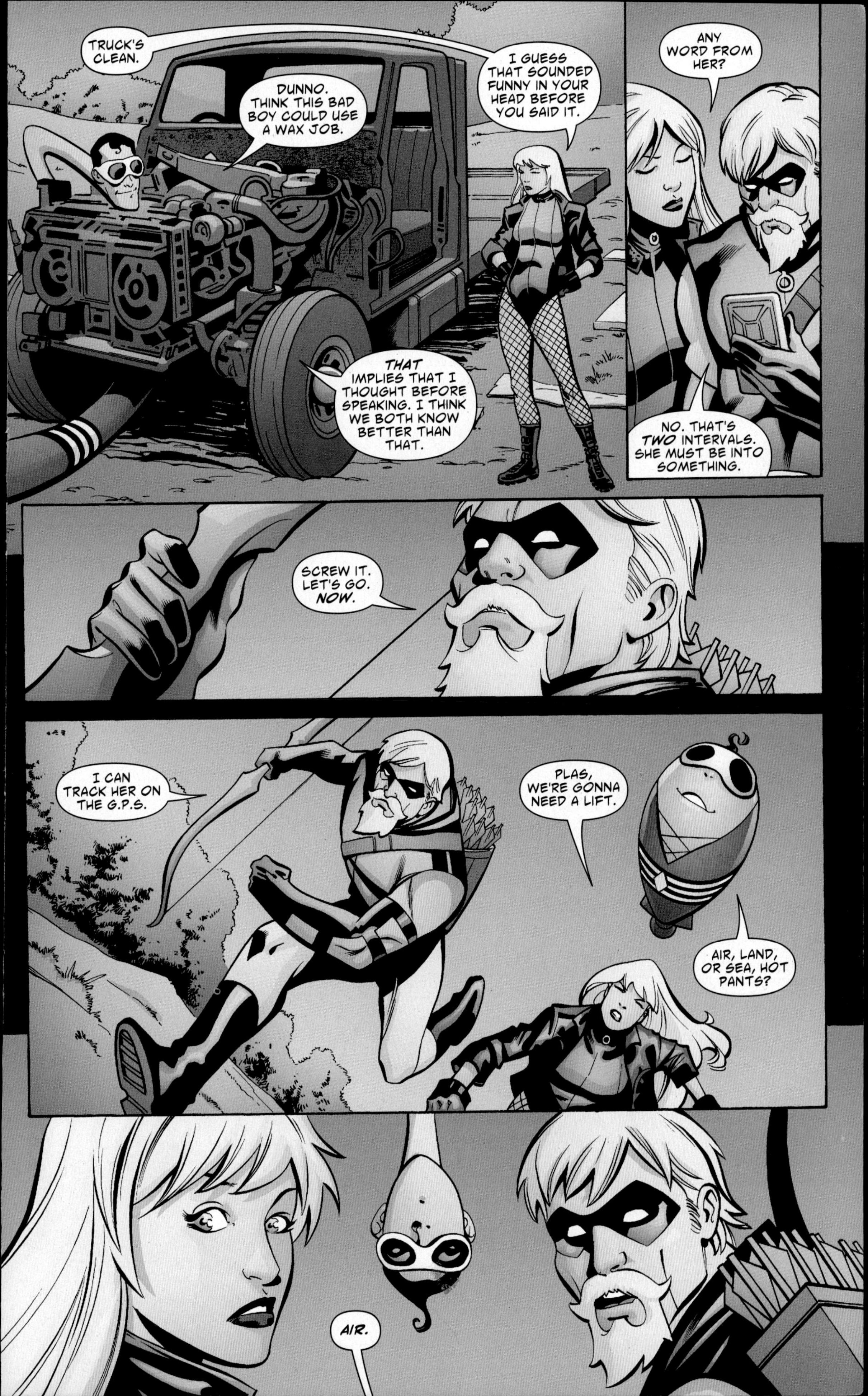
TRUCK'S CLEAN.
DUNNO. THINK THIS BAD BOY COULD USE A WAX JOB.
I GUESS THAT SOUNDED FUNNY IN YOUR HEAD BEFORE YOU SAID IT.
THAT IMPLIES THAT I THOUGHT BEFORE SPEAKING. I THINK WE BOTH KNOW BETTER THAN THAT.
ANY WORD FROM HER?
NO. THAT'S TWO INTERVALS. SHE MUST BE INTO SOMETHING.
SCREW IT. LET'S GO. NOW.
I CAN TRACK HER ON THE G.P.S.
PLAS, WE'RE GONNA NEED A LIFT.
AIR, LAND, OR SEA, HOT PANTS?
AIR.

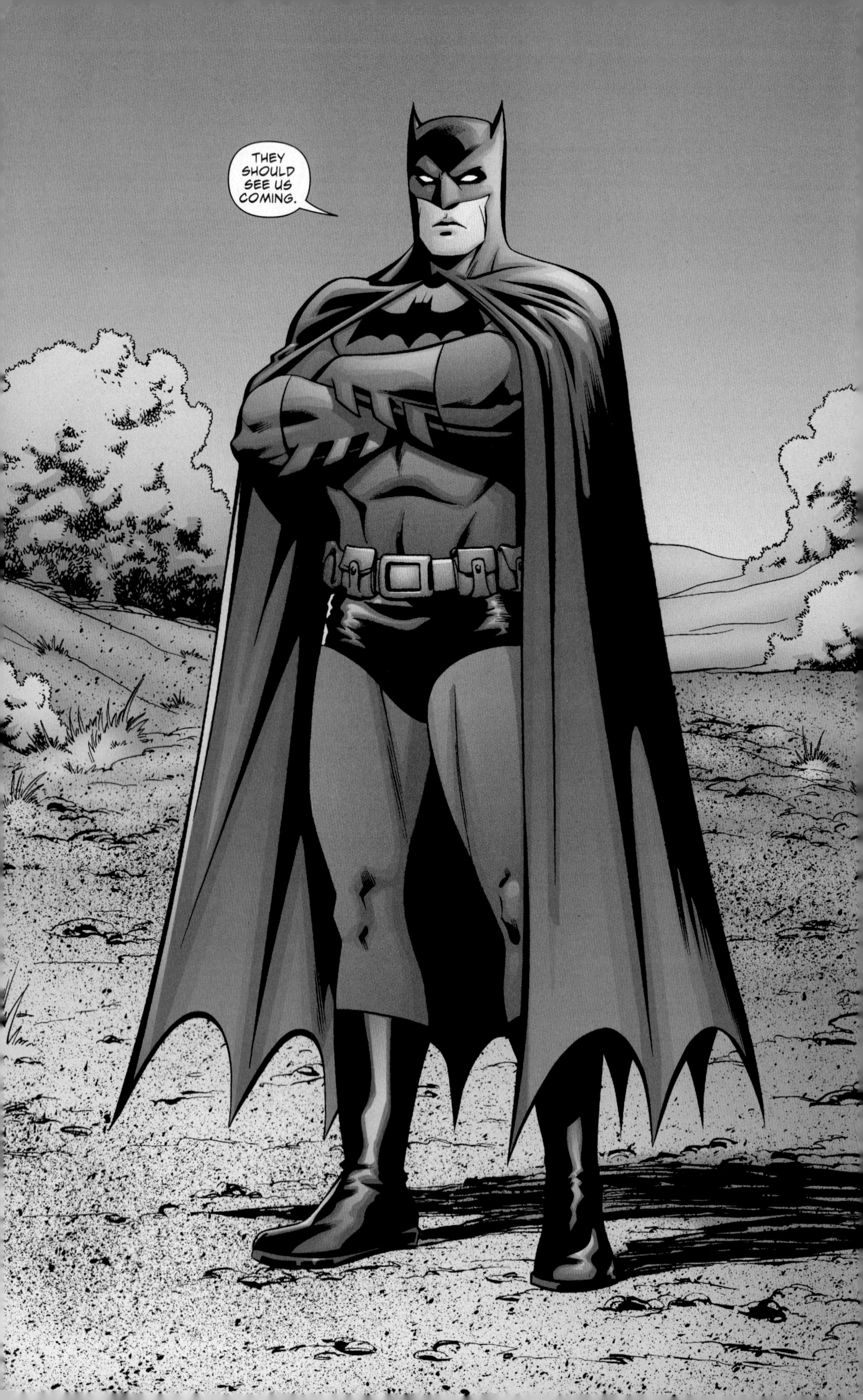
THEY SHOULD SEE US COMING.

GREEN ARROW AND BLACK CANARY 10

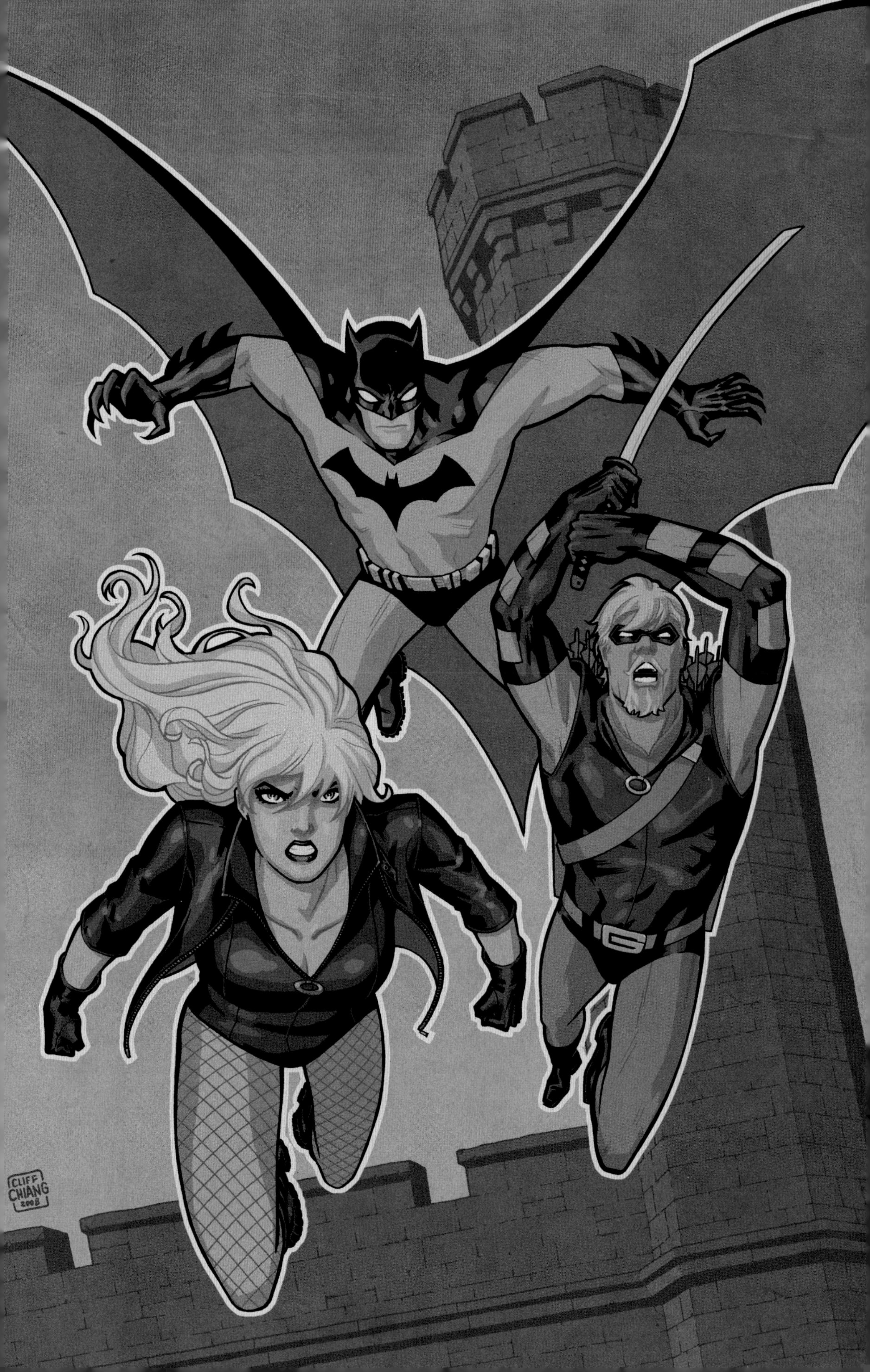
CLIFF
CHIANG
2008

A LEAGUE OF THEIR OWN

PART 2: STEP UP TO THE PLATE AND SWING AWAY

JUDD WINICK
STORY

MIKE NORTON / WAYNE FAUCHER
ART

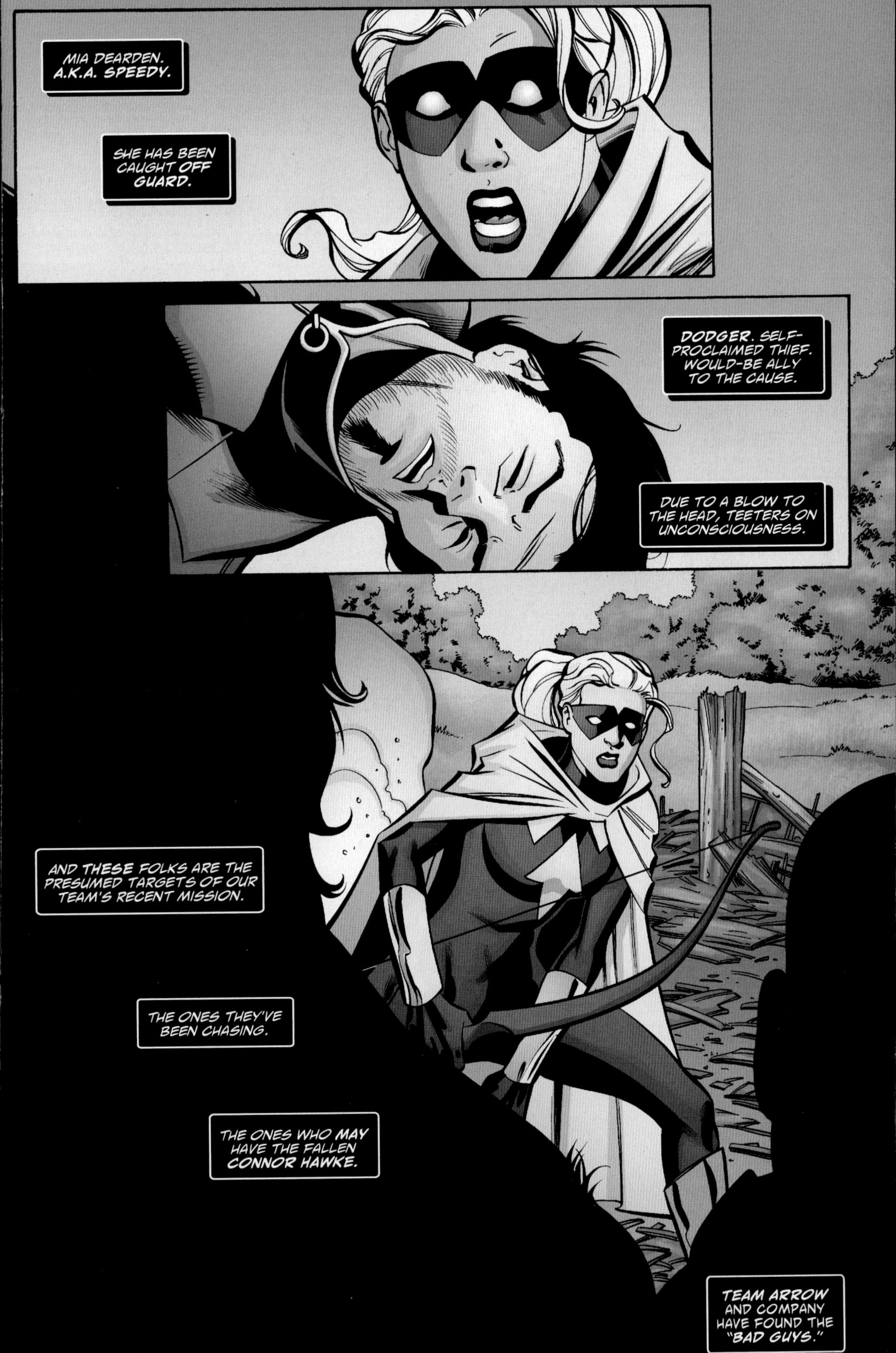
MIA DEARDEN. A.K.A. SPEEDY.
SHE HAS BEEN CAUGHT OFF GUARD.
DODGER. SELF-PROCLAIMED THIEF. WOULD-BE ALLY TO THE CAUSE.
DUE TO A BLOW TO THE HEAD, TEETERS ON UNCONSCIOUSNESS.
AND THESE FOLKS ARE THE PRESUMED TARGETS OF OUR TEAM'S RECENT MISSION.
THE ONES THEY'VE BEEN CHASING.
THE ONES WHO MAY HAVE THE FALLEN CONNOR HAWKE.
TEAM ARROW AND COMPANY HAVE FOUND THE "BAD GUYS."

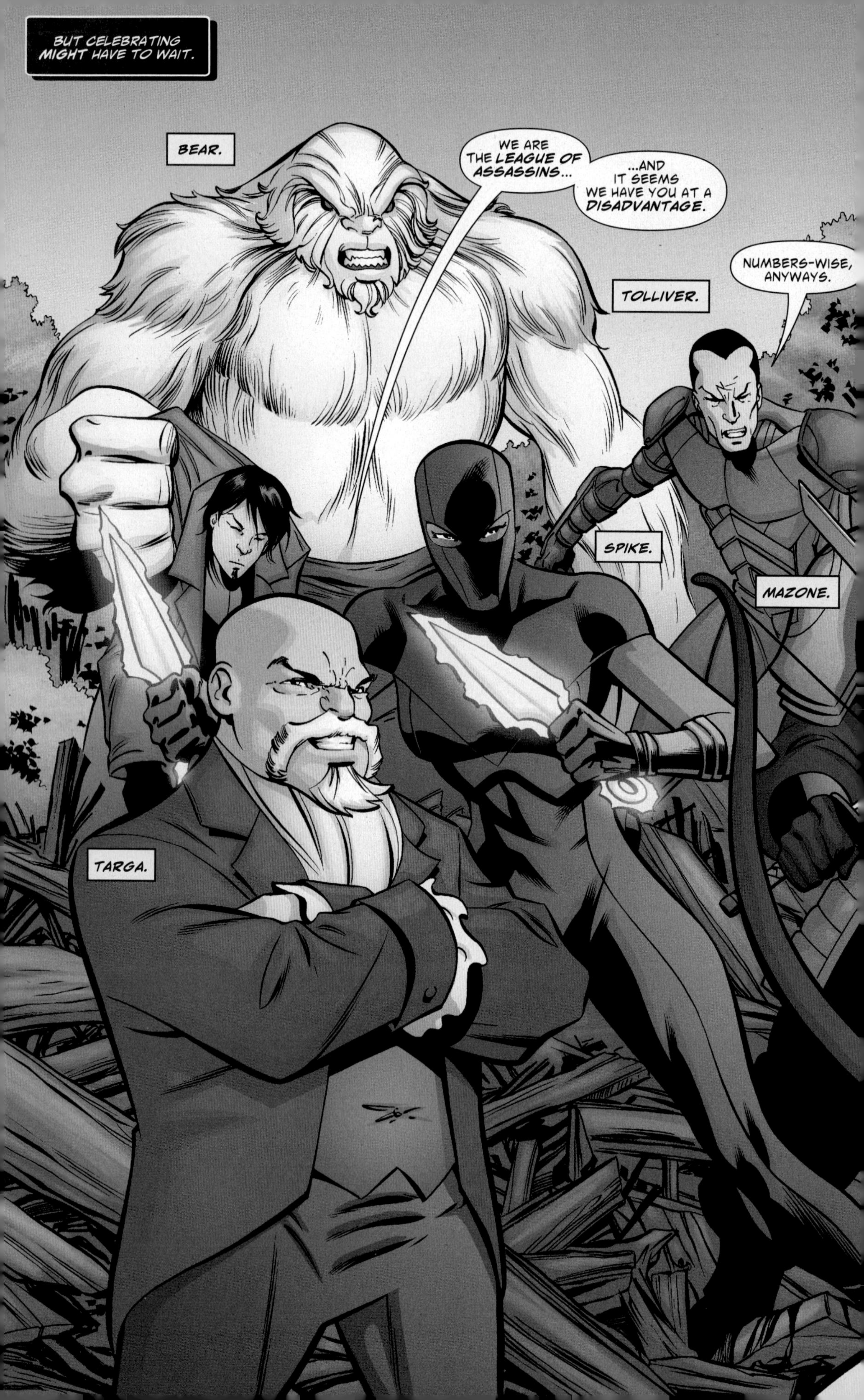
BUT CELEBRATING MIGHT HAVE TO WAIT.
BEAR.
WE ARE THE LEAGUE OF ASSASSINS...
...AND IT SEEMS WE HAVE YOU AT A DISADVANTAGE.
TOLLIVER.
NUMBERS-WISE, ANYWAYS.
SPIKE.
MAZONE.
TARGA.

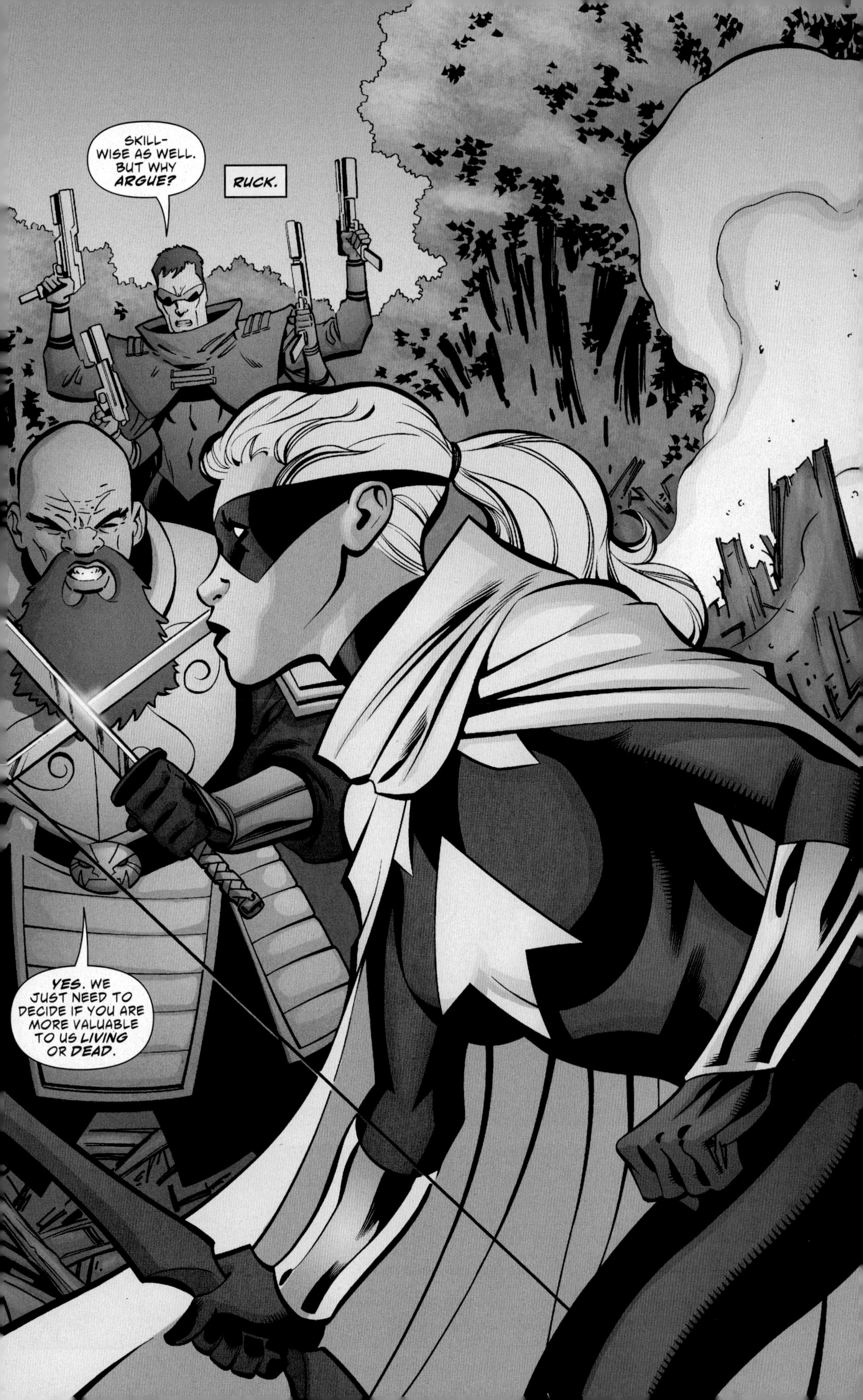
SKILL-WISE AS WELL. BUT WHY ARGUE?
RUCK.
YES. WE JUST NEED TO DECIDE IF YOU ARE MORE VALUABLE TO US LIVING OR DEAD.

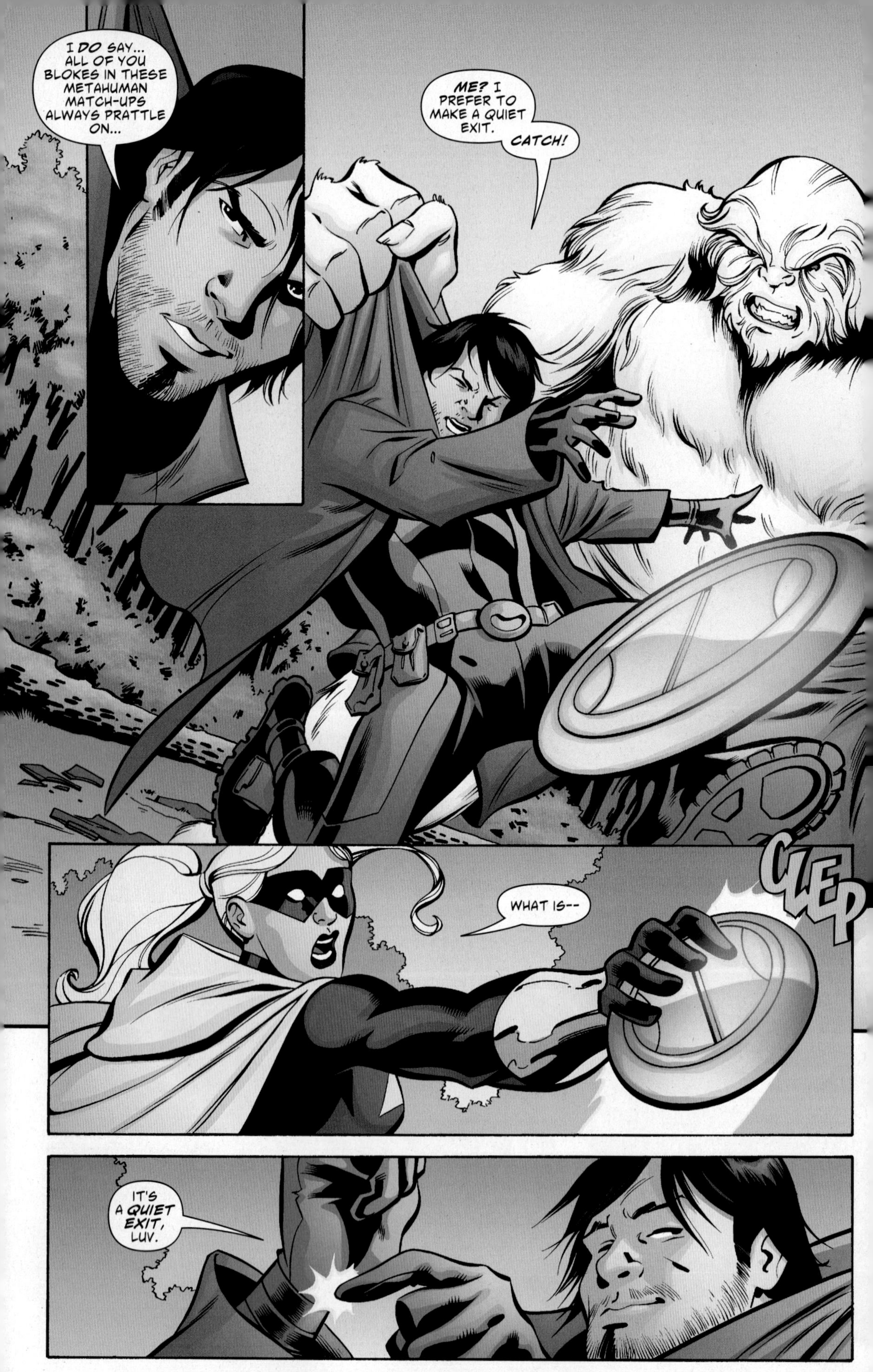
I DO SAY... ALL OF YOU BLOKES IN THESE METAHUMAN MATCH-UPS ALWAYS PRATTLE ON...
ME? I PREFER TO MAKE A QUIET EXIT.
CATCH!
CLEP
WHAT IS--
IT'S A QUIET EXIT, LUV.

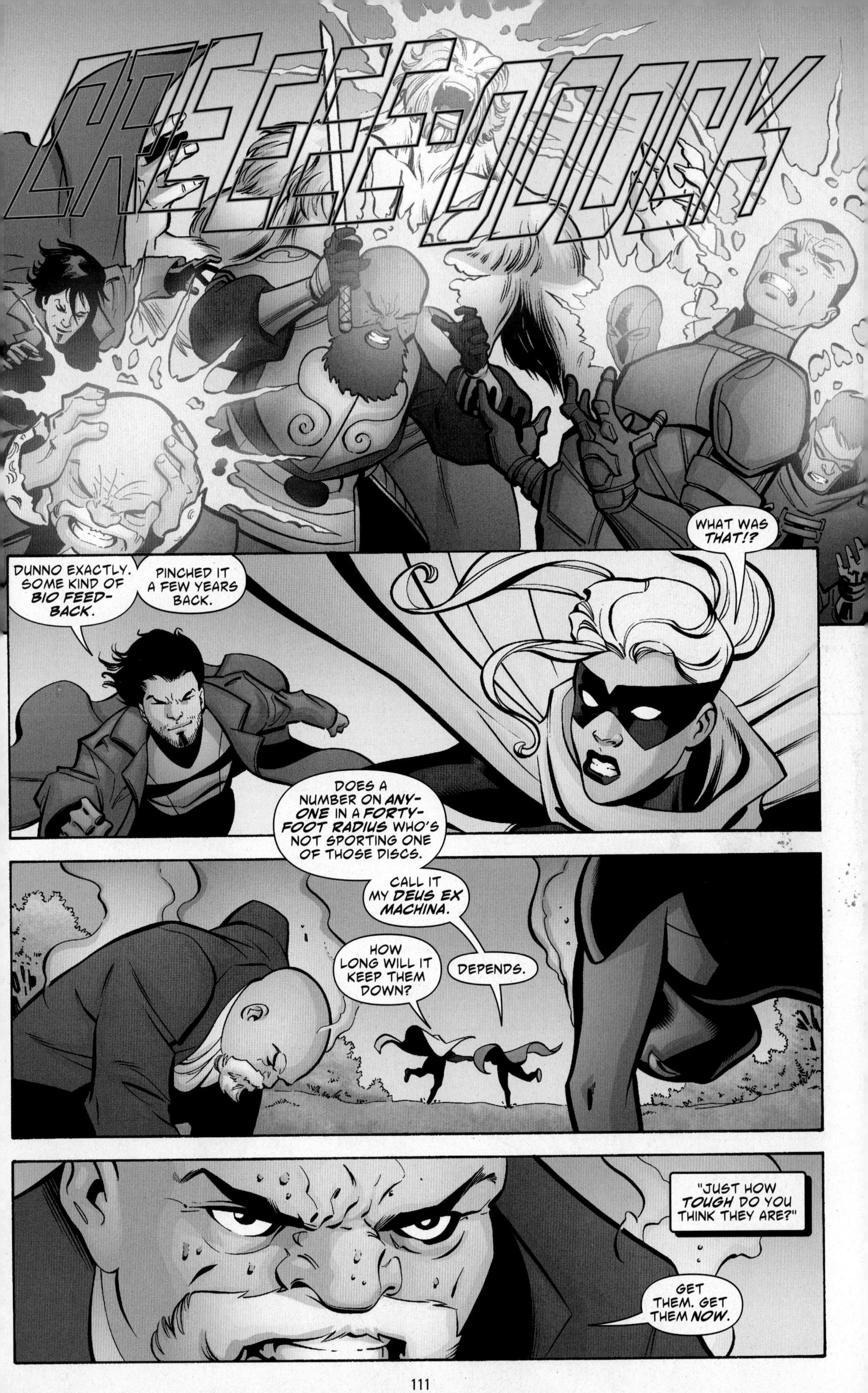
CREEEE-DOOOCK
WHAT WAS THAT!?
DUNNO EXACTLY. SOME KIND OF BIO FEED-BACK.
PINCHED IT A FEW YEARS BACK.
DOES A NUMBER ON ANY-ONE IN A FORTY-FOOT RADIUS WHO'S NOT SPORTING ONE OF THOSE DISCS.
CALL IT MY DEUS EX MACHINA.
HOW LONG WILL IT KEEP THEM DOWN?
DEPENDS.
"JUST HOW TOUGH DO YOU THINK THEY ARE?"
GET THEM. GET THEM NOW.

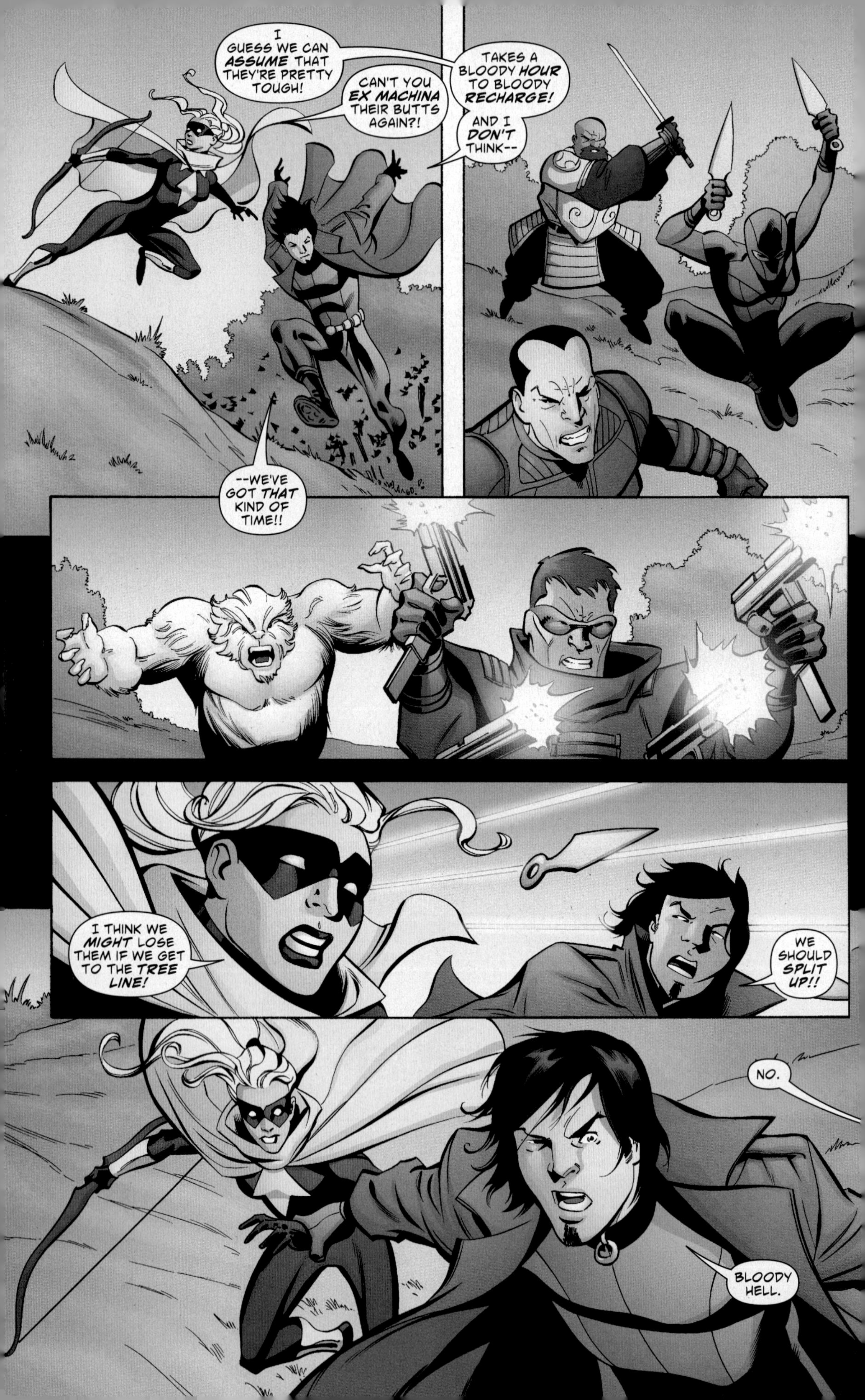
I GUESS WE CAN ASSUME THAT THEY'RE PRETTY TOUGH!
CAN'T YOU EX MACHINA THEIR BUTTS AGAIN?!
TAKES A BLOODY HOUR TO BLOODY RECHARGE!
AND I DON'T THINK--
--WE'VE GOT THAT KIND OF TIME!!
I THINK WE MIGHT LOSE THEM IF WE GET TO THE TREE LINE!
WE SHOULD SPLIT UP!!
NO.
BLOODY HELL.

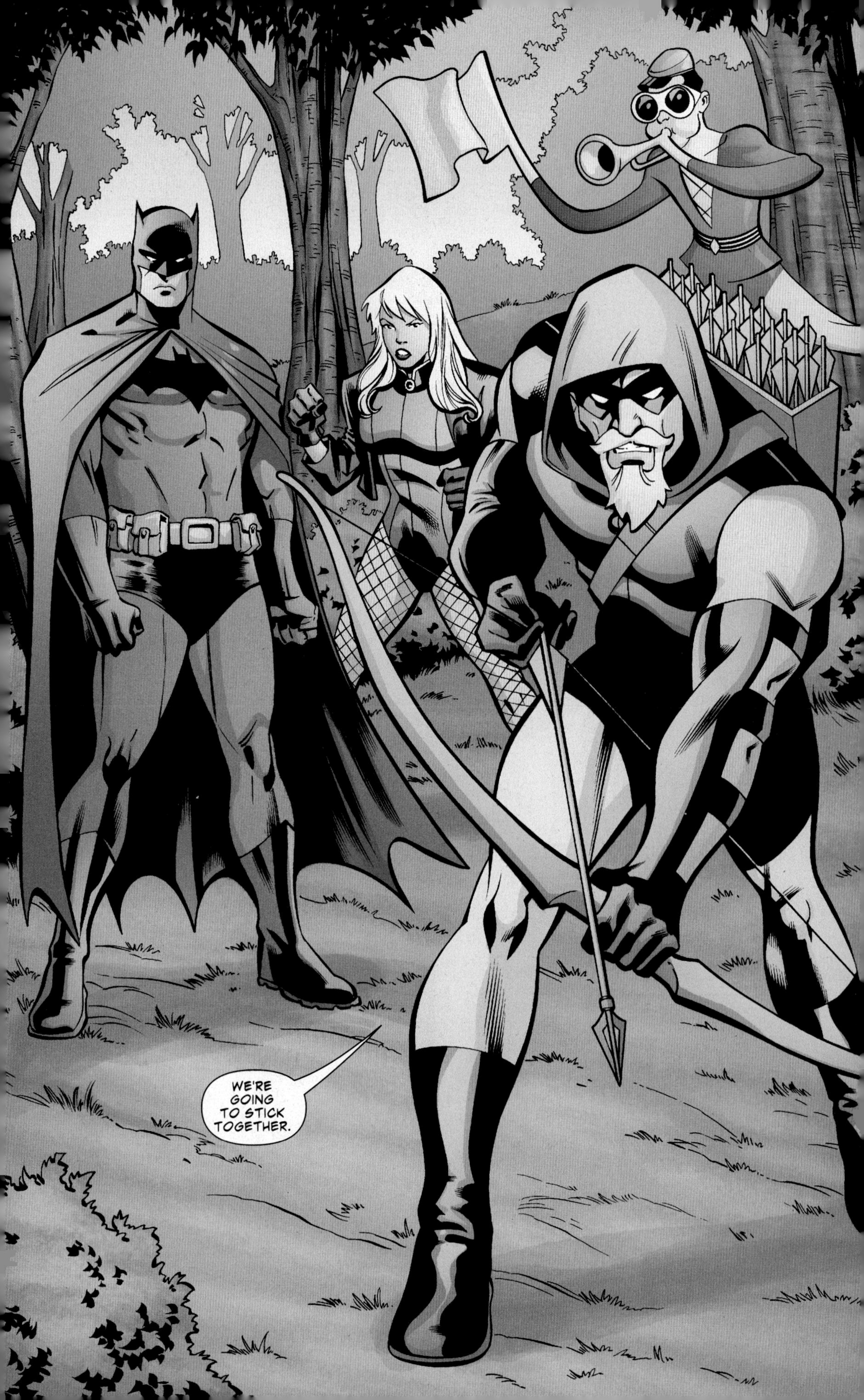
WE'RE GOING TO STICK TOGETHER.

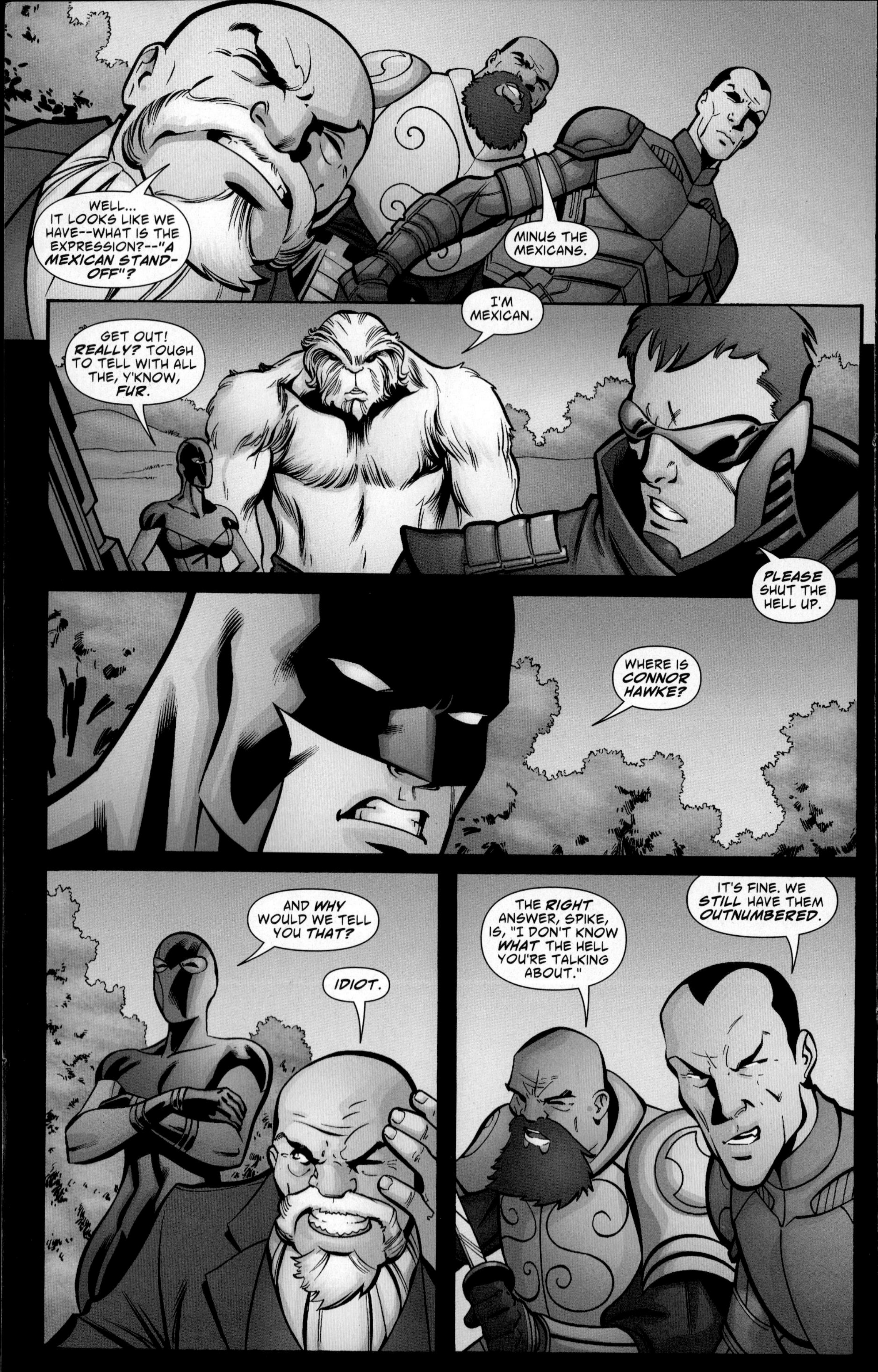
WELL... IT LOOKS LIKE WE HAVE--WHAT IS THE EXPRESSION?--"A MEXICAN STAND-OFF"?
MINUS THE MEXICANS.
I'M MEXICAN.
GET OUT! REALLY? TOUGH TO TELL WITH ALL THE, Y'KNOW, FUR.
PLEASE SHUT THE HELL UP.
WHERE IS CONNOR HAWKE?
AND WHY WOULD WE TELL YOU THAT?
IDIOT.
THE RIGHT ANSWER, SPIKE, IS, "I DON'T KNOW WHAT THE HELL YOU'RE TALKING ABOUT."
IT'S FINE. WE STILL HAVE THEM OUTNUMBERED.

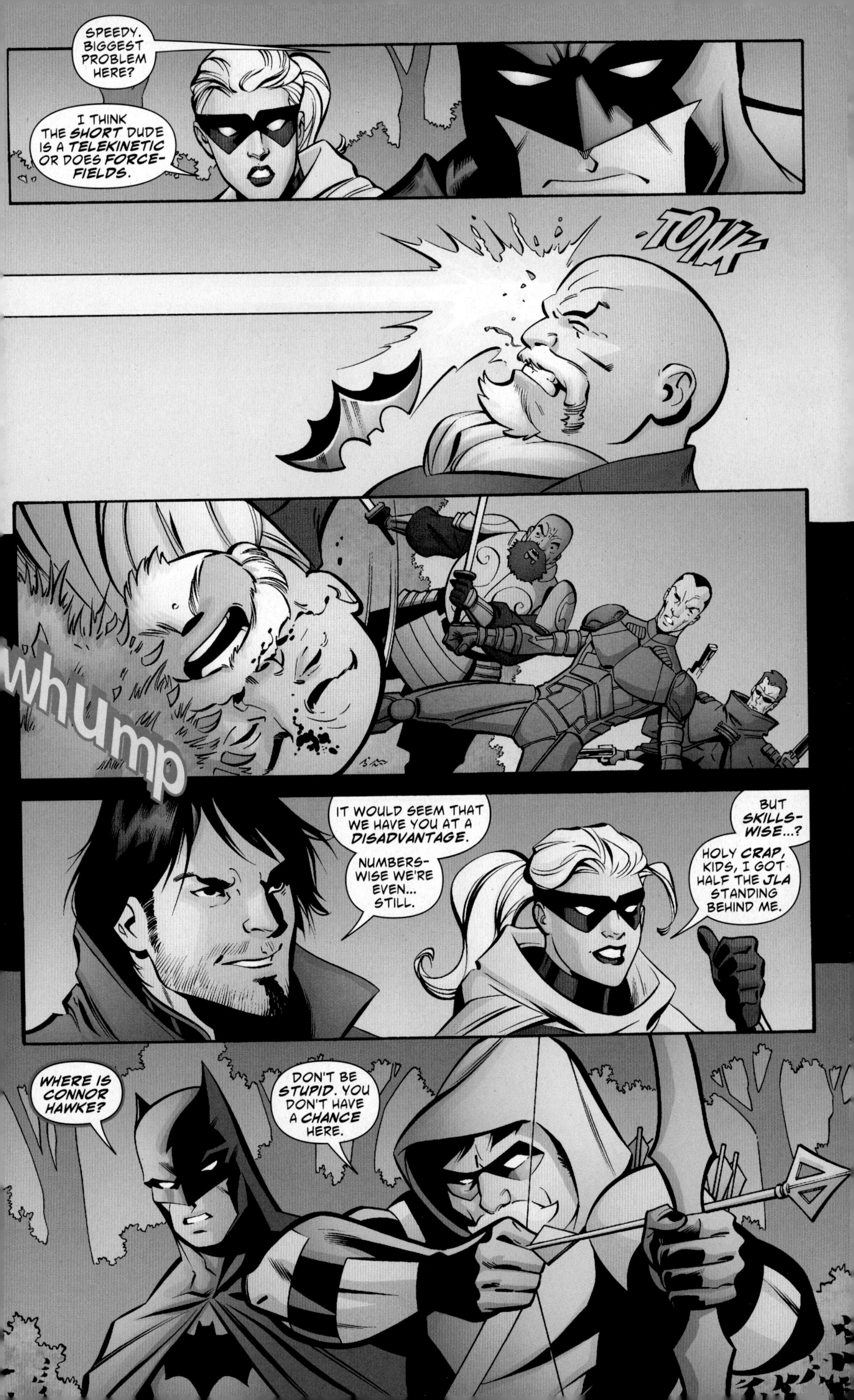
SPEEDY. BIGGEST PROBLEM HERE?
I THINK THE SHORT DUDE IS A TELEKINETIC OR DOES FORCE-FIELDS.
-TONK
whump
IT WOULD SEEM THAT WE HAVE YOU AT A DISADVANTAGE.
NUMBERS-WISE WE'RE EVEN... STILL.
BUT SKILLS-WISE...?
HOLY CRAP, KIDS, I GOT HALF THE JLA STANDING BEHIND ME.
WHERE IS CONNOR HAWKE?
DON'T BE STUPID. YOU DON'T HAVE A CHANCE HERE.

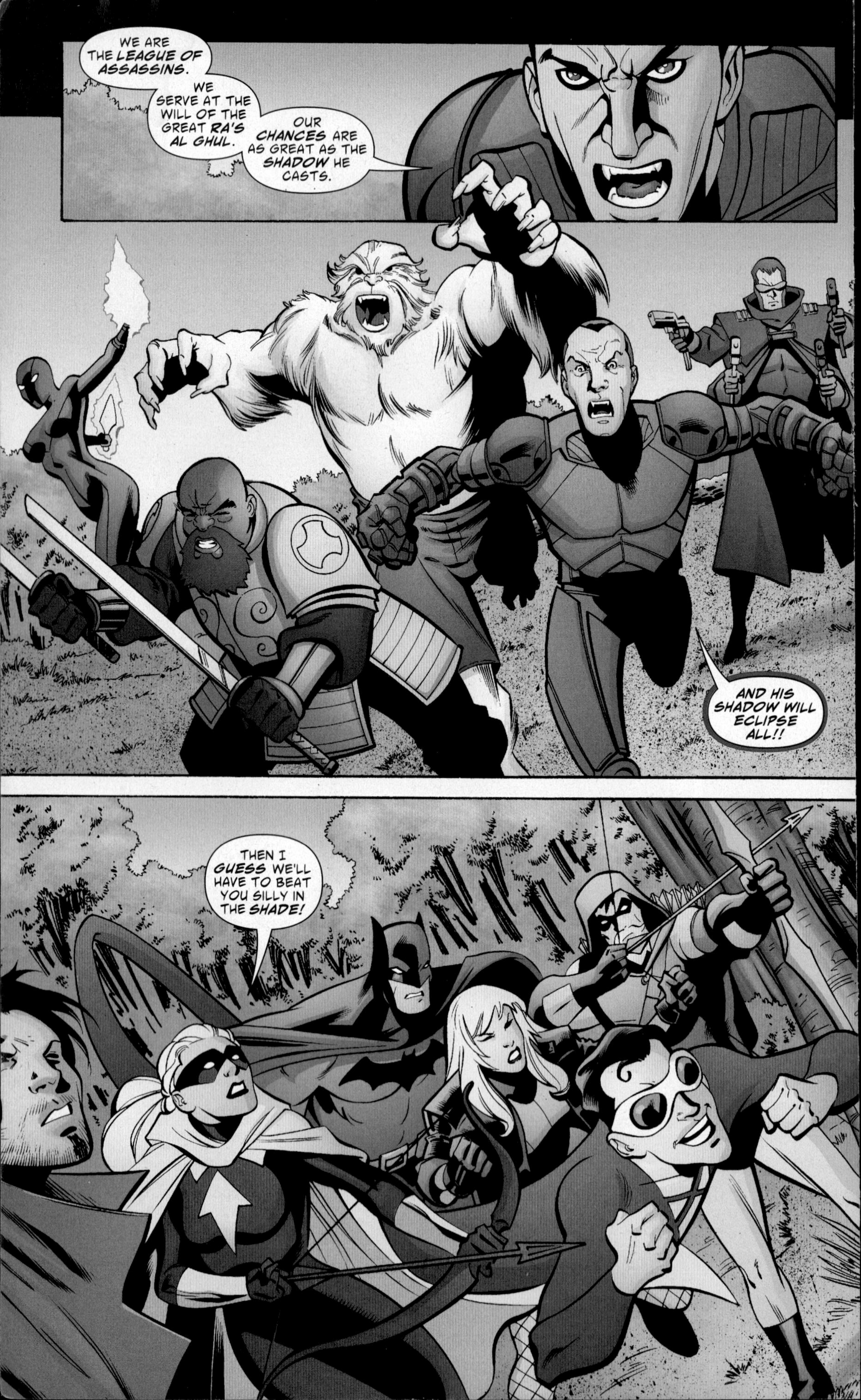
WE ARE THE LEAGUE OF ASSASSINS.
WE SERVE AT THE WILL OF THE GREAT RA'S AL GHUL.
OUR CHANCES ARE AS GREAT AS THE SHADOW HE CASTS.
AND HIS SHADOW WILL ECLIPSE ALL!!
THEN I GUESS WE'LL HAVE TO BEAT YOU SILLY IN THE SHADE!

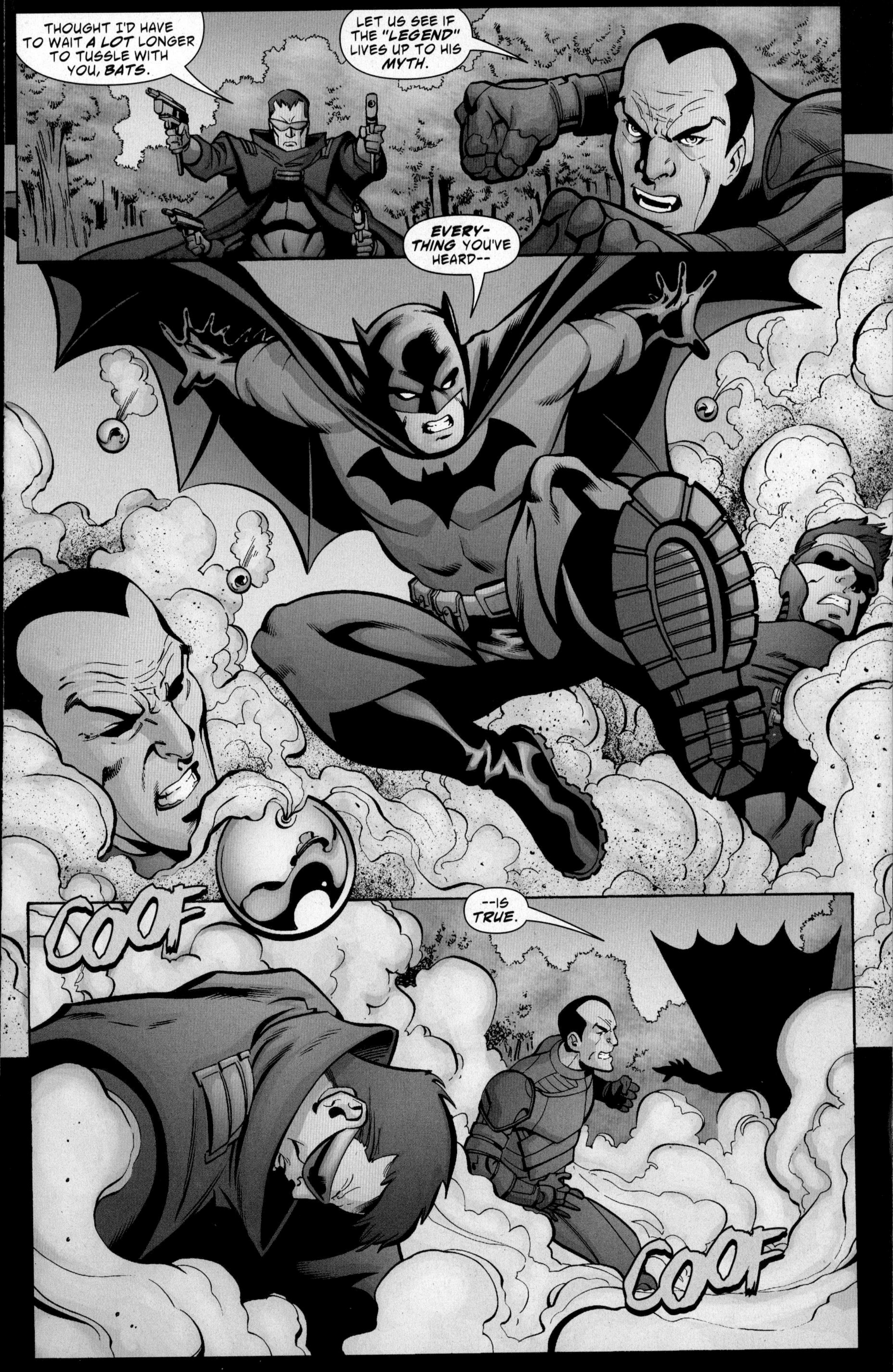
THOUGHT I'D HAVE TO WAIT A LOT LONGER TO TUSSLE WITH YOU, BATS.
LET US SEE IF THE "LEGEND" LIVES UP TO HIS MYTH.
EVERY-THING YOU'VE HEARD--
COOF
--IS TRUE.
COOF

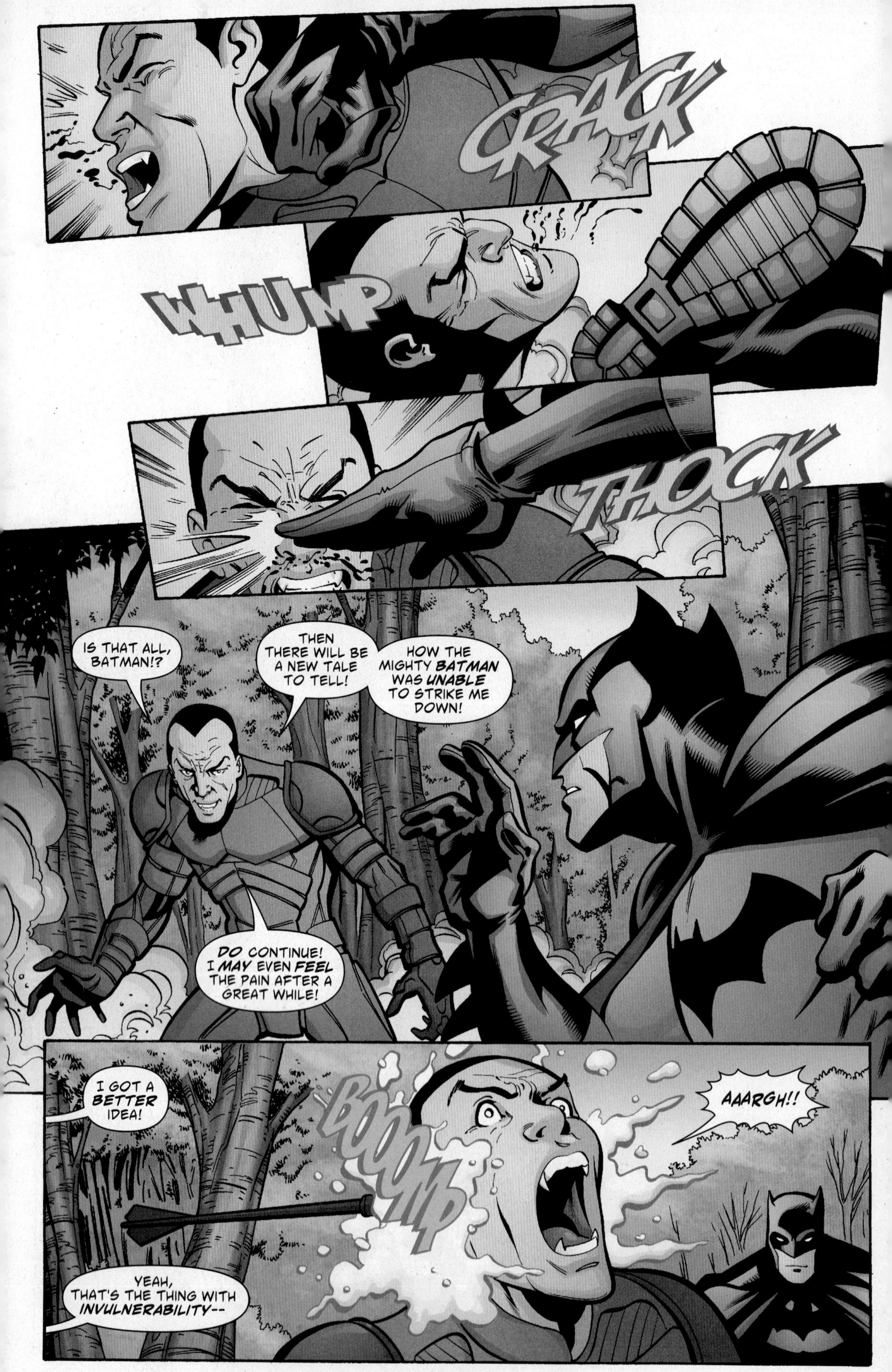
CRACK
WHUMP
THOCK
IS THAT ALL, BATMAN!?
THEN THERE WILL BE A NEW TALE TO TELL!
HOW THE MIGHTY BATMAN WAS UNABLE TO STRIKE ME DOWN!
DO CONTINUE! I MAY EVEN FEEL THE PAIN AFTER A GREAT WHILE!
I GOT A BETTER IDEA!
BOOOMP
AAARGH!!
YEAH, THAT'S THE THING WITH INVULNERABILITY--

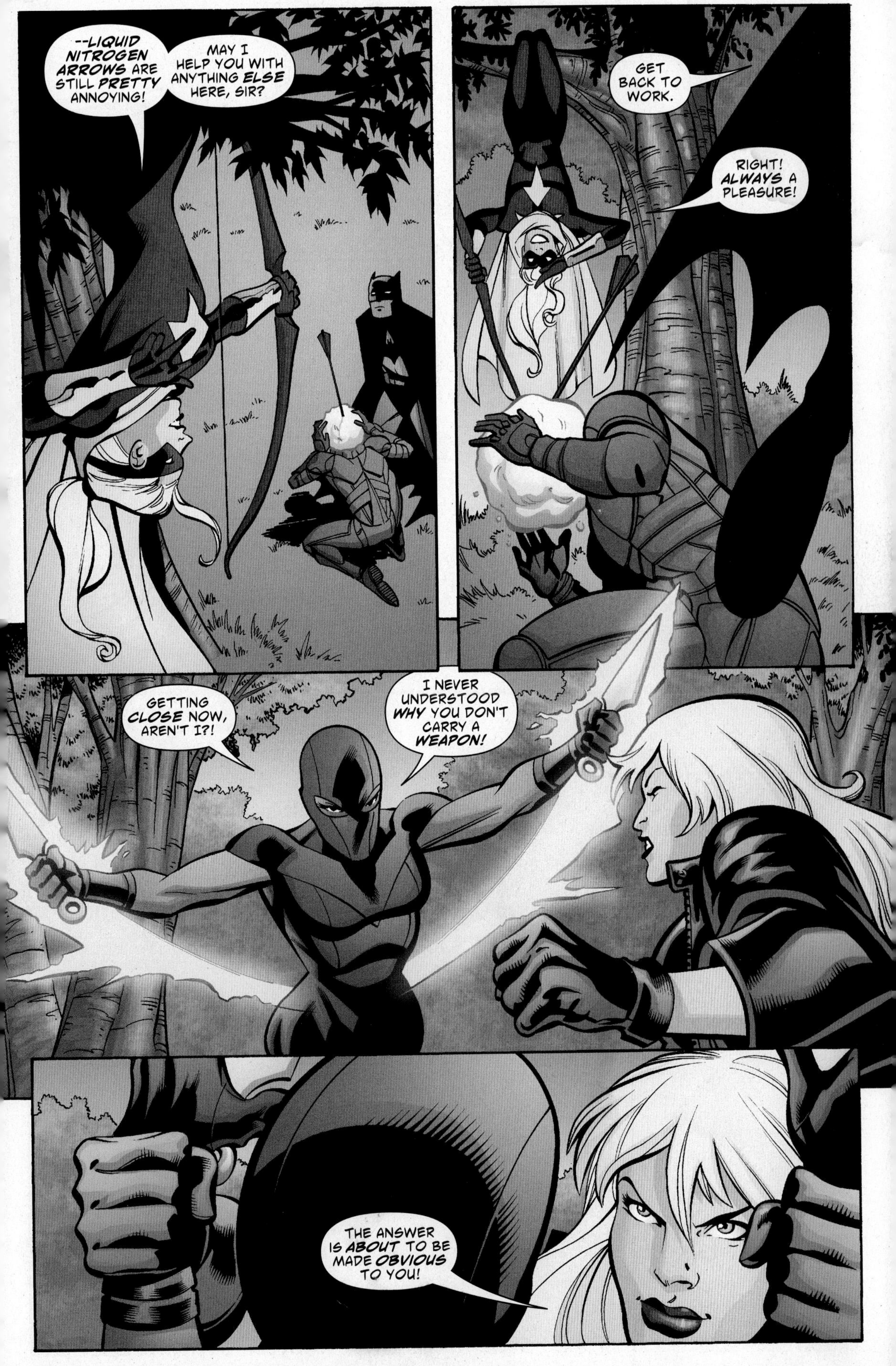
--LIQUID NITROGEN ARROWS ARE STILL PRETTY ANNOYING!
MAY I HELP YOU WITH ANYTHING ELSE HERE, SIR?
GET BACK TO WORK.
RIGHT! ALWAYS A PLEASURE!
GETTING CLOSE NOW, AREN'T I?!
I NEVER UNDERSTOOD WHY YOU DON'T CARRY A WEAPON!
THE ANSWER IS ABOUT TO BE MADE OBVIOUS TO YOU!

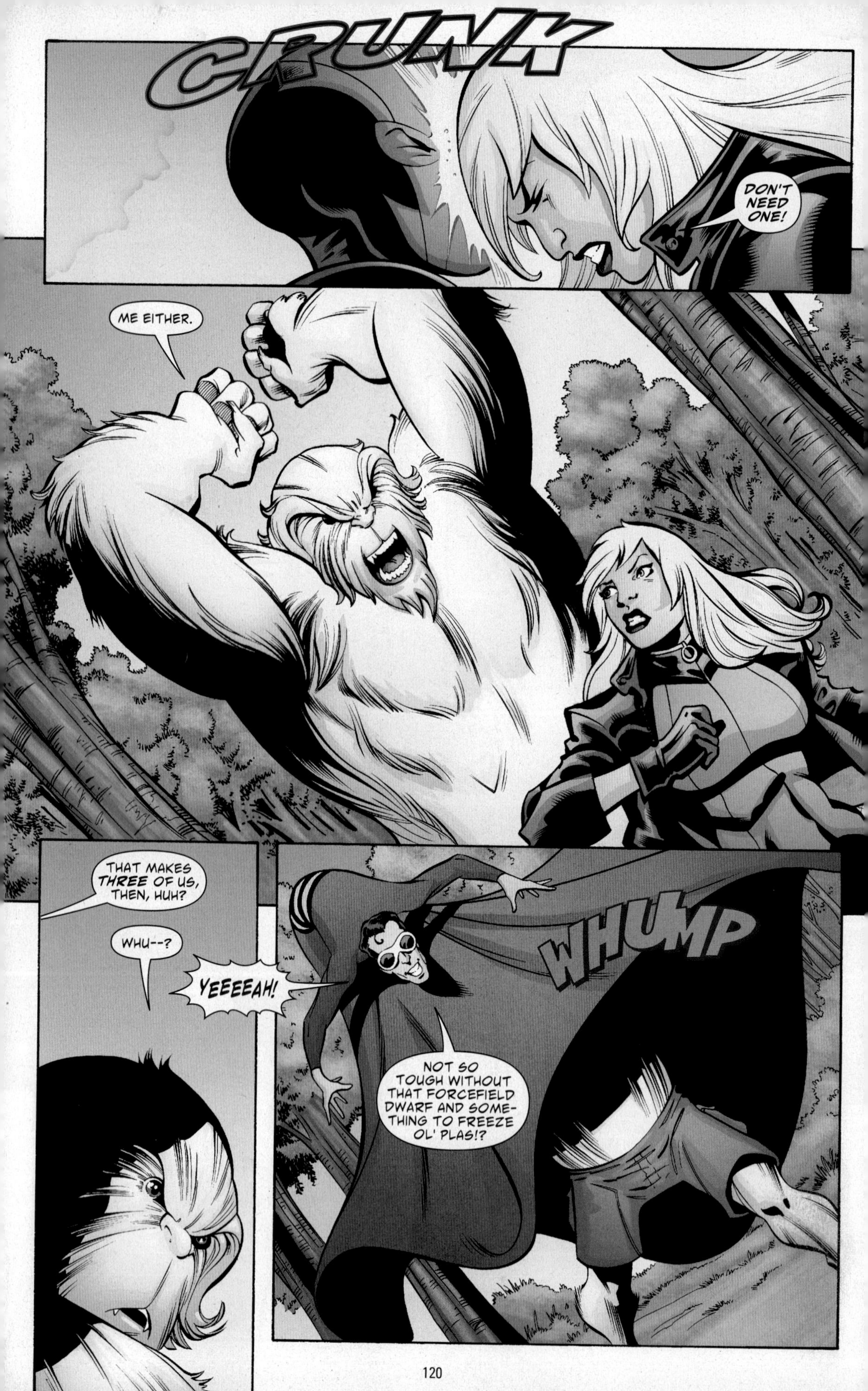
CRUNK
DON'T NEED ONE!
ME EITHER.
THAT MAKES THREE OF US, THEN, HUH?
WHU--?
YEEEEAH!
WHUMP
NOT SO TOUGH WITHOUT THAT FORCEFIELD DWARF AND SOMETHING TO FREEZE OL' PLAS!?

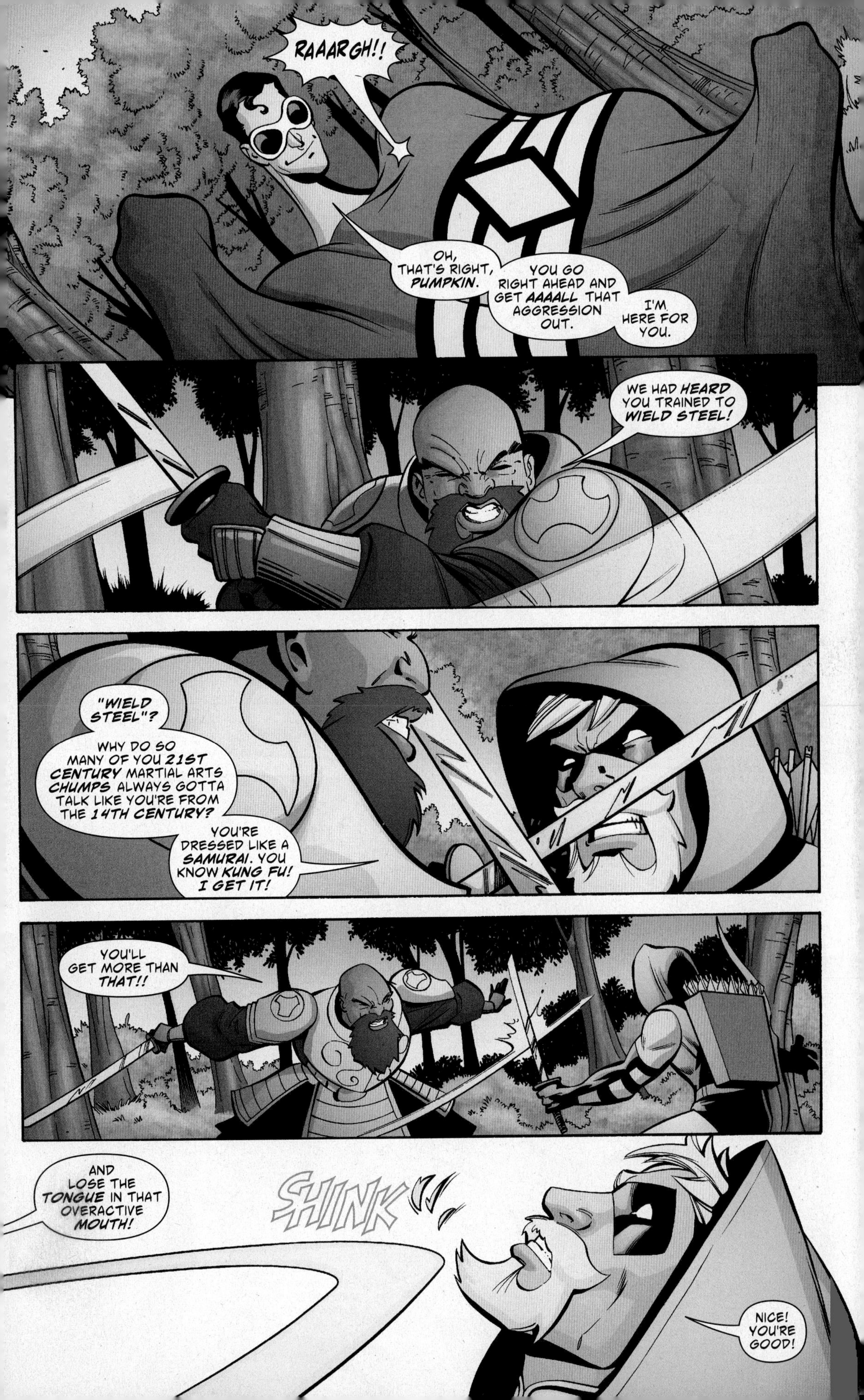
RAAARGH!!
OH, THAT'S RIGHT, PUMPKIN.
YOU GO RIGHT AHEAD AND GET AAAALL THAT AGGRESSION OUT.
I'M HERE FOR YOU.
WE HAD HEARD YOU TRAINED TO WIELD STEEL!
"WIELD STEEL"?
WHY DO SO MANY OF YOU 21ST CENTURY MARTIAL ARTS CHUMPS ALWAYS GOTTA TALK LIKE YOU'RE FROM THE 14TH CENTURY?
YOU'RE DRESSED LIKE A SAMURAI. YOU KNOW KUNG FU! I GET IT!
YOU'LL GET MORE THAN THAT!!
AND LOSE THE TONGUE IN THAT OVERACTIVE MOUTH!
SHINK
NICE! YOU'RE GOOD!

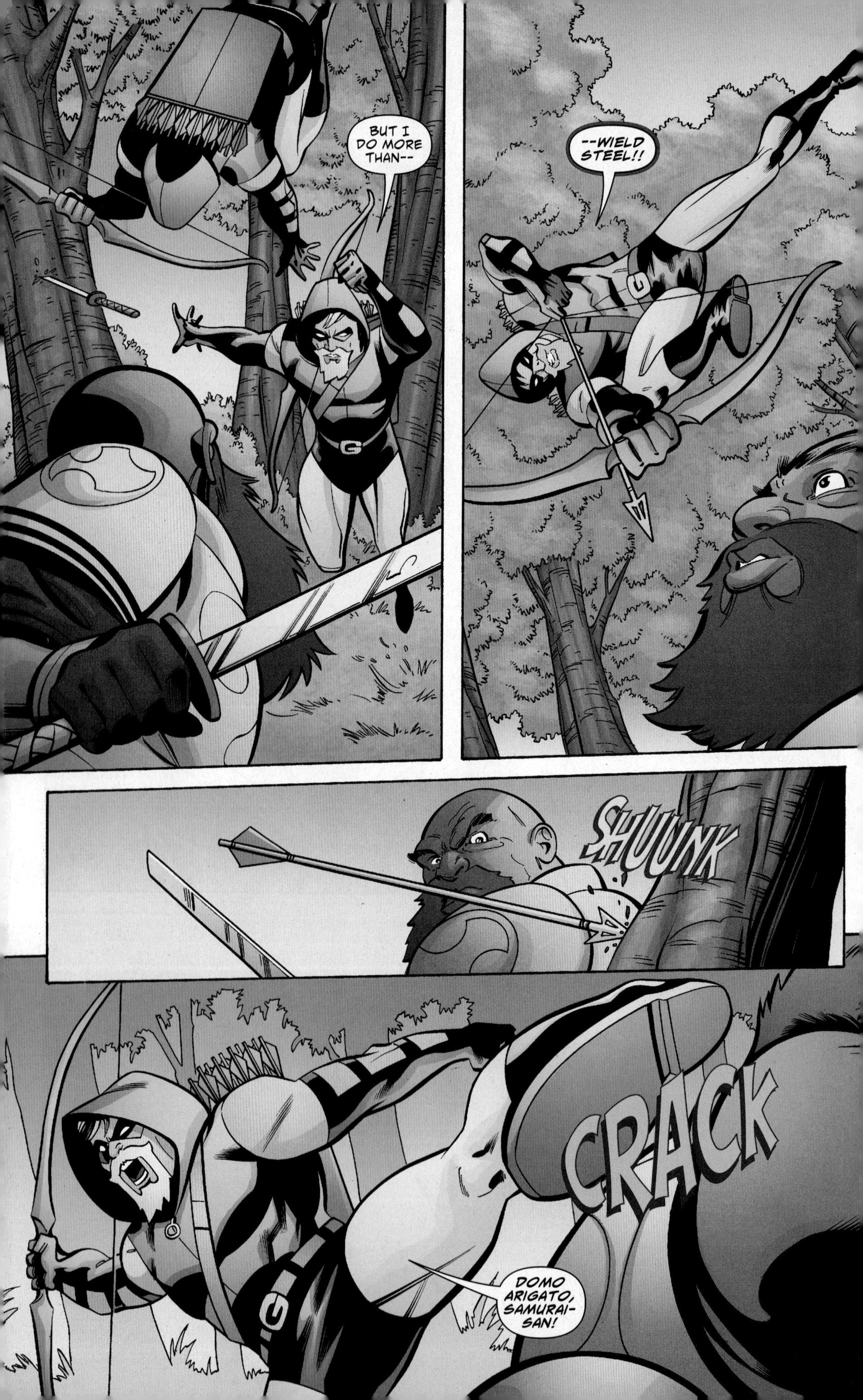
BUT I DO MORE THAN--
--WIELD STEEL!!
SHUUNK
CRACK
DOMO ARIGATO, SAMURAI-SAN!

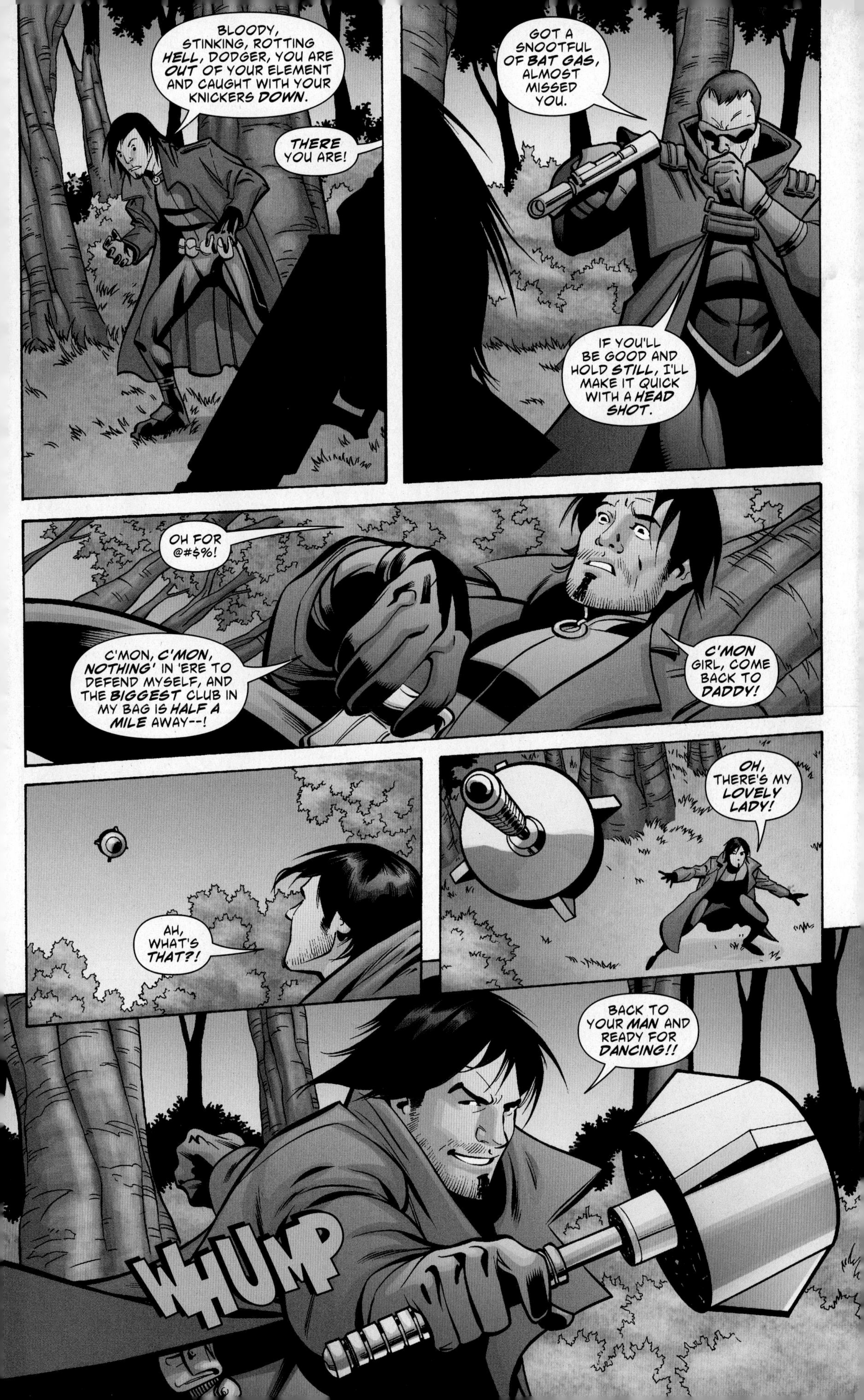
BLOODY, STINKING, ROTTING HELL, DODGER, YOU ARE OUT OF YOUR ELEMENT AND CAUGHT WITH YOUR KNICKERS DOWN.
THERE YOU ARE!
GOT A SNOOTFUL OF BAT GAS, ALMOST MISSED YOU.
IF YOU'LL BE GOOD AND HOLD STILL, I'LL MAKE IT QUICK WITH A HEAD SHOT.
OH FOR @#$%!
C'MON, C'MON, NOTHING' IN 'ERE TO DEFEND MYSELF, AND THE BIGGEST CLUB IN MY BAG IS HALF A MILE AWAY--!
C'MON GIRL, COME BACK TO DADDY!
AH, WHAT'S THAT?!
OH, THERE'S MY LOVELY LADY!
BACK TO YOUR MAN AND READY FOR DANCING!!
WHUMP

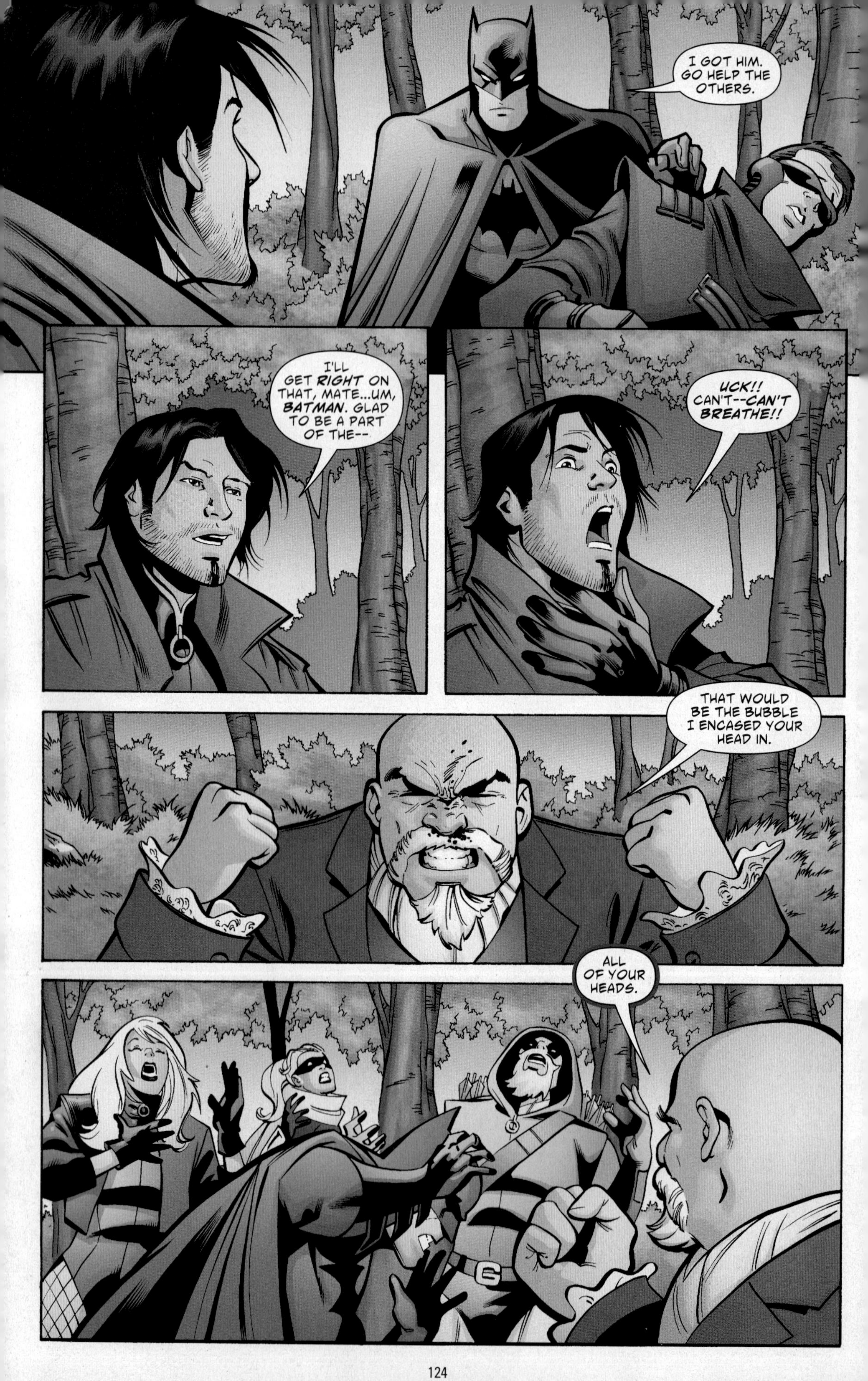
I GOT HIM. GO HELP THE OTHERS.
I'LL GET RIGHT ON THAT, MATE...UM, BATMAN. GLAD TO BE A PART OF THE--
UCK!! CAN'T--CAN'T BREATHE!!
THAT WOULD BE THE BUBBLE I ENCASED YOUR HEAD IN.
ALL OF YOUR HEADS.

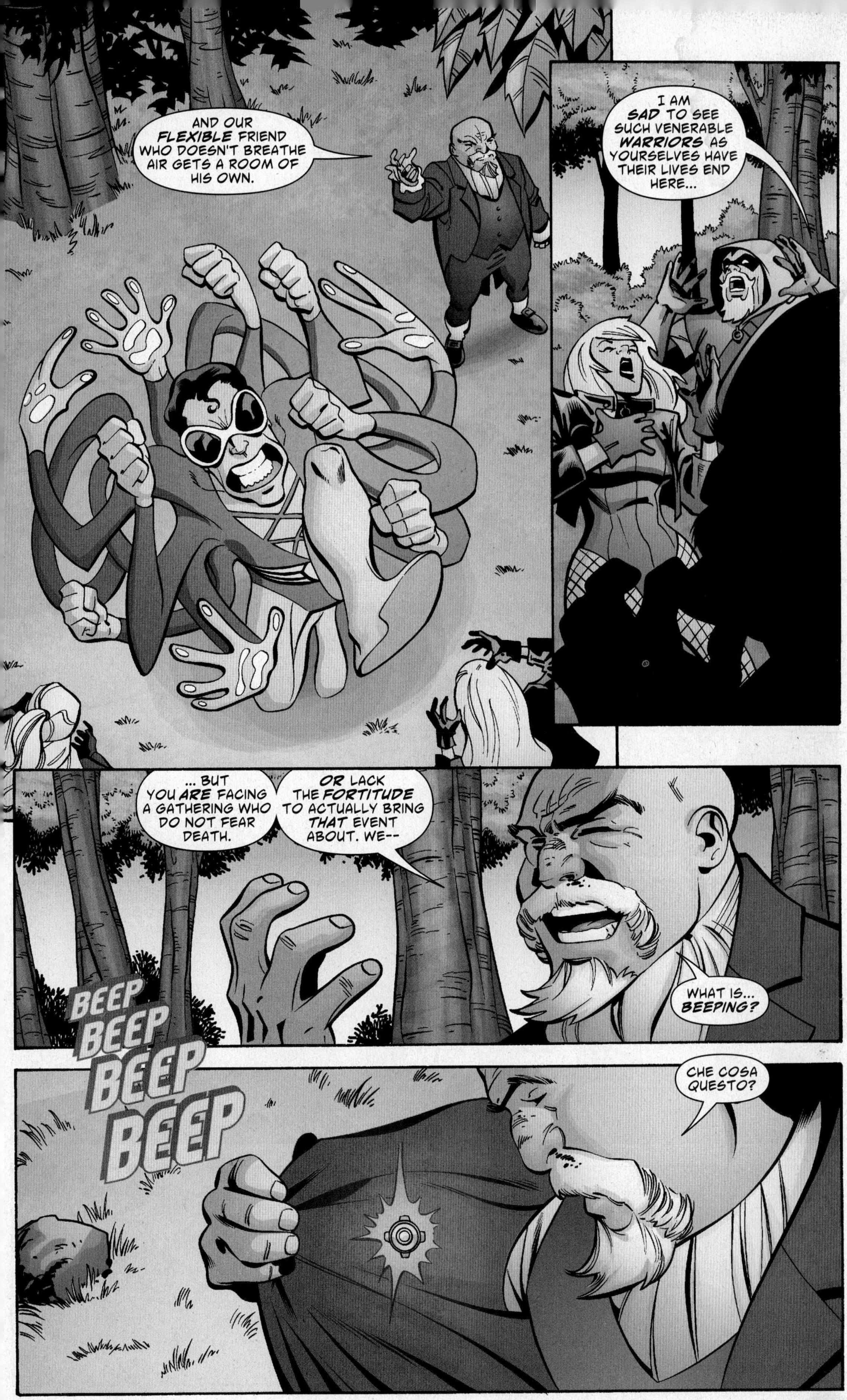
AND OUR FLEXIBLE FRIEND WHO DOESN'T BREATHE AIR GETS A ROOM OF HIS OWN.
I AM SAD TO SEE SUCH VENERABLE WARRIORS AS YOURSELVES HAVE THEIR LIVES END HERE...
... BUT YOU ARE FACING A GATHERING WHO DO NOT FEAR DEATH.
OR LACK THE FORTITUDE TO ACTUALLY BRING THAT EVENT ABOUT. WE--
WHAT IS... BEEPING?
BEEP BEEP BEEP BEEP
CHE COSA QUESTO?

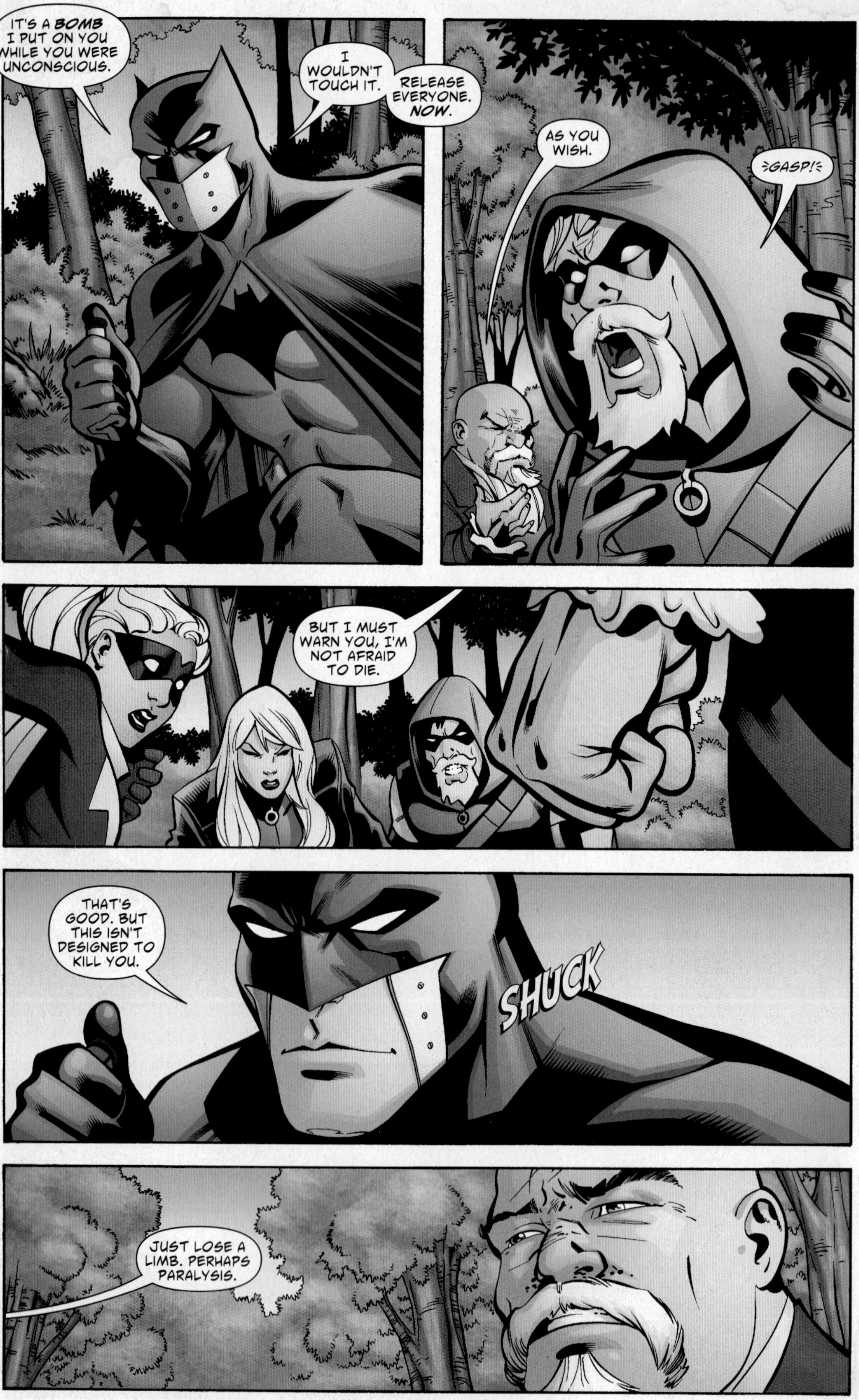
IT'S A BOMB I PUT ON YOU WHILE YOU WERE UNCONSCIOUS.
I WOULDN'T TOUCH IT.
RELEASE EVERYONE. NOW.
AS YOU WISH.
GASP!
BUT I MUST WARN YOU, I'M NOT AFRAID TO DIE.
THAT'S GOOD. BUT THIS ISN'T DESIGNED TO KILL YOU.
SHUCK
JUST LOSE A LIMB. PERHAPS PARALYSIS.

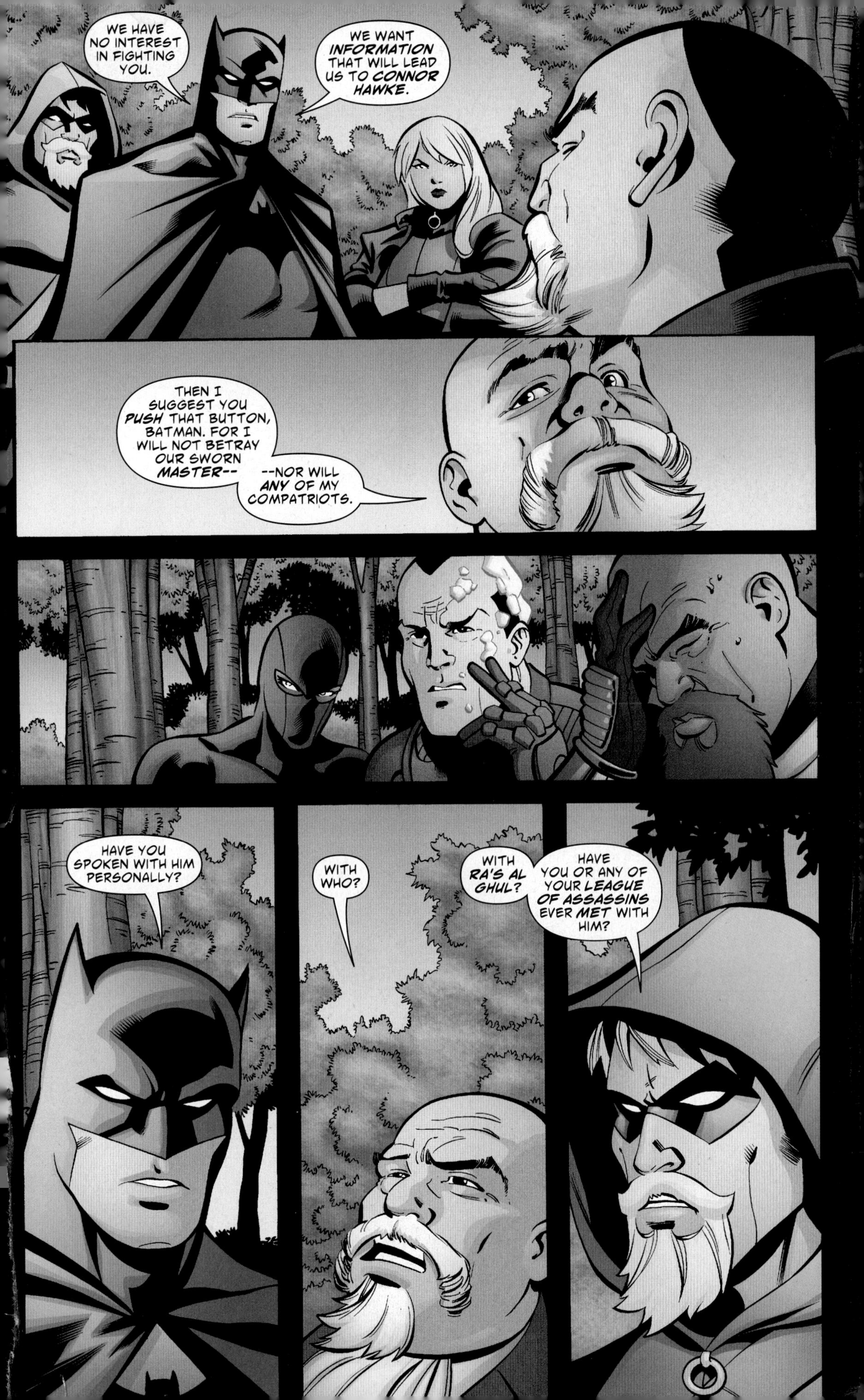
WE HAVE NO INTEREST IN FIGHTING YOU.
WE WANT INFORMATION THAT WILL LEAD US TO CONNOR HAWKE.
THEN I SUGGEST YOU PUSH THAT BUTTON, BATMAN. FOR I WILL NOT BETRAY OUR SWORN MASTER--
--NOR WILL ANY OF MY COMPATRIOTS.
HAVE YOU SPOKEN WITH HIM PERSONALLY?
WITH WHO?
WITH RA'S AL GHUL?
HAVE YOU OR ANY OF YOUR LEAGUE OF ASSASSINS EVER MET WITH HIM?

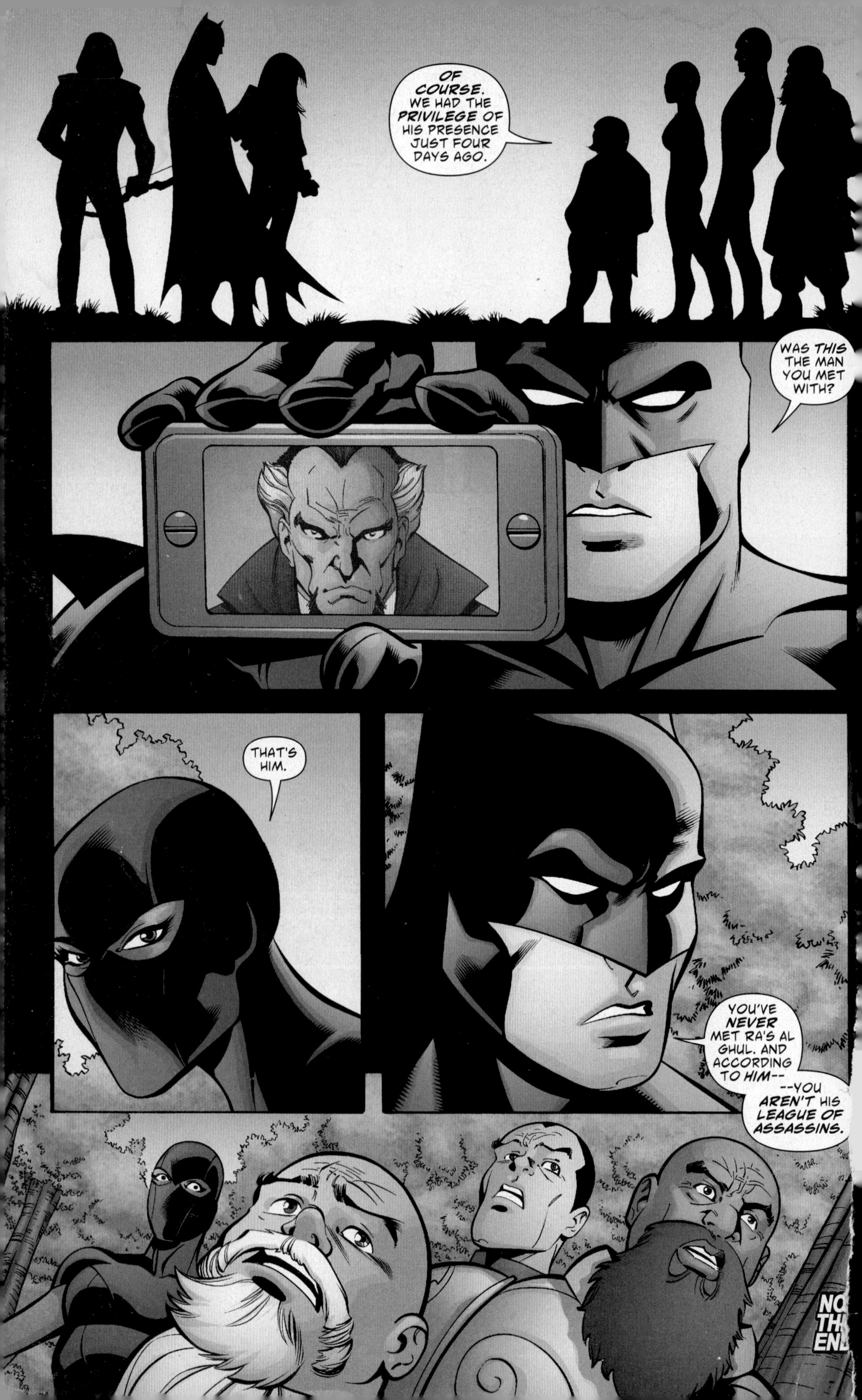
OF COURSE. WE HAD THE PRIVILEGE OF HIS PRESENCE JUST FOUR DAYS AGO.
WAS THIS THE MAN YOU MET WITH?
THAT'S HIM.
YOU'VE NEVER MET RA'S AL GHUL. AND ACCORDING TO HIM--
--YOU AREN'T HIS LEAGUE OF ASSASSINS.